LUCRETIUS

DE RERUM NATURA

BOOK III

EDITED BY

E. J. KENNEY

*Reader in Latin Literature and Textual Criticism
in the University of Cambridge*

CAMBRIDGE

AT THE UNIVERSITY PRESS

1971

Published by the Syndics of the Cambridge University Press
Bentley House, 200 Euston Road, London N.W.1
American Branch: 32 East 57th Street, New York, N.Y.10022

© Cambridge University Press 1971

Library of Congress Catalogue Card Number: 75–158555

ISBN: 0 521 08142 4

Printed in Great Britain
at the University Printing House, Cambridge
(Brooke Crutchley, University Printer)

CONTENTS

Man will never attain his full powers as a moral being until he has ceased to believe in a personal God and in the immortality of the soul.

WINWOOD READE, *The martyrdom of Man*

'I don't know why, but one doesn't exactly approve of being annihilated. Though when it's happened, nothing could matter less.' C. P. SNOW, *Last things*

PREFACE

The conscientious commentator will offer his work to the public in a mood of doubt and self-questioning. As an Editor of the series in which this edition appears I have felt a special duty to keep in the forefront of my mind its declared aim: 'to provide the student with the guidance that he needs for the interpretation and understanding of the book as a work of literature'. The amount of guidance here provided may, however, strike some readers as excessive. If so, it is because it has seemed to me that in the past Lucretius' interpreters have not always taken enough pains to disentangle and follow his argument as he intended it to be followed, and this, whatever shortcomings may be found in the execution, is what I have attempted to do. The *De Rerum Natura*, in spite of the lucid style of which the poet was rightly proud, is a difficult book, and I have often preferred the risk of telling the reader what he already knows to that of leaving him in the lurch – the besetting sin of commentators. It may also be felt that there is here too much expatiation on the poetical techniques of Lucretius. In this department the existing commentaries seem to leave much to be desired. In spite of the lead given by H. Sykes Davies in his *Criterion* article of 1931 and in spite of more recent contributions in this field such as Professor David West's excellent *The imagery and poetry of Lucretius* (1969), the conventional idea of Lucretius' art still persists: *ingenio maximus, arte rudis*. Cicero knew otherwise; but posterity has yet to be convinced. The student who finds some notes inordinately long may care to note that an effort has been made to, so to say, 'grade' their contents so that the essential information is usually presented at the beginning.

It would have been tedious in the extreme to record each and every debt to my predecessors. My general obligation to the commentaries of, in particular, Munro, Ernout–Robin and Bailey will be evident. I must make specific mention, however, of the way in which my approach to the under-standing and exegesis of Book III has been influenced by the superb edition of Richard Heinze – unworthily neglected by Bailey, who makes quite inadequate use of it. I have not been able to bring myself to reproduce any existing text; in pre-paring my own I have relied principally on Bailey's reports of the manuscripts.

It is a pleasure to record my thanks, for help and advice of various kinds, to Dr M. Baltes, Dr H.-D. Blume, Dr R. D. Dawe, Dr G. E. R. Lloyd, Mr Roland G. Mayer, Dr D. O'Brien, Mr N. H. Reed and Professor H. Tränkle. I am particularly indebted to my editorial colleague Mrs Easterling for suggestions leading to a number of important improvements in both presentation and substance. Professer R. G. M. Nisbet kindly agreed to read the proofs, and a number of weaknesses have been exposed by his acute criticisms. I regret only that it was not possible to incorporate more of his suggestions. His and Mrs Easterling's vigilance has saved me from more errors than I care to remember; those that remain must be laid at my door, where they belong.

March 1971   E. J. K.

NOTE. For the full titles of works cited by author only see the Bibliography, pp. 245–7.

INTRODUCTION

1. THE DOCTRINE

Ab Epicuro principium: Lucretius utters his allegiance in unambiguous terms (Commentary 2 n.). Yet this allegiance was perhaps to an idea as much as to a man. Epicurus (341–271 B.C.) was no Socrates; and he lacked both the poetic gifts and the humour to be his own Plato. What excited Lucretius to produce the most passionate didactic poem ever written was the Epicurean philosophy itself. Diogenes Laertius (10. 9) speaks of the 'siren-charms' of Epicurean doctrine; to Lucretius it seems to have come as a revelation, the only philosophical system which, by abolishing fear of the gods and of death, allowed mankind to achieve release from spiritual bondage. However, much of the appeal of the system must have derived from the character and personality of its founder. In the first place he was self-taught (D.L. 10. 13), a fact which perhaps helps to explain the originality of his doctrines taken as a whole and their essentially practical nature.[1] He was also a man of blameless life and singular sweetness of disposition, as his letters to his disciples testify; it is small wonder that they venerated him. The Homeric heroes were honoured by their peoples 'as gods' (Hom. *Il.* 5. 78, 10. 33, 12. 312, etc.); divine honours were on occasion paid to earthly rulers even before the Hellenistic period; and Empedocles had claimed that he walked among men 'as an immortal god, no longer mortal'.[2] Such were the precedents according to which it was natural that the followers of Epicurus should acclaim him as the true, the only Saviour, σωτήρ:[3] greater than the powers which, through

---

[1] Festugière 27–8; Martha remarks (9) that the Epicurean philosophy represents an attempt to systematize the temperament of a single individual: 'S'il est vrai que les doctrines font les mœurs, n'est-il pas vrai aussi que les mœurs font les doctrines?' The point is valid for most, if not all, ancient philosophies, but particularly so for the Epicurean. Cf. Boyancé 301.

[2] ἐγὼ δ'ὑμῖν θεὸς ἄμβροτος, οὐκέτι θνητὸς | πωλεῦμαι (31 B 112.4–5 DK).

[3] Cf. Festugière 63 n. 1; for the growth of 'individual' religion and the quest for personal salvation in post-classical Greece see Festugière, ch. 1 'Le fait religieux au seuil de l'ère hellénistique'; W. Tarn and G. T. Griffith, *Hellenistic civilization*[3] (1952), ch. x 'Philosophy and Religion'; E. R. Dodds, *The Greeks and the irrational* (1951), ch. VIII 'The fear of

sheer force of mind, he had vanquished. *deus ille fuit, deus* proclaims
Lucretius (5. 8); and the evangelistic fervour and single-minded
impetus of the *De Rerum Natura* make it singularly tempting to see in
the poem the document of a conversion. Certainly it is hardly an
exaggeration to say that this self-styled enemy of religion was 'in the
profounder sense that transcends creeds and forms, the greatest religious mind of pagan Rome',[1] as he contemplated the revelation
achieved by reason with an awe that can only be called religious,
diuina uoluptas atque horror (cf. Comm. 28–30n.). It has often been
remarked that the Epicurean school of philosophy (and the same is
true of the Stoic) had many of the characteristics of a church: 'a
sacred founder, and sacred books, and a credo of memory verses from
those books',[2] congregations of the faithful, and a tradition that was
more concerned to preserve and gloss than to build upon and develop
the founder's doctrine.[3] Dogma and orthodoxy pervade the *D.R.N.*
Lucretius' purpose was to help men to attain happiness, which he
describes (3. 322) as *dignam dis degere uitam*; but the godlike existence
to which he encourages his readers to aspire is closer to that of
Epicurus than to the detached and ineffectual gods of the *intermundia*.
To those gods he owed of necessity a duty of formal piety as exemplified by Epicurus himself (6. 67–79),[4] but no more; their appearance
in Book III (18–24) serves, not to introduce the contemplation of their
virtues, but to lend force (by way of contrast to the non-existence of
Hell) to the idea that inspires the poet's true religious feelings – the
operation of the laws of Nature, dictating inexorably the motions of
the atoms in the void, *quaecumque infra per inane geruntur* (27). The
vehicle of this revelation is the Epicurean doctrine, sprung – the
analogy with the mythical birth of Athena from the head of Zeus is
unmistakably hinted at – from the divine mind of Epicurus (3. 14–15);
and it is Epicurus, not the gods of the *intermundia*, whom Lucretius

freedom'; G. Murray, *Five stages of Greek religion* (1935), ch. IV 'The failure
of nerve'.

[1] Leonard 76. Cf. J. S. Mill, *Autobiography* ch. 2: 'the best among
[unbelievers]...are more genuinely religious, in the best sense of the word
religion, than those who exclusively arrogate to themselves the title'.

[2] Leonard 80.

[3] Cf. Martha 10–12, 346; Festugière 31 n. 2; and on the points of
resemblance between Epicurus and St Paul ibid. 36 n. 3.

[4] Cf. Festugière 74–5.

invokes throughout the poem in terms borrowed from, and clearly intended to recall, the conventional invocation of deity. Here, not in the anthropomorphic figments of priests and poets, was the true divinity.

In the *D.R.N.* we are offered, not an account of the Epicurean system (cf. §3 below), but the personal testament of the poet. For a full exposition of the Epicurean faith and of what it demanded of its adherents we must look elsewhere.[1] However, if Book III is to be read with understanding, certain preliminary points must be made. In particular the associations that cling to the word 'Epicurean' in modern usage must be ignored. The Epicurean philosophy was materialistic: its account of the universe, based on the theories of the earlier atomists Democritus and Leucippus, taught that all phenomena are produced by the motions, according to certain laws, of solid and and indestructible bodies (atoms) in the void. Nothing is created out of nothing; nothing is resolved into nothing; everything, except the individual atoms themselves, is subject to change. The human soul, like the human body, is composed of atoms and is mortal. The gods exist but do not regulate either natural phenomena or human affairs. There is no life after death; the business of man is to achieve happiness as best he can in this life, according to the dictates of reason. Happiness is defined as wellbeing of body and mind, and consists fundamentally in the avoidance of pain and anxiety (ἀπονία, ἀταραξία).[2] This bald summary may, it is hoped, assist comprehension of Lucretius, but it is totally inadequate to describe what Epicureanism really was and the part which it played in the lives of its devotees, particularly the emphasis, of which we hear little in the *D.R.N.*, which was laid on friendship and a common life. Various features of the physical doctrines are open to criticism and were attacked in antiquity by rival schools, and in particular the self-centred gods of Epicurus were a favourite target; but the most vulnerable aspect of the system as a whole clearly lay in its emphasis on happiness and pleasure, as opposed to the Stoic insistence on virtue. It is this emphasis that, in trivialized

---

[1] See the works of Martha Festugière, De Witt and Farrington; Leonard 36–55; W. Schmid, art. 'Epikur' in *Reallexicon für Antike und Christentum* v (1962) 681–819.

[2] Cf. the 'Quadruple Remedy' (*Tetrapharmakon*) of Philodemus (quoted by Festugière 46 n. 1): 'The gods are not to be feared, death is without danger, good is easy to possess, evil is easy to bear bravely.'

and degraded forms, has come to be synonymous with Epicureanism in the minds of many, to whom of course 'pleasure' means something quite different from what it meant to Epicurus. This misunderstanding was already well established in Lucretius' day. Nothing in fact could be more misleading than the equation of Epicurean doctrine with mere hedonism. Rather the reverse is the case: the trouble with Epicureanism, and the main reason perhaps why it never enjoyed the general success of Stoicism, was not that it was too easy, but that it was too difficult, too austere, too unworldly.[1] It is hard for an ordinary man, at the same time as he is forbidden to pursue the usual goals of worldly ambition, to accept that he must live well now because there will be no other chance for him to live at all, and that the good life must be lived for its own sake without any prospect of either reward or punishment in the hereafter.[2] At its best the austerity and nobility of the Epicurean life as it was lived by the founder and by its highest representatives compels admiration; but it was a style of life that, essentially, rejected life. 'There is a strange shadow of sadness hanging over this wise and kindly faith, which proceeds from the essential distrust of life that lies at its heart. The best that Epicurus has really to say of the world is that if you are very wise and do not attract its notice – Λάθε βιώσας – it will not hurt you. It is a philosophy not of conquest but of escape.'[3] And admirable as certain aspects of Epicurean ethics are, the connexion between the physical premisses of the system and its moral conclusions is sometimes loose.[4] Lucretius has occasionally been criticized for expending so much moral energy in the denunciation of

---

[1] Cf. the apology placed in the mouth of Torquatus by Cicero: ...*ut*... *intellegatur*...*ea, quae uoluptuaria, delicata, mollis habeatur disciplina, quam grauis, quam continens, quam seuera sit* (*De Fin*. 1. 37).

[2] 'Here we have one of the deepest implications of the Epicurean doctrine of nihilism – the moral obligation laid upon us by the brief span of our existence to live a rich and abundant life of sense and spirit, of the body and of the soul, that one might withdraw, at the appointed hour, *plenus vitae conviva*, with equanimity, and even nobly and proudly' (Hadzits 138–9).

[3] Murray, op. cit. (p.1 n. 3) 110.

[4] '...in Epicureanism (as so commonly in other naturalistic or behaviorist systems), ideals of the good life are smuggled in from without the system – as it were, even from the very folklore of ethics, those ancient notions of what is decent for a true man, recorded long ago in Hesiod and Homer, and doubtless invoked even by a Boeotian blacksmith when he praised or pummeled his neighbor' (Leonard 44); cf. Festugière 52–3.

old wives' tales which the educated Romans of his day – for whom, as the style of his poem shows, he must have been writing – could not conceivably have taken seriously; and, conversely, it has been regretted that he did not devote some part of the poem to expounding Epicurean ethics.[1] Such criticisms rest on a misconception of the poet's aims. In limiting himself to a negative and destructive approach (based, it should be stressed, on positive physical teaching) Lucretius was both following the promptings of his own nature and writing for the world and for posterity. He was anything but a fool, and we are bound to assume that he was aware that his enlightened contemporaries did not require to be undeceived about Hades. In attacking these popular notions he was attacking a particular manifestation of something universal and eternal, or at all events coeval with the human species: 'the poet is not so much concerned to refute a popular belief as to point its moral, if rightly understood'.[2] An intelligent reader, trained to draw general conclusions from particular cases, can see all the innumerable superstitions of the Hellenistic and Greco-Roman worlds[3] imaged in Lucretius' great diatribe; but to convey his point forcefully it was necessary for him to choose examples that would carry emotional conviction through their familiarity. Tantalus, Tityos, Sisyphus are demolished, not because Memmius and his peers believed in them, but because other men had believed in them, did believe in them – and would believe in them, or in fresh variations of them, again.[4] The charge that Lucretius was battering at an open door could with equal justice be levelled against each and every writer who in any age has attacked folly and superstition.[5]

[1] So, for instance, Hadzits 153.

[2] Sikes 127–8.

[3] Cf. Murray, loc. cit. (p. 1 n. 3); Leonard 73–4.

[4] Cf. Hadzits 141: 'Little could Lucretius...anticipate the diseased imaginations and the cruelties imposed upon later centuries by fears of everlasting punishment.' Perhaps not; but these things would have confirmed his worst fears of what men will do to themselves once they have rejected the guidance of reason and true philosophy.

[5] Cf. Festugière 78 n. 1. One form of superstition (as Lucretius must have seen it) that flourished in the first century B.C. as it had flourished in Hellenistic Greece (cf. p. 1 n. 3) was the romantic expectation of a political σωτήρ or Messiah: for contemporary exploitation of this idea see E. Norden, *Kl. Schriften zum klass. Altertum* (1966) 369 n. 26. For the period as one favourable to mysticism see also E. R. Dodds, *Pagan and Christian in an age of*

2. THE POET

Little is known about Lucretius. This is by no means a disadvantage
for the interpretation of his poem, which can and should be understood without reference to the personal circumstances of the poet.[1]
Since however in Lucretius' case the biographical question has had a
certain nuisance value it must receive some discussion. St Jerome has
transmitted under the year 94 B.C. the following notice: *Titus Lucre-*
tius poeta nascitur, qui postea amatorio poculo in furorem uersus, cum aliquot
libros per interualla insaniae conscripsisset quos postea Cicero emendauit,
proprio se manu interfecit anno aetatis XLIIII (*Eusebii Pamphili Chronici*
Canones, p. 231 Fotheringham). This would place Lucretius' death in
51 B.C., a date which fails to square with a statement in the *Life* of
Virgil ascribed to Donatus (but generally thought to be based on
Suetonius' *De uiris illustribus*) that he died in the year in which Virgil,
aged 17, assumed the *toga uirilis*, i.e. 53 B.C. These and other incon-
sistencies make secure dating impossible: for the reader of the *D.R.N.*
it is enough to know that the poet was born in the 90s and died, a
comparatively young man, in the late 50s of the first century B.C.[2] A
more intractable problem is posed by St Jerome's account of the love-
philtre and the poet's madness and suicide. Few scholars have either
accepted or rejected this tradition outright,[3] and even those who are
disinclined to trust the unsupported word of a Christian saint in such
a matter as the obviously edifying death of a pagan and a blasphemer
are inclined to allow that some features of the *D.R.N.* are consistent
with what St Jerome tells us. Both Santayana and Bailey use the
phrase 'strange vehemence' of Lucretius' manner in certain passages,

anxiety (1965) 100 n. 1. Lucretius' purpose was to declare the true Messiah:
Epicurus.
   [1] See the fundamental essay of H. F. Cherniss, 'The biographical fashion
in literary criticism', *Univ. Cal. Publ. Class. Philol.* 12 (1943) 279–92,
reprinted in *Critical essays on Roman literature: Elegy and Lyric*, ed. J. P.
Sullivan (1962).
   [2] For a fuller discussion see Bailey 3–5; his favourable assessment of the
Vita Borgiana should be discounted. There is no evidence as to Lucretius'
birthplace. If, as seems not improbable, it was Rome, he is one of the very
few Latin poets or men of letters not to hail from the provinces: cf. Watts,
G. & R. n.s. 18 (1971).
   [3] See Bailey 8–12; Boyancé 18. On some of the weaknesses of the case
against St Jerome's veracity see Gain, 'The life and death of Lucretius',
Latomus 27 (1969) 545–53.

and Bailey sees evidence of actual derangement in the famous excursus in Book v on the use of animals in warfare (1308–49). This line of argument, however, would hardly have been started if St Jerome's statement had not given a lead, and should be regarded with great caution.[1] The 'vehemence' remarked by Santayana and Bailey is real enough, but vehemence does not necessarily connote derangement; and in the *D.R.N.* it is, so far from being 'strange', an essential feature of the diatribe style (see §4(*a*) below), as also of the poet's emotional involvement in the terrible history of his country (Comm. 48–86n.). Nor is the 'high melancholy' of which Santayana speaks evident to all readers of the poem who approach it without preconceptions of the poet's manner. It is just over a century since M. Patin in his *Études sur la poésie latine* (1868) launched the theory of 'l'Antilucrèce dans Lucrèce': the idea that Lucretius is fundamentally unconvinced by what he is saying and that a deep native pessimism is constantly breaking through the doctrinaire optimism that he is committed to preaching. This theory is by no means universally discarded and still colours some assessments of Lucretius; it is based in the main on the interpretation of selected passages taken out of their context in the argument of the poem.[2]

A second problem is raised by St Jerome's reference to Cicero. It must be read together with a well-known passage in Cicero's letters to his brother Quintus, written in February of 54 B.C.: *Lucreti poemata, ut scribis, ita sunt, multis luminibus ingeni, multae tamen artis (ad Q.F.* 2. 10 (9). 3). The stylistic judgement implied in this sentence is discussed below (§4(*b*)); it is very difficult to deduce from it any reliable chronological or biographical data. It need not imply that Lucretius was dead when the words were written,[3] and it certainly implies nothing

---

[1] This is not the place to expatiate on 5. 1308–49; it is enough to say that the verses, if read carefully in their context, offer no foundation whatever for any suspicions as to the poet's sanity. McKay (*A.J.P.* 85 (1964) 124–35) is right to suggest (125) that the vivid descriptions are based on Lucretius' experience of *uenationes*; but his attempt (134) to fit the passage into the argument rests on a misunderstanding of the (very carefully written) sequence 5. 1341–9. See now Schrijvers 296–305.

[2] See the useful discussion by Kinsey, 'The melancholy of Lucretius', *Arion* 3. 2 (1964) 115–30; and cf. E. de Saint Denis, 'Lucrèce, poète de l'infini', *L'inf. litt.* 15 (1963) 17–24; Wormell, *G. & R.* n.s. 7 (1960) 54–65.

[3] See Bailey 4, repeating the important arguments of Sandbach, *C.R.* 54 (1940) 72–7.

about any editorial activity on the part of either Cicero or his brother. The *D.R.N.* was clearly left in an unfinished state at the poet's death (§3 below); but the ancient practice was always to allow incomplete but publishable work to appear with the barest minimum of correction.[1] The term *emendo* was no doubt used by St Jerome, who was well acquainted with the details of book production, in its technical sense, which signified something not much more ambitious than proof-correcting in modern times: it amounted to little more than the elimination of copying errors. Some such process would have had to be carried out by the person, whoever he was, who 'published' the *D.R.N.* after the poet's death, but it is unlikely to have entailed anything that a literate slave could not have managed; and in view of Cicero's outspoken contempt for Epicureanism it seems inherently unlikely that he would have been willing to spend his own time performing the operation.[2] In any event it is hazardous to use these two notices as evidence for the character of the relationship between Cicero and Lucretius; they could hardly have been oblivious of each other's existence,[3] but more than that one may hardly say.

The poem itself, as one might expect, offers no direct and very little indirect information about the poet. It is dedicated to a certain Memmius who, whether or not he is identical with the well-known Gaius Memmius,[4] was certainly an aristocrat, as is shown by the terms in which he is addressed: 1. 26 *Memmiadae nostro*, 42 *Memmi clara propago*. This fact does not of course entail that the poet was Memmius' social equal. On the other hand the *D.R.N.* is obviously the work of a well-educated man, widely read in the literatures of both Greece and Rome, a 'lord of language', who used Latin masterfully and as to the manner born, and who spoke as a Roman to Romans. None of this proves anything about Lucretius' birth or social status, but a

[1] The Virgilian half-lines are a striking example: see *Vit. Donat.* 41 *edidit...Varius, sed summatim emendata, ut qui uersus etiam inperfectos sicut erant reliquerit.*

[2] It has been suggested (Giussani xvi) that Cicero accepted nominal responsibility but entrusted the actual work to a secretary or to one of the staff of copyists maintained by his friend Atticus. Why however should he have felt obliged to become involved at all?

[3] Cicero was not above borrowing a striking phrase from Lucretius: see Comm. 993 n.

[4] See Catull. 10. 13 and Fordyce's note.

comparison with the manner of Horace tempts one to guess that the authority with which Lucretius addressed his fellow-countrymen was rooted in something more than confidence in his role of philosopher-poet. His repeated insistence on the hazards of ambition, though a central feature of Epicurean doctrine, takes on added significance when viewed against the contemporary background of civil strife. These read as the sentiments, not of a detached observer out of the *sapientum templa serena* (2. 8), but of a man who had witnessed and indeed been a party to the demoralization of a class in whose fate he was deeply interested. The agonies he describes sound like those of his own friends and kindred.[1]

3. THE POEM

(a) SCOPE

It is important to grasp at the outset the fact, already stressed, that the *D.R.N.* does not set out to present a complete account of the Epicurean system. Lucretius' ultimate aim is positive, to put his readers in the way of achieving happiness: this is acknowledged, not, one feels, without a hint of irony – for such certainties were not for the poet of the *Aeneid* – in Virgil's famous apostrophe.[2] His immediate aim, however, is negative: to destroy the barriers that obstruct man's path to self-fulfilment, the illusions that stand between him and enlightenment – fear of the gods, fear of the afterlife, fear of death. In order for these illusions to be destroyed they must be shown to be inconsistent with a correct understanding of the physical universe (cf. Comm. 40 n.). Thus the physical doctrines, though they are fundamental and though the exposition of them occupies most of the poem, are in the design of Lucretius' great enterprise functionally subservient to its main end: the scientific argument provides the premiss for the destructive argument which in turn provides the premiss for the final positive ethical conclusions – the statements about how men ought to live. But those final conclusions are not drawn, the statements are not made: the last link in the chain of

---

[1] Cf. Sellar 290–91; Hadzits 5 (drawing attention to 1. 41, 5. 36); Martha 25–9.

[2] *G.* 2. 490–92 *felix qui potuit rerum cognoscere causas | atque metus omnis et inexorabile fatum | subiecit pedibus strepitumque Acherontis auari.*

argument Lucretius takes as read or leaves for others to provide. Thus, though the argument often takes a particular Epicurean ethical position for granted, there is very little in the poem that may be called ethical doctrine.[1] This great omission has of course excited remark. It has been suggested that these limitations reflect a personal limitation of interest in Epicurean philosophy, which Lucretius saw less as a way of life than as the means to an end which was not precisely the end envisaged by the founder.[2] That the stimulus to write the *D.R.N.* was personal and deeply felt is extremely probable, indeed is the overwhelming impression that the poem makes on the great majority of readers; but it does not follow that Lucretius was not interested in the parts of the system which he does not choose to develop. It is important to emphasize that the *D.R.N.* is a poem, for the fact carries certain implications. It belonged of necessity, according to ancient ways of thinking about literature, to a specific genre (εἶδος, γένος, *genus*), that of the didactic epos (see §4(*a*) below), and that tradition, as represented in particular by Parmenides and Empedocles (to whom Lucretius was obviously indebted), did not offer a model for the exposition of ethical doctrine. Hesiod, who stood at the head of the whole tradition, has something to say in the *Works and Days* about Justice and of the rules which should govern the behaviour of men to the gods and to each other, but what he says is couched in the primitive style of 'wisdom-literature', not as systematic and constructive exposition. Is a metrical account of Epicurean ethics (which were fundamentally very simple) imaginable?[3] Poetry, especially poetry such as Lucretius', cannot thrive upon an unmixed diet of abstractions; it must have its roots in and be nourished by bodily images and concrete associations. On the other hand, the Epicurean cosmos,

---

[1] Thus in the *D.R.N.* the traditional subordination of Canonics (as the Epicureans called rational philosophy) and Physics (natural philosophy) to Ethics (moral philosophy) is reversed: cf. Hadzits 11. On the other hand, as is shown by (e.g.) the famous description of the sacrifice of Iphigenia (1. 80–101), Lucretius' objections to religion were moral, as were those of James Mill and indeed of all reflective unbelievers. Cf. R. Robinson, *An atheist's values* (1964) 130.

[2] So Boyancé 301: 'Lucrèce n'a adhéré à l'épicurisme que parce qu'il y a découvert l'explication d'un mal dont l'importance ne pouvait lui apparaître que parce que lui-même il en souffrait.'

[3] Lucilius' well-known fragment on Virtue (1326–38 M.) is as dull as ditchwater; and no writer is in general more lively and pungent.

machina mundi, a complex but wholly material organization, provided a theme for which models already existed in the tradition and which was calculated to call forth the full force of Lucretius' unique creative powers. Moreover, it offered a great technical challenge. The importance of this point is apt to be overlooked by a modern reader; but ancient poets were from first to last preoccupied with technique, and Lucretius, though he should certainly not be pigeonholed *tout court* as a New Poet, was fully aware of the requirements of Alexandrian *doctrina* and all that they implied.[1] The scope of the *D.R.N.* must be seen as conditioned by the tradition in which it was written: Lucretius' predecessors in that tradition – Hesiod, Parmenides, Empedocles – offered both models for didactic poetry of a certain kind, the exposition of complex cosmogonical and physical theory, and also an incentive to demonstrate superiority in this kind of writing. The Epicurean system itself, with its emphasis on phenomena and the evidence of the senses, afforded a splendid stimulus to Lucretius' superb powers of observation and description, both of what he could see and of what he could not see but could visualize – the minute but all-potent motions of the atoms. Generic influences can be seen at work also in another profoundly important characteristic of the poem, its satire, the roots of which we may trace as far back as Hesiod. 'We may see in the underlying moral earnestness [of Hesiod] the origins of a *mood* which pervaded the later masterpieces of didactic poetry and was perhaps an essential element in their success as works of art: for poetry seems most easily to combine with a didactic purpose when teaching rises to *preaching*.'[2] This potentiality for satire that was latent in the didactic and philosophical tradition had been exploited by Xenophanes, who was celebrated for the biting expression of his contempt for the views of his fellow-men, and by Democritus, known throughout antiquity as the Laughing Philosopher. Yet it was, it seems, Lucretius who first harnessed the power of satire and applied it to the systematic exposure of error, folly and superstition. The manner in which he did so will be discussed below ($\S4(a)$); at present it is sufficient to establish the point that the limitations in scope and intention of the *D.R.N.* were designed by the poet, for the best, and that viewed in the light of the tradition in which Lucretius found himself called to work they

[1] See Kenney 369–72.
[2] Cox 126.

make sense.[1] They are not necessarily to be taken, as they sometimes are, as the index of a deficiency in Lucretius.

(*b*) STRUCTURE

Though on close investigation a good many complexities can be detected the structure of the *D.R.N.* in its broad outlines is simple:

The atoms ⎰ I The atoms and the void; rival theories refuted
⎰ II The properties of atoms; their secondary qualities in combination

The soul ⎰ III The soul is proved to be mortal
⎰ IV Thought and sensation

The world ⎰ V The creation and history of the world
⎰ VI Celestial and terrestrial phenomena

Various correspondences, thematic and formal, underline this symmetry.[2] The outermost pairs of books, I–II and V–VI, are linked in so far as they demonstrate that all phenomena must be explained in material terms and that no intervention of divine or supernatural agencies may be postulated; hence these four books may be seen as directed, ultimately, against the fear of the gods. This identity of purpose is explicitly recognized by the statement, repeated at the beginning of each book, that in the Epicurean universe gods are not needed.[3] Books I and V, the first of their pairs, are further linked by repetition of the *leitmotiv* I. 76–7 = 5. 89–90,[4] with which may be compared the often-remarked correspondences in Virgil's *Aeneid* between the beginnings of Books I and VII. This type of responsion was a

[1] A qualification, however, may be admitted. These self-imposed limitations go some way to explain why the poem had more influence on the history of Latin poetry than on the history of philosophy. See Crawley, esp. 17–18.

[2] For further discussion of structure see Bailey 31–7; Boyancé 69–83; and the articles of Minadeo and Owen. The details of these and other schemata are open to question, but there can be no quarrelling with the general conclusion, that Lucretius planned and executed the poem with immense care. That he cannot therefore have been insane of course does not follow: Leonard 14–15.

[3] 1. 146–58, 2. 167–81, 5. 76–90, 6. 50–79.

[4] Cf. also 1. 80 *ne forte rearis* ∼ 5. 78 *ne forte...reamur.*

standard device to articulate long poems. Within this framework the two central books III–IV are directed against fear of the afterlife; and once again the point is emphasized by correspondences at the beginning of each book.[1] Symmetrical disposition of this kind about a centre is 'natural' in the sense that it seems to suggest itself spontaneously in architecture and the visual arts, but in large-scale works of literature it can be achieved only through careful planning and execution. Other literary examples show that the principle of 'centrality' was deliberately cultivated.[2] Together with this static pattern of arrangement the poem exhibits a dynamic movement: in Books I and II the foundations are laid for the questions that are explored in Books III–IV, V–VI. Moreover the reappearances of Epicurus, progressively presented as man (1. 66), father (3. 9) and god (5. 8), imply an articulation in three pairs of books and, connected with this articulation, a crescendo in the development of the poem.[3] This combination of symmetry and movement is characteristic of much Latin poetry.[4]

That the *D.R.N.* had not received its final revision at the poet's death is proved unequivocally by 5. 155, where Lucretius promises to treat fully of the nature of the gods. That promise is nowhere redeemed. Many other passages have also been used as evidence for this question, but there is considerable disagreement between interpreters and a growing disposition among recent critics to accept that certain repetitions may have been deliberate and were not inserted merely as stopgaps. Occasionally passages have been condemned as incomplete or misplaced through misunderstanding of the argument (Comm. 607–14n.). However, when all allowances of this kind are made, enough difficulties remain to support the view that, had he lived to complete his design, Lucretius would have altered the version of his poem that has come down to us substantially though not radically.[5]

---

[1] 3. 31–40 ~ 4. 26–44.

[2] Moritz, 'Some "central" thoughts on Horace's *Odes*', *C.Q.* N.S. 18 (1968) 116–31; G. Williams, *Tradition and originality in Roman poetry* (1968) 233–9.

[3] Cox 135; cf. Wormell (*ap.* Dudley) 43.

[4] See W. A. Camps, *An introduction to Virgil's Aeneid* (1969), ch. VI 'Principles of structure; continuity and symmetry'.

[5] See Comm. at (e.g.) 620–21, 806–18nn.; and cf. Boyancé 79–83.

4. THE POETRY

(a) THE TWO TRADITIONS AND THE TWO STYLES

Ancient writers, critics and readers were, as has already been indicated, used to thinking of literature in terms of established 'kinds' or types (εἴδη, γένη, *genera*: hence 'genre'). The *D.R.N.* belonged formally to the genre of didactic epos, a 'high' and 'literary' genre. Epicurus was notoriously hostile to poetry, holding that the truth should be communicated in plain words (Comm. 133–4n.); hence Lucretius' choice of the poetical medium for his message has occasioned much comment and speculation.[1] It entailed not only the rejection of an Epicurean position, but a positive commitment: acceptance of the standards appropriate to the chosen genre and the continuance – not interpreted as slavish dependence – of the tradition established by the poet's predecessors. These predecessors fall into three groups: (1) Hesiod; (2) the philosophical poets, notably Parmenides and Empedocles; (3) Hellenistic didactic poets, above all Aratus. Lucretius' most obvious debt might seem to be to Empedocles' Περὶ Φύσεως (On Nature), and Empedocles is in fact eulogized at 1. 716–33. However in literary terms the influence of Hesiod and the Hellenistic poets is scarcely less important. This is less a matter of specific indebtedness in this or that detail[2] than of the poet's self-consciousness vis-à-vis his art and of his expressed sense of personal involvement. Such self-consciousness is a peculiarly Hellenistic trait, which manifests itself in such well-known passages as the Prologue to Callimachus' *Aetia*; but it derives ultimately from Hesiod. Lucretius' awareness of and participation in this and other aspects of the literary tradition can be seen in such passages as 1. 926–50, which have been discussed elsewhere.[3] For the present purpose it is enough to emphasize that the *D.R.N.* is a poem in the fullest sense: a literary production belonging in a literary tradition and written in complete awareness of the laws and conventions shaping the tradition. It appears, to judge at all events from the silence of our sources, that Lucretius was, so far as his philosophy went, a lone wolf: that is to say, he seems to have had no

[1] See Waszink, 'Lucretius and poetry', *Med. d. Konink. Ned. Akad.* N.S. 17 (1954) 243–57; Boyancé 57–68; and the articles of Classen and Amory.

[2] Among the numerous translations of Aratus' *Phaenomena* was one by Cicero, with which Lucretius seems to have been acquainted: Bailey 29–30.

[3] Kenney 369–71.

contact with contemporary Epicureanism,[1] of which he may indeed have disapproved. This isolation has no counterpart in the literary sphere: Lucretius did not live or write in a cultural vacuum, and his poem, because it is supremely original, is not therefore to be regarded as an oddity, a kind of literary 'sport'.

Another extremely potent influence, however, must be reckoned with; and it is precisely the combination of this second, subliterary (as it may be called), tradition with the main literary tradition of didactic epos that explains the peculiar character of the *D.R.N.* By this brilliant combinatory stroke Lucretius not only produced a profoundly original poem; he also laid the foundations of a tradition of satirical writing that has flourished down to modern times. One of the most striking features of the *D.R.N.* is the discrepancy in tone and emotional impact between the scientific, or expository, and the non-expository passages. As has already been remarked, Epicurean physics provided the premisses for Lucretius' views about the relationship of man to his environment, the universe, and to other men; and this fundamental role dictates that the exposition of the system should occupy a large part of the poem.[2] But these premisses were subordinate to the conclusions which could be drawn from them, and it is when Lucretius confronts his readers with these great conclusions that the poem reaches its highest poetical and emotional levels. Nowhere is this better exemplified than in Book III: the elaborate exposition of the *animus* and *anima* that takes up most of the book is shown by the *igitur* of v. 830 (see §5(*a*) below) to have been preliminary to the real message, that death is not to be feared and that there is no life, and no punishment, after death. Thus it is not entirely appropriate to style passages of the non-expository type 'digressions' or 'excursuses'.[3] Neither type of passage is meaningful without the other; they are complementary to each other in the grand strategy of the poem, and in both the poet is in full control of his aims and of the means which he has chosen to achieve those aims.

The fundamental characteristic that distinguishes the non-ex-

---

[1] Boyancé 12; Crawley 11–12.

[2] It is clear, however, that the physics had fired his imagination and that he saw in this part of the doctrine much more than inevitable but somewhat tedious preliminaries: cf. Festugière 52–3; Amory 167–8.

[3] Sellar 322; Cox 134, also styling them 'calculated *intrusions*'.

pository passages is their emotional effect, what ancient rhetoricians and critics called πάθος or τὸ παθητικόν. In contrast the expository passages, though occasionally enlivened by flashes of sarcastic wit at the expense of a rival viewpoint or by an odd stroke of satire, are for the most part rationally and logically argumentative; they are not devoid of emotion, but emotion is not the main driving force. These stylistic differences reflect a difference of ends: for rational persuasion a low-keyed style is suitable, for emotional conviction a highly-charged style. The distinction was a basic one in ancient rhetorical theory, as expressed in the doctrine of the three styles of speaking, *genera dicendi*: a low, a middle, and a high, corresponding with the three chief aims of the orator, to instruct, to please, and to play on the emotions of his audience – *docere, delectare, mouere*.[1] In practice the so-called 'middle' or 'florid' style is of little importance: between two extremes it is pedantry to select any one intermediate position as more significant than the others, and it was the two extremes that provided the real points of reference. These were the *genus tenue*, the 'slender' style suited to explanation and information; and the *genus grande* (*amplum, acre*), the grand style by which the hearer is swept off his feet and *compelled* to feel with the orator (or poet) by the sheer force and weight of the utterance. It was also standard doctrine that the accomplished speaker must be prepared to move from one stylistic level to another as his material required: *is est...eloquens, qui et humilia subtiliter et alta grauiter et mediocria temperate potest dicere* (Cic. *Or.* 100). Such a differentiation is exemplified even in the Elder Pliny's *Natural History*, where the moralizing excursuses (as Pliny's truly are) are consistently written in a much more elaborate and 'literary' Latin than the body of the work.[2] It is exemplified much more subtly, as might be expected, in the *Georgics*: the bulk of the poem, as with the *D.R.N.*, is taken up by what purports to be technical instruction, but the full range of Virgil's poetical resources is reserved for the 'excursuses' in which, in fact, the real message of the poem, which is

[1] See, for instance, *M. Tulli Ciceronis Brutus*, ed. A. E. Douglas (1966) xxxiv–xxxv; '*Longinus' on the Sublime*, ed. D. A. Russell (1964) xxxiv–xxxvii.

[2] A good example is *N.H.* 14. 1, where the subject of trees leads into a representative specimen of the *locus communis de diuitiis*. On the combination of 'demonstration' and 'exhortation' in prose treatises cf. A. Michel, *Le 'Dialogue des Orateurs' de Tacite et la philosophie de Cicéron*, Ét. et Comm. 44 (1962) 19.

only formally about agriculture, is enshrined. In Virgil the distinction between the two types of passage is still perceptible, but much less sharply defined than in either Pliny or Lucretius.[1]

Among the means employed by Lucretius to convey his message satire figures prominently, and the point has not gone unremarked.[2] What however has not been adequately assessed is the part that his poem played in the foundation of the Roman satirical tradition, particularly by the incorporation in it of so many of the characteristics of the diatribe. In an often-quoted passage (1. 935–50 = 4. 10–25) Lucretius compares the poetry in which his message is conveyed to the honey which is smeared on a cup of bitter medicine to induce a child to drink it. This type of homely comparison, which goes back at least to Plato's *Laws* (659e), is also used by Horace (*Sat.* 1. 1. 25–6). Though Lucretius wrote for cultivated readers, who must be prepared to take a good deal of trouble if they are to follow him, yet his approach, on its higher level, is the same as that of more popular philosophers, in that it too relies heavily on a certain sweetening of the pill – in his case the clothing of his message in poetry (for the 'honey' cannot be taken to refer to the non-expository or 'pathetic' passages alone). There is a closer relationship still with the popular tradition, however, which is seen in Lucretius' use of stylistic devices and techniques drawn from that tradition – in particular from the diatribe.

Diatribe, διατριβή, is defined by a writer on rhetoric as 'the expansion of a brief moral thought',[3] but in practice it approached the status of a subliterary genre, one of a number of such genres of a generally homiletic type. Its most famous exponent was one Bion of Borysthenes or Olbia (a Milesian colony on the Black Sea), who lived from about 325 to 255 B.C. Most of what is known about him is to be found in Book IV of Diogenes Laertius' *Lives of the philosophers* and in the few surviving fragments of his diatribes which are embedded in the work of a later writer in the same field, Teles.[4] Bion's

---

[1] Cf. L. P. Wilkinson, *The Georgics of Virgil* (1969) 183.

[2] Dudley, 'The satiric element in Lucretius', *ap.* Dudley 115–30; Murley, 'Lucretius and the history of Satire', *T.A.P.A.* 70 (1939) 380–95; Waltz, 'Lucrèce satirique', *Lettres d'humanité* 8 (1949) 78–103.

[3] Hermogenes, *Meth.* 5, p. 418 R. βραχέος διανοήματος ἠθικοῦ ἔκτασις.

[4] See Hense; a good many isolated *dicta* attributed to Bion are found in Stobaeus. For further specimens of the genre see the texts edited in *Mus. Helv.* 16 (1959) 77–142.

status as what might be called the poor man's Socrates is well illustrated by the remark attributed to Eratosthenes that he was the
first to dress philosophy in brightly-coloured clothes:[1] that is to say,
he used all the resources of contemporary rhetoric to make philosophy
palatable to the common man.[2] He was not a philosopher as Plato or
Zeno or Epicurus were philosophers; in so far as he belonged to any
school he was a Cynic, but there was no exclusiveness in his doctrines.
He was a travelling lecturer, a communicator rather than an origi-
nator, the C. E. M. Joad of his day; his philosophy aimed at helping
the man in the street and 'treats of ordinary human problems in a
common-sense spirit'.[3] This entailed the constant use of rhetorical
and stylistic devices that were all designed to command and retain,
if necessary by shock tactics, the attention of audiences that were all
too vulnerable to any species of distraction. The style of the performance was semi-dramatic;[4] the interlocutor of the Platonic dialogues
survived in an attenuated form as an anonymous butt, whose objections, invariably futile, were prefaced merely by a φησί, 'he says',
and afforded opportunities for the speaker to display his wit and
sharpen his point. The argument was illustrated by striking images
drawn from the experience of the audience; the tone was hectoring,
relying more on pithy exhortation than on urbane persuasion; the
expression was vivid, pungent, sometimes obscene. Formal logic and
systematic arrangement were little regarded; the intention of these
sermons was to inculcate a few simple lessons of conduct in memorable terms, and the speaker concentrated on enlisting the sympathies
of his audience, so that it should appear as clear to them as it did to
him that those who did not agree with the point of view expressed

[1] D.L. 4. 52 πρῶτος Βίων τὴν φιλοσοφίαν ἀνθινὰ ἐνέδυσεν. On Socrates
cf. Cic. *Tusc.* 5. 10 *primus philosophiam deuocauit e caelo et in urbibus conlocauit
et in domus etiam introduxit et coegit de uita et moribus rebusque bonis et malis
quaerere.*

[2] For a sketch of Bion's life and work see D. R. Dudley, *A history of
Cynicism* (1937) 62–6.

[3] Dudley, op. cit. (preceding note) 65–6.

[4] The lecture as a dramatic performance, a thing not indeed unknown in
our own day, was highly relished throughout antiquity. Seneca (*Ep.* 108. 6)
complains that people came to philosophy lectures to be entertained rather
than instructed, and the substance of his complaint can be extensively
documented from other sources.

were fools – 'stultitiam arguit uulgi', as the Horatian scholiast put it.[1]

Though Bion's own sympathies were fundamentally Cynic, the diatribe was, as a vehicle for philosophy, non-sectarian: it was above all suited to attack, to the deflation of folly and the destruction of error. Horace, who refers (*Ep.* 2. 2. 60) to the 'talks and biting wit of Bion', *Bioneis sermonibus et sale nigro*, was clearly influenced by the diatribe, as Lucilius had been before him and as Seneca (a doctrinaire Stoic) was after him. The Christian sermon too was indebted to this popular homiletic tradition.[2] What was original to Lucretius was the marriage of these techniques with the high style that was mandatory for didactic epos so as to produce, in his 'pathetic' passages, a unique and individual fusion. The power of the satire which resulted from this union was clearly appreciated by Horace (Comm. 1068–9 n.), but it may be suggested that the most important outcome of this Lucretian amalgamation of genres was the foundation of a new school of satirical writing in the 'high' or 'tragic' vein. Horace, with his relatively gentle and urbane approach to satire, contented himself with limited borrowing of specific motifs; it was left for Juvenal to exploit to the full the possibilities of this new type of satirical poetry. To return to Lucretius himself, the point to be grasped is that he did not write satirically merely because his mind had a satirical bent which would not be denied and had to be given its head, even in a didactic poem; the satirical approach was suggested – indeed dictated – by the work in hand, the attack on folly, error and superstition. *Indignatio* – not 'indignation' but a refusal to acquiesce in popular illusion – is not peculiar to Juvenal (1. 79); it was precisely Lucretius' *indignatio* of what he had read and of what he saw and heard around him that motivated the writing of the *D.R.N.* in the first place.[3] If such very different writers as Horace and Seneca and Juvenal all

[1] Ps.-Acro *ad* Hor. *Ep.* 2. 2. 60. On the diatribe the standard work is still A. Oltramare, *Les origines de la diatribe romaine* (1926); it is unfortunately inadequate on Lucretius.

[2] Cf. E. Norden, *Die antike Kunstprosa*[5] (1958) 556, drawing attention to diatribe-characteristics in the Epistles of St Paul (1 Cor. 15. 35–6, Rom. 9. 19–20).

[3] A loose fashion of writing ascribes to Juvenal and indeed to Lucretius (e.g. Sikes 30; Leonard 28; Dudley 126) the *saeva indignatio* that rightly belongs to Jonathan Swift.

share certain satirical traits with Lucretius, the explanation is not to be sought merely in temperamental similarities, but is a matter of *generic* relationship: that is to say, all these writers had more or less the same end in view, all were to a greater or lesser extent indebted to the same tradition, and all adopted similar techniques belonging to that tradition to achieve their ends. It is only against this historical background that the originality of Lucretius can be clearly discerned.[1]

(b) LANGUAGE AND METRE

Cicero's comment (p. 7 above) means: 'what you say in your letter is quite right: Lucretius' poetry displays great originality, but also very careful workmanship.'[2] *tamen* emphasizes what Cicero recognized as a paradox, that Lucretius' work exemplified *both* original genius *and* literary craftsmanship. Conventional assessments tended to emphasize either the *ars* or the *ingenium* of a poet, yet here was one who displayed both; and Statius' reference to *docti furor arduus Lucreti* (*Silv.* 2. 7. 76) appears to echo the same judgement.[3] Any attempt to describe and evaluate Lucretius' poetry should begin by considering ends and means. Lucretius frequently insists on the idea of clarity (cf. Comm. 1 n.): at 1. 933–4 he contrasts the difficulty of his subject-matter with the lucidity of his verse: . . . *obscura de re tam lucida pango | carmina, musaeo contingens cuncta lepore.* This claim is on the whole justified: when all allowances have been made for numerous and often thorny problems of interpretation, the preponderant impression of Lucretius' style is of its simplicity and clarity. These characteristics were deliberately planned and achieved; they are the result of considered stylistic decisions which were then executed with extreme care.[4] The style which resulted is often labelled 'archaic'; and it is true that by comparison with Lucretius the didactic verse of his contemporary Cicero seems, technically speaking, slick and 'modern' –

---

[1] On the diatribe element in Lucretius see further, besides Oltramare (p. 19 n. 1), Vallette, 'Lucrèce et la diatribe', *R.É.A.* 42 (1940) 532–41, with particular reference to 3. 870 ff. More illustrations will be found in the Commentary.

[2] *luminibus ingeni* is usually rendered 'flashes of genius', but this cannot be right: *lumina* must refer to 'high lights' or 'brilliant passages' in the poem (cf. Sikes 38–9).

[3] Cf. Kenney 366–7.

[4] Cf. 3. 419 *conquisita diu dulcique reperta labore,* and see Comm. *ad loc.*

modern, moreover, in the sense that the Augustan poets appear to have followed the technical lead that Cicero offered.[1] But a comparison which takes only means into account and neglects ends is invalid. Cicero has in fact recorded, by implication, his view of how didactic poetry should be written in the *De Oratore*: *etenim si constat inter doctos hominem ignarum astrologiae ornatissimis atque optimis uersibus Aratum de caelo stellisque dixisse; si de rebus rusticis hominem ab agro remotissimum Nicandrum Colophonium poetica quadam facultate non rustica scripsisse praeclare: quid est cur non orator de rebus eis eloquentissime dicat, quas ad certam causam tempusque cognorit?*(1. 69). Crassus, of whose speech this forms part, goes on to say in so many words that poet and orator have the same ends in view and, *mutatis mutandis*, employ the same means: *est enim finitimus oratori poeta*. That the poet, like the orator, seeks to convince Lucretius must have accepted; but the other implications of Cicero's argument he would have rejected with contempt. The notion that a poet can and should be prepared to transmute any material whatsoever into polite literature belongs to a different and less noble conception of life and poetry than Lucretius'. It would have been technically feasible for him to sacrifice clarity to elegance of a Hellenistic sort, much as Cicero did himself in his didactic poetry. Such a sacrifice would have entailed some loss of force, but that was not the main reason for not making it. Lucretius would not and could not compromise: his mission was too important. What was at stake was nothing more nor less than personal salvation, and nothing could be suffered to impair the clarity of the message; there must be no room for misunderstanding. If, after reading the *D.R.N.*, a man declined to be saved, it should not be said that it was because the call to salvation had been obscure. Thus, when Bailey writes (117) that 'his rhythm is to a great extent dictated by his vocabulary', this perfectly true remark is not to be interpreted as an adverse criticism. This 'dictation' was something willed by the poet in the interests of clarity – of that σαφήνεια which we are told Epicurus so much prized (D.L. 10. 13).[2] He was in fact by no means a helpless victim of that *patrii sermonis egestas* of which he complains (1. 892; 3. 260: see n.): for it is often

---

[1] See the most recent discussion, with immense wealth of statistical detail, by G. E. Duckworth, *Vergil and classical hexameter poetry* (1969) 43.

[2] This is a different matter from being 'forced' (Smith 159) to use this or that form.

overlooked that these complaints are made in the context of specific technical problems and are not symptomatic of a general inability to cope with the linguistic difficulties of his undertaking.

We must, then, be on our guard against what has been well described as the 'heresy...of characterizing and estimating an author too much in terms of his predecessors and, worse still, his successors, and too little in terms of his own objectives and his chosen methods'.[1] If Lucretius' style, compared with that of Cicero, seems 'archaic', that is no more than a summary and somewhat misleading way of saying that he adhered to certain usages and forms which were already being discarded in his own day because by doing so he was able to communicate what he had to say more directly and forcibly.[2] A well-known example is the practice of eliding final -s after a short vowel and before a consonant (cf. Comm. 52n.): this usage, described by Cicero (*Or.* 161) as 'countrified', *subrusticum*, occurs in Cicero's own earlier poetry but is discarded in his later work.[3] Similarly, to avoid circumlocution and paraphrase, Lucretius allowed himself an amount of morphological variation which to Augustan taste would have seemed excessive: thus in four verses (4. 491–4) he uses three different forms of the adverb *sorsum*, 'separately', obviously for metrical convenience.[4] The same considerations dictated his use of (for example) the archaic termination *-ai* for *-ae* (Comm. 83n.) Again, in the matter of repetition, Lucretius' practice was dictated partly by his

---

[1] Maguinness *ap.* Dudley 71.

[2] '...historically speaking there is no such thing as archaic literature; only archaistic literature, that is, writings which are self-consciously old-fashioned at the time of composition' (J. C. Bramble, *Farrago* (Journal of Cambridge University Classical Society) no. 5 (1969) 3–4). See also Bramble's excellent remarks on the pernicious influence of metaphors of growth, maturity and senility; of ascent to and descent from a pinnacle; of cycles and ages of bronze, gold and silver. In the Commentary 'archaic' is employed as a descriptive term for the sake of convenience; it does not connote a stylistic judgement.

[3] This point does not emerge clearly from Bailey's discussion: see W. W. Ewbank, *The poems of Cicero* (1933) 70–71.

[4] *sorsum* (– –), admissible in several places of the verse; *seorsum* (∪ – –), fitting at the end; *sorsus* (– ∪), fitting in the antepenultimate place. Cf. Smith 140–57, 159–66. Even among the Augustans there is variance in such things from poet to poet: Virgil, for instance, is more restrained than Ovid, who permits himself the variant forms *eburnus* and *eburneus* in consecutive verses (*Met.* 10. 275–6). Cf. Comm. 798n. and Index s.v. 'Variation'.

desire for clarity, but also by the need for emphasis.[1] We must accordingly beware of setting up an arbitrary norm and labelling deviations
from it as either 'archaic' or 'decadent': each poet must to some
extent be allowed to be a law unto himself. That Lucretius was technically capable when he wished of writing verse that is 'correct' by
Ciceronian or Augustan standards is shown by the observation that
in, for example, his famous description of the Sacrifice of Iphigenia
(1. 80–101), one of the most impassioned pieces of writing in the
entire poem, there is not a single 'irregular' verse-ending. Bailey's
remark, quoted above, applies predominantly to the expository parts
of the poem, where the combination of technical subject-matter and the
need for clarity exercised a limiting influence. In the non-expository
passages Lucretius could and did allow his genius a freer rein.
It is in the light of these considerations that the indispensable cata-
logues of Lucretian usage compiled by modern investigators must be
studied and evaluated.[2] The freedom with which Lucretius handled
the Latin language and the great flexibility of choice which he allowed
himself went too far for Augustan tastes, which emphasized above all
balance, restraint and moderation.[3] Yet without Lucretius Augustan
poetry could not have been what it was. From the immense
range of possibilities that he opened up his successors chose at will;
above all Ovid, who of all Roman poets alone approached and
at times surpassed Lucretius in his experimental attitude to
language.[4]

The fundamental stylistic problem in Latin hexameter poetry concerns the relationship between the metrical unit, the hexameter verse,
and the units of discourse – phrase, clause, sentence and period. No
Latin poet holds the balance with more perfect mastery than Virgil,
and the history of the Latin hexameter during the first century B.C.

[1] Cf. Maguinness *ap.* Dudley 73–5. In the matter of repetitions the practice
of poets of all periods differs very widely: see the bibliography at *C.Q.* N.S. 9
(1959) 248 n. 1 (add B. L. Gildersleeve, *Brief Mention* (1930) 161; *Euripides
Phaethon* ed. J. Diggle (1970) 91–2).

[2] Bailey 72–171; Smith 129–86; and the works listed by Boyancé
345–6.

[3] Well documented by F. Cupaiuolo, *Tra poesia e poetica* (1966); and by
Williams, op. cit. (p. 13 n. 2).

[4] A single instance will make the point, that of Ovid's use of noun-
formations in *-men* and *-tus*; cf. Bailey 134–5.

may profitably be studied in terms of the evolution of a verse 'period'
analogous to the period of artistic prose. However, such a study should
not be conducted on deterministic premisses. Lucretius' treatment of
the problem is not necessarily inferior because it is different from
Virgil's. For him, in general, the individual verse and its main sub-
divisions coincide with and indeed constitute the units and the
sub-units of discourse. This generalization is more consistently true of
the expository than of the 'pathetic' parts of the *D.R.N.*; in the latter
enjambment, the carrying over of sense and construction from one verse
to the next, is considerably more frequent.[1] Moreover, within the verse
(more particularly in the expository passages) Lucretius is in general
much less preoccupied than Virgil or even Cicero with that balancing
of complementary elements, such as the halves of adjective–noun
phrases, that distinguishes the developed Augustan hexameter.[2]
This sort of arrangement of the elements of the utterance has more than
formal value: it produces a feeling of suspense, a creation of expectancy
in which the reader is induced to look forward to the syntactical and
semantic dénouement of phrase, clause or sentence. The result is what
we may call 'tension' in the writing. The principle is one that holds
good in developed Latin prose writing, particularly that of Cicero.[3]
It is a technique that is essentially emotional – hence the Ciceronian
employment of it in oratory – but it does not necessarily assist, and
may actually obscure, intellectual comprehension. To the orderly
progress of the difficult argument that Lucretius was faced with con-
ducting, this sort of device, employed as we meet it in Cicero or Virgil
or Ovid, would have constituted an impediment. In the interests of
his all-dominant desire for clarity he rejected this style of writing:
in the expository passages the movement of the utterance is essentially

[1] See Bailey 120–23, summarizing the important work of K. Büchner,
Beobachtungen über Vers und Gedankengang bei Lukrez (Hermes Einzelschr. 1,
1936); but see also the weighty criticisms of W. Schmid, *Gnomon* 20 (1944)
5–10.

[2] Conveniently illustrated by Pearce 162–6: thus verses of the type
'*sensifer* unde oritur primum per uiscera *motus*' (3. 272), with its variations,
are much fewer in Lucretius (about one in 225) than in Cicero's *Phaenomena*
(about one in 34) or in Catullus 64 (about one in 15). Cf. also Maguinness
ap. Dudley 77–8.

[3] An excellent example in the first sentence of the *De Oratore*, where the
role of the 'enclosing' technique in engendering expectation is very clearly
demonstrated.

'linear', as we may call it,[1] accommodating itself closely to the ends of the verses and to their main caesural divisions. This technique, taken together with the repetitions which Lucretius employs to drive home his points, as Sinker remarks (xxx), 'intensifies the cumulative effect of the arguments that he advances'. Criticism of style must spring from an understanding of ends. The 'unperiodic' style of Lucretius is not to be appraised as 'archaic' or undeveloped in comparison with Virgil's: the two poets were attempting very different things.

In its simplest form the Lucretian style of writing follows the structure of the verse extremely closely: thus 6. 356 *dissoluunt nodos omnis* || *et uincla relaxant,* or 4. 556 *seruat enim formaturam* || *seruatque figuram.* But even in cases such as these the apparent simplicity may be deceptive. In the first instance there is chiasmus; and since *omnis,* though in grammatical agreement with *nodos,* also modifies *uincla* in sense (ἀπὸ κοινοῦ construction), there is in fact a stricter symmetry than at first appears:

dissoluunt nodos || omnis || et uincla relaxant.

This is not unsophisticated writing. In the second case the anaphora *seruat...seruatque* is effective, and the effect, as often in Lucretius, is reinforced by alliteration and assonance. The technique of 'theme and variation', particularly associated with Virgil,[2] was familiar to Lucretius: so at 5. 980–1 ...*nec diffidere ne terras aeterna teneret* | *nox in perpetuum detracto lumine solis.* Here it will be seen that enjambment is discreetly used to diversify, as also at (for example) 3. 136–9:

nunc animum atque animam || dico coniuncta teneri
inter se || atque unam naturam conficere ex se,
sed caput esse quasi || et dominari in corpore toto
consilium || quod nos || animum mentemque uocamus.

[1] The distinction is made by Postgate in a stimulating paper, 'Flaws in classical research', *Proc. Brit. Acad.* 3 (1908) 161–211. His dictum that 'the modern sentence, to put it roughly, is an arrangement in line, the ancient one within a circle' (167) must be understood as referring principally to certain kinds of poetry and artistic prose; it is not true, as the discussion in the text indicates, of Lucretius.

[2] See J. Henry, *Aeneidea* 1 (1873) 206–7, 745–51; it should be noted that Henry neither states nor implies that the technique was invented by Virgil, indeed he emphasizes that it is 'almost inseparable from poetry' and is equally at home in prose (745–6, 750).

The tendency to adjust the utterance to fill the verse is most clearly seen in duplicated phrases of the type *seiungi seque gregari* (1. 452) or *disiectis disque sipatis* (1. 651); but even in these phrases there is a significant amplification of the sense.[1]

The point that it is sought to make may emerge more clearly from a comparative analysis of two passages from Book III:

(i) *Expository style: 323–49*

In this 'paragraph' Lucretius demonstrates the indissoluble connexion of body and soul, and the stylistic texture must be seen as reflecting the movement of the argument. **323–4** Statement of thesis: theme (323) + variation, in the form of a statement of its converse (324: *est custos = tenet ~ 323 tenetur*). The syntax of 323 is 'linear' in the sense that it follows a simple order of subject – verb – adverbial phrase; and the structure of the variation is also simple (pair of nouns + dependent genitives), but the order is artful: emphatic *ipsa* beginning the verse and the twin phrases arranged chiastically, with the effect reinforced by alliteration. **325–6** First corroboration of thesis: positive theme (325) + negative variation (326). **327–30** Illustration: divided equally into 'protasis' (327–8) and 'apodosis' (329–30), each constructed in parallel fashion with substantized infinitive as subject + *quin*-clause. Monotony is avoided by a slight variation: whereas the subject phrase and predicate of the 'protasis' each occupy a whole verse, in the 'apodosis' *extrahere* is enjambed. **331–2** Resumption of the argument so far: statement of theme in atomic terms (*implexis...fiunt*) + metaphorical variation (see Comm.). **333–6** The impossibility of separate sensation by mind and body: theme (333–4) negatively expressed (*nec...sine...sorsum*) + variation positively expressed (*communibus... conflatur utrimque*). In the variation there is 'enclosing' word-order (*communibus...motibus,*[2] *accensus...sensus*[3]), perhaps designed to reinforce the idea of the atomic interconnexions (cf. Comm.). **337–8** The impossibility of the body's coming into being or existing after death by itself: simple tripartite enumeration, varied only by the metrical cliché *durare uidetur*. **339–43** Illustration, parallel to that of 327–30,

---

[1] Cf. Bailey 145–6, many of whose examples have been borrowed for the present discussion.

[2] Cf. Pearce 163; he does not notice this instance.

[3] Pearce 307–10.

but *ex converso*: the behaviour of water as an antitype of the behaviour of body and soul. The development is simply articulated (*non*...*ut*...*sed* ...*non*...*sic*...*sed*; with the *sed* that prefaces each 'apodosis' beginning its verse), but there is enjambment between 339 and 340[1] and between 341 and 342; the period ends with a variation of the type already discussed, *pereunt conuulsi conque putrescunt*, reinforced by alliteration. **344–7** A virtual restatement of what has previously been said, but with emphasis on *ex ineunte aeuo*, so that *sic* is displaced from its obvious articulatory position at the beginning of the verse. The construction of 344–6 is perhaps slightly awkward, and the 'golden' line 345 is not typically Lucretian writing (see Comm.), but the development is still 'linear': 346 stands for a separate clause, i.e. the participial phrase = '*even when* hidden' (so that the verse expands and varies *ex ineunte aeuo*); and the conclusion has a verse to itself, strongly and simply articulated, *discidium ut nequeat* || *fieri* || *sine peste maloque*. **348–9** Summary: the last two verses of the 'paragraph', by a technique illustrated throughout the Commentary ('ring-composition'), repeat its doctrine and refer back to its beginning (*causa salutis*...*naturam* ∼ *natura*... *causa salutis*). The syntax is simple, with the logical relationship between the *quoniam*-clause and its apodosis clearly marked by the repetition *coniunctast*...*coniunctam*.

(ii) '*Pathetic*' *style: 1025–52*

This passage is a harangue in terms indebted to the diatribe (Comm. 1024–52 n.).[2] The argument is simple: 1025–44 convey the demonstrative premiss, that even great men have died; and 1045–52 the conclusion, that the person addressed has no call to chafe at the inevitability of death, especially as he has little to live for in any case. The logic is emotional rather than rational, and the style is correspondingly 'tense': specific points to note are the longer sentences, the greater frequency of enjambment, and the use of 'enclosing' word-order and syntactical anticipation. **1025–6** Exploitation of the separative possibilities of Latin word-order: *lumina*...*reliquit, multis*... *rebus* (with *tu*...*improbe* scornfully sandwiched between and the necessary but unexpressive *fuit* further sandwiched between *tu* and

---

[1] Partial enjambment, in fact: the syntax of the half-clause *ut*...*uaporem* is complete, to the reader's ear, by the end of the verse.

[2] A good discussion by Conte, *S.I.F.C.* 37 (1965) 114–32.

improbe). **1027–8** Enjambment and 'framing' of the verse by the sonorous perfect forms. **1029–33** A particularly impressive sentence: the subject *ille quoque ipse* is announced immediately, but is not completed by its predicate until 1033; the intervening 3 + verses enlarge the stature of the man – who is then shown to be as mortal as other men. The sentence-structure is designed to carry the reader on: *strauit iterque dedit...ac...docuit...et contempsit*; in detail note (1029–30) 'tension' (*uiam...strauit*) + enjambment, (1031) *pedibus* looking forward to *super ire, salsas* to *lacunas*,[1] (1032) *contempsit* to *murmura ponti*, (1033) *animam* to *fudit*. Nowhere can the reader pause at the main caesura with a complete syntactical subunit safely, so to say, negotiated; always he is drawn on. **1034–5** Momentarily 'linear' writing: subject in one verse, predicate in the next; but the structure of 1034 exemplifies a well-known rhetorical device, the 'tricolon crescendo': *Scipiadas* || *belli fulmen* || *Carthaginis horror*. **1036–8** Anaphora (*adde...adde*); enjambment + 'tension' (*eadem...quietest*). **1039–41** Enjambment + 'tension'; (1041) alliteration + assonance + enclosure (*sponte sua... ipse*). **1042–4** Enjambment + striking imagery (see Comm.). **1045–52** The harangue ends with a longer and fast-moving sentence: syntactically 1046–52 depend on 1045. Predominantly the effects are secured by enjambment, sometimes very strong (1050–51) and 'tension' (fully enclosing word-order at 1049 *sollicitam...mentem*); but monotony is carefully avoided, and the movement of 1047–9 is varied with some subtlety:

qui *somno* PARTEM MAIOREM *conteris* AEVI (tension)

et uigilans stertis || nec somnia cernere cessas ('linear'

                 articulation)

*sollicitam*que geris CASSA FORMIDINE *mentem* (tension).

Within these larger developments attention is also paid to the smaller-scale effects, as in 1052, a very skilfully disposed verse:

incerto FLVITANS *errore* VAGARIS.

If the foregoing analyses are to be useful, their scope must be made clear. They have been chosen to represent two extreme cases: an expository passage in a low key is contrasted with a rhetorical harangue highly charged with feeling. Between these extremes there is a wide range of intermediate possibilities; and the analyses have shown that even in these two passages there is no rigid differentiation of style:

[1] Notice here the effect of the rhyme.

enjambment occurs in the expository passage, 'linear' writing in the 'pathetic'. Thus there can be no question of a hard-and-fast distinction on stylistic grounds between different types of passage, no application of, so to say, a litmus-paper test, no 'either–or'. Analysis must always be based on the context and the end in view.

In conclusion something should be said about Lucretius' imagery. Commentators and interpreters have frequently remarked on his extraordinarily vivid powers of description and on his faculty (shared among modern writers only by Kipling) for transferring a sense of colour and movement to the written page. It is this faculty which gives Lucretius' images their peculiar quality. A full discussion is not necessary here: the subject has been well treated by West and is dealt with at the appropriate places in the Commentary. What should be noted in the context of the matters discussed above is that in Lucretius both description and imagery, like all his other stylistic characteristics, are *functional*: they assist to carry conviction by illuminating the argument, and they are employed throughout the poem, in expository and 'pathetic' passages alike, for this purpose.[1] The illustrative role of simile and metaphor is of course their real *raison d'être*, and among Lucretius' predecessors Empedocles in particular was noted for his metaphors;[2] what is unique to Lucretius is the astonishing clarity and particularity of his vision and of its translation into words. In this respect the prophet of σαφήνεια was its actual embodiment.

5. BOOK III

(a) SUBJECT, STRUCTURE AND ARGUMENT

Books III and IV, as was said above (§3), are central in the structure, and hence in the argument, of the entire poem. There are two reasons why Book III seems to deserve special study. In the first place the problem that it poses is still as urgent and inescapable for humanity as it ever was, and perhaps never more so: for the second half of the twentieth century is a time when advances in the techniques of both

---

[1] This is what Dr C. J. Carter (in a letter to the editor) has strikingly called 'the pervasive community of metaphor'. See Sykes Davies 29–38.

[2] Cf. Longrigg, *C.R.* N.S. 20 (1970) 8–9: Aristotle said of Empedocles that he was versed in the use of metaphor and all other poetical devices (D.L. 8. 57).

the termination and the prolongation of life seem to have outstripped man's capacity to reckon with their ethical implications.[1] Some, admittedly, of the premises of Lucretius' argument may seem to have lost whatever relevance they ever had: the gods in whose power he so passionately disbelieved are even more unreal to us than they must have been to the majority of his educated contemporaries. (Their place, however, has been taken by other gods and idols, not all obviously preferable.) In spite of such reservations the central problem persists: every human being must die, and nearly every human being fears to die. One of the means by which many people still try to come to terms with this fear is the concept of an afterlife, whether viewed with hope or with apprehension or with terror. The problem must be faced;[2] and Lucretius' solution to it deserves respect. It may in fact be judged to be no solution; but it is at least a beautiful, eloquent and courageous attempt. Secondly, of all the books of the *D.R.N.*, Book III appears to be the most highly finished, neatly constructed, and the best able to stand on its own.[3] In its main structural outlines it follows a simple plan:

1–93	Introduction
94–829	Argument:
	94–416 the soul is material –
	417–829 and hence mortal
830–1094	Conclusion: death is not to be feared.[4]

This scheme is both intellectually and emotionally satisfying. The short Introduction is marked by the panegyric of Epicurus as signalling a fresh start in the development of the poem. In it Lucretius

[1] See A. Toynbee and others, *Man's concern with death* (1968), passim.

[2] 'Si on considère le sujet, il n'en est pas de plus capable d'émouvoir la pensée, plus digne d'être médité et plus entouré de mystères tristement séducteurs' (Martha 171).

[3] As an intellectual and imaginative achievement Book V must be awarded the palm.

[4] It was argued by Rand, 'La composition rhétorique du troisième livre de Lucrèce', *R.Ph.* sér. 3. 8 (1934) 243–66, that Lucretius followed traditional rhetorical doctrine in the structure of Book III: thus 1–93 = *Prooemium*, 94–416 *Narratio*, 417–829 *Argumentatio*, 830–1094 *Peroratio*. The distinction between *Narratio* and *Argumentatio* is perhaps somewhat artificial. Owen accepts Rand's argument and detects the same basic structure in every book of the poem (123–6).

states concisely and powerfully the theme of the book. There then follows the Argument, a long and careful exposition of the scientific proofs of (i) the corporeal nature and action of the soul, (ii) its mortality and coduration with the body: this forms the great and ineluctable premiss on which the Conclusion of the book is founded.[1] The logical relationship between these two great divisions of the book, Argument and Conclusion, is marked by the simple but immensely pregnant *igitur* at v. 830: in this one word the whole preceding section is summed up. Their relationship is further emphasized by a fundamental stylistic difference between them: the Argument is conducted in what we have called the 'expository' style, the Conclusion in the 'pathetic'. Though the discussion of the *animus* and *anima* is essential to the argument, it is theoretical: the premiss must be established beyond all possibility of cavil, or the whole edifice of reasoning will collapse, but passion, though Lucretius could not resist the occasional flirt of irony or sarcasm, does not play a predominant part. The Conclusion, by contrast, is essentially an essay in practical philosophy, couched in arguments whose validity of course depends on the doctrines established in the first part of the book, but which are aimed at men's common sense and humanity as much as at their intellects. Hence two connected phenomena: a rise in both emotional and poetic 'temperature' as Lucretius sets himself to enforce, in the service of reason and humanity, the great truth that death is not a thing to fear; and the change to a style of argument appropriate to popular philosophical teaching and particularly indebted, as explained above (§4(*a*)), to the diatribe. There is something peculiarly satisfying about this balance between the long, reasoned, comparatively passionless exposition and the relatively short but intense conclusion: neither element is complete without the other, and it is the successful integration of the two that makes the reading of Book III a memorable experience.

(*b*) THE 'CONSOLATIO'

As was said above, the purpose of the Conclusion of Book III is practical: Lucretius demonstrates, in the light of the facts now established, that

---

[1] 'Toute cette physique lentement accumulée n'est qu'un immense ouvrage de guerre, une sorte de savante circumvallation, par laquelle le poëte investit la foule confuse de nos terreurs, qu'il va maintenant dissiper par quelques poétiques assauts' (Martha 135).

death is not to be feared. It has also been shown (§4(a)) that in such 'pathetic' passages as this Lucretius drew freely on the popular homiletic tradition, particularly on the diatribe. In Book III yet another extra-Epicurean influence may be seen at work, that of the *consolatio*.[1] This was a stock literary-philosophical genre, designed to fortify men against the contingencies of existence – particularly death and exile – by marshalling the available arguments which might serve to console and comfort. Epicurus himself seems to have made little use of this type of argument (which he possibly disdained?), and it is probable that Lucretius has imparted an Epicurean colouring to some treatise On Death, Περὶ Θανάτου, such as that which served as the basis of Plutarch's *Consolatio ad Apollonium*.[2] Be that as it may, his debt to the genre is unmistakable. Such treatises, artificial as they may now seem, had a strictly practical aim and were taken perfectly seriously, as can be seen from the witness of Cicero and Seneca. The Tenth Satire of Juvenal is a *consolatio*, and was praised as such by Byron: 'I should think it might be read with great effect to a man dying without much pain, in preference to all the stuff that ever was sung or said in churches.' Byron's qualification 'without much pain' is shrewd as well as sardonic, for it implies a fundamental question: how effective can formal consolatory writing ever be for those who stand most in need of it? The genre is little practised, if at all, today, but some effort must be made to criticize Lucretius' (or any other) *consolatio* in terms of its practical efficacy, for this was writing designed to serve a specific purpose. It should of course be acknowledged that the argument of the Conclusion of Book III is directed at the emotions and is conducted in emotional terms; such is the very essence of the *consolatio*. Considered then as emotional argument, how effective is it? It is difficult to improve on the answer given to this question by Santayana, who must be quoted *in extenso*:

> Nothing could be more futile... than to marshal arguments against that fear of death which is merely another name for the energy of life, or the tendency to self-preservation. Arguments involve premises, and these premises, in the given case, express some particular form of the love of life; whence it is impossible to conclude that death is in

---

[1] See *O.C.D.*, s.v. *consolatio*, for the connexion with the diatribe; and Nisbet and Hubbard 279–81.

[2] Cf. Heinze 45.

no degree evil and not at all to be feared. For what is most dreaded is not the agony of dying, nor yet the strange impossibility that when we do not exist we should suffer for not existing. What is dreaded is the defeat of a present will directed upon life and its various undertakings. Such a present will cannot be argued away, but it may be weakened by contradictions arising within it, by the irony of experience, or by ascetic discipline. To introduce ascetic discipline, to bring out the irony of experience, to expose the self-contradictions of the will, would be the true means of mitigating the love of life; and if the love of life were extinguished, the fear of death, like smoke rising from that fire, would have vanished also.[1]

The same point is made, more briefly, by Cornford:

Epicurus, it is true, abolished the terrors of hell; but he also abolished the joys of heaven...I do not know how common the horror of death may be among normal people; but, where it exists, is it not often the prospect of extinction that horrifies them? If so, the fear of death, which Epicurus claimed to have banished, is actually increased by the denial of immortality. Is it Plato's fault that Western humanity has, on the whole, rejected the Epicurean consolation?[2]

The fault, if there is one, belongs to Epicurus. If Lucretius is seen at his greatest as a poet in Book III, the faith that he professes is here seen at its weakest. For there are more questions still to be asked. When man has cast out the fear of death – if he can – what is he left with? This question Lucretius makes no real attempt to answer, and his failure to do so cannot be attributed entirely to the limitations of his own enterprise. His readers were bound to ask: death disposed of, what follows? The great paean of triumph which concludes Book III contrasts strangely with the answer which Lucretius would have had to give if to do so had lain within the scope of his design: the promise of a cautious and muted happiness that awaited those who had finally overcome superstition and fear. But for Lucretius the all-important undertaking was the battle against ignorance and error: what life might be like for mankind if the battle were ever to be won he does not tell us and perhaps could not imagine. To say as much is not to admit that after all Lucretius was a pessimist; the weakness was in the

[1] Santayana 52–3. Cf. Seneca, *Ep.* 82. 15.
[2] F. M. Cornford, *The unwritten philosophy and other essays* (1950) 136–7.

Epicurean faith, and it was because of that weakness that 'the Lucretian argument could not prevail over instinctive human hopes and,
therefore, Platonic reason, that supplanted that hope, Stoic persuasion
and Christian faith won the victory over the European heart and mind'.[1]

6. THE TEXT[2]

Our knowledge of the text of Lucretius depends principally on two
manuscripts now in the University Library at Leiden in Holland,
Oblongus (O) and Quadratus (Q), so called from their formats. Both
were written in France in the ninth century A.D. and their texts go
back (through how many intermediate stages is disputed) to a common
original written in capital script and hence to be dated to the end of
antiquity. Fragments of two other ninth-century copies (G–V, U) are
preserved at Copenhagen and Vienna; their text is allied to that of
Q.[3] A fifth Carolingian manuscript [P], now lost, was discovered,
possibly at Murbach in Alsatia, and copied by the Italian humanist
Poggio in 1418. Poggio's copy [p] is also lost, but the copy made from
[p] by another humanist, Niccolò de' Niccoli, survives in the
Laurentian Library at Florence (L). From [p] and L descend all
the many copies of Lucretius made in Italy during the fifteenth
century, and also the early printed editions. The most difficult
problem which confronts the historian and the critic of Lucretius'
text is that of establishing the text of the lost [P] from its descendants
and then determining the relationship of [P] as reconstructed to the
extant witnesses OQG–VU. This problem has not yet been defini-
tively solved and perhaps never will be,[4] but its practical importance

---

[1] Hadzits 99.

[2] For the history of Lucretius' text and its editing down to modern times
students should read the incomparable account of Munro, in the Introduction to vol. I of his great edition. His narrative, especially as regards the
contribution of Lachmann, must however be corrected by reference to
Timpanaro, op. cit. (n. 4 below). See also Bailey 37–51; Smith
95–128. For the bibliography of the printed editions see C. A. Gordon,
A bibliography of Lucretius (1962).

[3] The leaves at Vienna (V) are in fact parts of two different MSS. The
first six leaves originally belonged to the same copy as those at Copenhagen,
and this combined source is termed G–V. The other four leaves (U) are
quite distinct. See list of Sigla, p. 36 below.

[4] See S. Timpanaro, *La genesi del metodo del Lachmann* (1963) 62-5.

for deciding what Lucretius wrote has often been overrated.[1] When the Italian branch of the tradition offers a reading different from and apparently superior to that of the older manuscripts, we have as a rule no reliable means of deciding whether it represents the reading of [P] or is the result of conjectural emendation by Italian humanists, who were prolific correctors of texts: such cases must be considered on their individual merits. No apology is offered for including discussion of textual points in the Commentary, for textual and literary criticism are inseparable and bear on one another;[2] it cannot be a matter of indifference whether Lucretius began what is in some ways the finest book of his poem with the sonorous interjection *o* or the anaemic preposition *e* (Comm. 1 n.). Moreover students should never be allowed to lose sight of the complex historical processes by which our knowledge of the past has come down to us. They should remember that a text is the outcome of such a process, not something 'given' that may be taken for granted. It is an injustice to the author to treat textual problems which have a real bearing on the sense or the poetry or both as if they did not exist. No special technical knowledge is required to follow these discussions; palaeography, often wrongly equated with textual criticism, plays a subordinate role, and no acquaintance with it is presumed in the reader.[3] The text of Book III presented in this edition is the best that the editor has been able to constitute from the evidence available to him in existing editions and other printed sources. In a very few cases, where the text offered by the manuscripts appears to be hopelessly garbled and no conjectural solution seems plausible enough to print, recourse has been had to the obelus or *crux desperationis* (†). It may well be salutary to remind students that some parts of the ancient record are now defaced past all human aid.

[1] See Timpanaro, op. cit. (preceding n.) 66; and cf. on the 'vetustus Politiani' of Statius' *Silvae* L. Håkanson, *Statius' Silvae* (1969) 15.
[2] Cf. P. Maas, *Textual criticism* (1958) 40–41: 'the core of practically every problem in textual criticism is a problem of *style.*'
[3] An excellent introduction to the history of the transmission of texts and to textual criticism is given by Reynolds and Wilson.

SIGLA

O = Leidensis Vossianus F. 30 (Oblongus), saec. ix
   O^s = eiusdem corrector qui uocatur Saxonicus, saec. ix
   O^1 = eiusdem corrector, saec. xi
   O^2 = eiusdem correctores recentiores
Q = Leidensis Vossianus Q. 94 (Quadratus), saec. ix
   Q^1 = eiusdem corrector, saec. xv
{ G = Schedae Haunienses olim Gottorpienses, saec. ix
{ V = Schedae Vindobonenses priores, saec. ix
U = Schedae Vindobonenses posteriores, saec. ix
(P) = Poggianus deperditus
L = Laurentianus xxxv. 30, saec. xv

Ceteri codices saec. xv nominatim laudantur

TITI LVCRETI CARI DE RERVM NATVRA LIBER TERTIVS

O TENEBRIS tantis tam clarum extollere lumen
qui primus potuisti inlustrans commoda uitae,
te sequor, o Graiae gentis decus, inque tuis nunc
ficta pedum pono pressis uestigia signis,
non ita certandi cupidus quam propter amorem   5
quod te imitari aueo: quid enim contendat hirundo
cycnis, aut quidnam tremulis facere artubus haedi
consimile in cursu possint et fortis equi uis?
tu pater es, rerum inuentor, tu patria nobis
suppeditas praecepta, tuisque ex, inclute, chartis,   10
floriferis ut apes in saltibus omnia libant,
omnia nos itidem depascimur aurea dicta,
aurea, perpetua semper dignissima uita.
nam simul ac ratio tua coepit uociferari
naturam rerum, diuina mente coorta,   15
diffugiunt animi terrores, moenia mundi
discedunt, totum uideo per inane geri res.
apparet diuum numen sedesque quietae,
quas neque concutiunt uenti nec nubila nimbis
aspergunt neque nix acri concreta pruina   20
cana cadens uiolat, semperque innubilus aether
integit et large diffuso lumine ridet.
omnia suppeditat porro natura, neque ulla
res animi pacem delibat tempore in ullo.
at contra nusquam apparent Acherusia templa   25
nec tellus obstat quin omnia dispiciantur,
sub pedibus quaecumque infra per inane geruntur.
his ibi me rebus quaedam diuina uoluptas

1 o *OV*: *om. Q*: e *Victorianus, edd. fere omnes*   11 libant *Auancius*: limant *OQV*   15 coorta *Orelli*: coortam *O*: coartam *QV*   21 semperque *L*: semper *OQV*   22 rident *Lachmann*   28 ibi *Pontanus*: ubi *OQV*

percipit atque horror, quod sic natura tua ui
tam manifesta patens ex omni parte retecta est.   30
    Et quoniam docui cunctarum exordia rerum
qualia sint et quam uariis distantia formis
sponte sua uolitent aeterno percita motu
quoue modo possint res ex his quaeque creari,
hasce secundum res animi natura uidetur   35
atque animae claranda meis iam uersibus esse
et metus ille foras praeceps Acheruntis agendus,
funditus humanam qui uitam turbat ab imo
omnia suffundens mortis nigrore neque ullam
esse uoluptatem liquidam puramque relinquit.   40
nam quod saepe homines morbos magis esse timendos
infamemque ferunt uitam quam Tartara leti
et se scire animi naturam sanguinis esse
aut etiam uenti, si fert ita forte uoluntas,   [46]
nec prorsum quicquam nostrae rationis egere,   45 [44]
hinc licet aduertas animum magis omnia laudis   [45]
iactari causa quam quod res ipsa probetur:
extorres idem patria longeque fugati
conspectu ex hominum, foedati crimine turpi,
omnibus aerumnis adfecti, denique uiuunt   50
et quocumque tamen miseri uenere parentant
et nigras mactant pecudes et manibu' diuis
inferias mittunt multoque in rebus acerbis
acrius aduertunt animos ad religionem.
quo magis in dubiis hominem spectare periclis   55
conuenit aduersisque in rebus noscere qui sit:
nam uerae uoces tum demum pectore ab imo
eliciuntur et eripitur persona, manet res.
denique auarities et honorum caeca cupido

29 sic natura *Auancius*: signatura *OQV*   31–4 = iv 45–48   33 aeterno
Naugerius: alterno *OV*: alterna *Q*   43 animi *O*: anime *QV, unde* animae
Lachmann   44 [46] *post* 43 *transp. Bentley*   47 causa *O*[1]: causam *OQV*
53 inferias *Q*[1]: inferia *OQV*   58 eliciuntur *Gifanius* et *L*: om. *OQV*
manet res *Laur. xxxv 31*: manare *OQV*

quae miseros homines cogunt transcendere finis   60
iuris et interdum socios scelerum atque ministros
noctes atque dies niti praestante labore
ad summas emergere opes, haec uulnera uitae
non minimam partem mortis formidine aluntur.
turpis enim ferme contemptus et acris egestas   65
semota ab dulci uita stabilique uidetur
et quasi iam leti portas cunctarier ante:
unde homines dum se falso terrore coacti
effugisse uolunt longe longeque remosse,
sanguine ciuili rem conflant diuitiasque   70
conduplicant auidi, caedem caede accumulantes,
crudeles gaudent in tristi funere fratris
et consanguineum mensas odere timentque.
consimili ratione ab eodem saepe timore
macerat inuidia ante oculos illum esse potentem,   75
illum aspectari, claro qui incedit honore,
ipsi se in tenebris uolui caenoque queruntur.
intereunt partim statuarum et nominis ergo;
et saepe usque adeo mortis formidine uitae
percipit humanos odium lucisque uidendae   80
ut sibi consciscant maerenti pectore letum
obliti fontem curarum hunc esse timorem,
hunc uexare pudorem, hunc uincula amicitiai
rumpere et in summa pietatem euertere fundo.
nam iam saepe homines patriam carosque parentis   85
prodiderunt, uitare Acherusia templa petentes.
nam ueluti pueri trepidant atque omnia caecis
in tenebris metuunt, sic nos in luce timemus
interdum nilo quae sunt metuenda magis quam
quae pueri in tenebris pauitant finguntque futura.   90

62–3 ~ ii 12–13   66 uidentur *Lambinus*   72 fratris *Macrobius Sat. VI*
ii 15: fratres *OQV*   78 statuarum *Laur. xxxv 31*: statum *OQV*   81 consciscant *L*: coniciscant *OQV*   84 pietatem *Laur. xxxv 31*: pietate *OQV*
fundo *Lambinus*: suadet *OQV*: fraude *Lachmann*: clade *Bernays*: suesse *Merrill*
e summa...sede *Bailey*   87–93 = ii 55–61, vi 35–41

hunc igitur terrorem animi tenebrasque necessest
non radii solis neque lucida tela diei
discutiant, sed naturae species ratioque.

PRIMVM animum dico, mentem quam saepe uocamus,
in quo consilium uitae regimenque locatum est,   95
esse hominis partem nilo minus ac manus et pes
atque oculi partes animantis totius exstant.

. . . . .

sensum animi certa non esse in parte locatum,
uerum habitum quendam uitalem corporis esse,
harmoniam Grai quam dicunt, quod faciat nos   100
uiuere cum sensu, nulla cum in parte siet mens;
ut bona saepe ualetudo cum dicitur esse
corporis, et non est tamen haec pars ulla ualentis.
sic animi sensum non certa parte reponunt,
magno opere in quo mi diuersi errare uidentur.   105
saepe itaque in promptu corpus quod cernitur aegret,
cum tamen ex alia laetamur parte latenti;
et retro fit uti contra sit saepe uicissim,
cum miser ex animo laetatur corpore toto;
non alio pacto quam si, pes cum dolet aegri,   110
in nullo caput interea sit forte dolore.
praeterea molli cum somno dedita membra
effusumque iacet sine sensu corpus onustum,
est aliud tamen in nobis quod tempore in illo
multimodis agitatur et omnis accipit in se   115
laetitiae motus et curas cordis inanis.
nunc animam quoque ut in membris cognoscere possis
esse neque harmonia corpus sentire solere,
principio fit uti detracto corpore multo

91–3 = i 146–8   94 quam *Charisius GL i 210. 5 K.*: quem *OQV*
95 locatum *Marullus*: uocatum *OQV, nimirum ex u.* 94   *post u.* 97 *lacunam
statuerunt edd. uett.*   106 aegret *Macrobius GL v 650. 33 K.*: aegrum
OQV   108 uti *Lambinus*: ubi *OQ*   113 honustum *Q¹*: honestum *OQV*
118 sentire *Wakefield*: interire *OQV*

saepe tamen nobis in membris uita moretur;   120
atque eadem rursum, cum corpora pauca caloris
diffugere forasque per os est editus aer,
deserit extemplo uenas atque ossa relinquit:
noscere ut hinc possis non aequas omnia partis
corpora habere neque ex aequo fulcire salutem,   125
sed magis haec, uenti quae sunt calidique uaporis
semina, curare in membris ut uita moretur.
est igitur calor ac uentus uitalis in ipso
corpore qui nobis moribundos deserit artus.
quapropter quoniam est animi natura reperta   130
atque animae quasi pars hominis, redde harmoniai
nomen, ad organicos alto delatum Heliconi,
siue aliunde ipsi porro traxere et in illam
transtulerunt, proprio quae tum res nomine egebat.
quidquid id est, habeant; tu cetera percipe dicta.   135
    Nunc animum atque animam dico coniuncta teneri
inter se atque unam naturam conficere ex se,
sed caput esse quasi et dominari in corpore toto
consilium quod nos animum mentemque uocamus.
idque situm media regione in pectoris haeret.   140
hic exsultat enim pauor ac metus, haec loca circum
laetitiae mulcent, hic ergo mens animusquest.
cetera pars animae per totum dissita corpus
paret et ad numen mentis momenque mouetur.
idque sibi solum per se sapit, id sibi gaudet,   145
cum neque res animam neque corpus commouet una.
et quasi, cum caput aut oculus temptante dolore
laeditur in nobis, non omni concruciamur
corpore, sic animus nonnumquam laeditur ipse
laetitiaque uiget, cum cetera pars animai   150
per membra atque artus nulla nouitate cietur.
uerum ubi uementi magis est commota metu mens,

135 id *Laur. xxxv 31*: *om. OQV*   145 id *alterum add. Wakefield*: *om. OQV*
146 ulla *Laur. xxxv 31 teste Büchnero*

consentire animam totam per membra uidemus
sudoresque ita palloremque exsistere toto
corpore et infringi linguam uocemque aboriri,   155
caligare oculos, sonere auris, succidere artus,
denique concidere ex animi terrore uidemus
saepe homines: facile ut quiuis hinc noscere possit
esse animam cum animo coniunctam, quae cum animi ui
percussast, exim corpus propellit et icit.   160
    Haec eadem ratio naturam animi atque animai
corpoream docet esse: ubi enim propellere membra,
corripere ex somno corpus mutareque uultum
atque hominem totum regere ac uersare uidetur,
quorum nil fieri sine tactu posse uidemus   165
nec tactum porro sine corpore, nonne fatendumst
corporea natura animum constare animamque?
praeterea pariter fungi cum corpore et una
consentire animum nobis in corpore cernis.
si minus offendit uitam uis horrida teli   170
ossibus ac neruis disclusis intus adacta,
at tamen insequitur languor terraeque petitus
suauis et in terra mentis qui gignitur aestus,
interdumque quasi exsurgendi incerta uoluntas.
ergo corpoream naturam animi esse necessest,   175
corporeis quoniam telis ictuque laborat.
    Is tibi nunc animus quali sit corpore et unde
constiterit pergam rationem reddere dictis.
principio esse aio persubtilem atque minutis
perquam corporibus factum constare. id ita esse   180
hinc licet aduertas animum ut pernoscere possis.
nil adeo fieri celeri ratione uidetur
quam sibi mens fieri proponit et incohat ipsa.

154 ita palloremque *L*: itaque pallorem *OQV*   159 ui *Itali*: uis *Nonius Marcellus p. 179 L.*: om. *OQV*   160 perculsa est *Non. Marc. ibid.*
170 teli *Marullus*: leti *OQV*   173 suauis] segnis *Munro*   183 sibi *Wakefield*: si *OQV*

ocius ergo animus quam res se perciet ulla,
ante oculos quorum in promptu natura uidetur. 185
at quod mobile tanto operest, constare rutundis
perquam seminibus debet perquamque minutis,
momine uti paruo possint impulsa moueri.
namque mouetur aqua et tantillo momine flutat
quippe uolubilibus paruisque creata figuris. 190
at contra mellis constantior est natura
et pigri latices magis et cunctantior actus:
haeret enim inter se magis omnis materiai
copia, nimirum quia non tam leuibus exstat
corporibus neque tam subtilibus atque rutundis. 195
namque papaueris aura potest suspensa leuisque
cogere ut ab summo tibi diffluat altus aceruus,
at contra lapidum conlectum spicarumque
noenu potest. igitur paruissima corpora proquam
et leuissima sunt, ita mobilitate fruuntur, 200
at contra quaecumque magis cum pondere magno
asperaque inueniuntur, eo stabilita magis sunt.
nunc igitur quoniam est animi natura reperta
mobilis egregie, perquam constare necessest
corporibus paruis et leuibus atque rutundis. 205
quae tibi cognita res in multis, o bone, rebus
utilis inuenietur et opportuna cluebit.
haec quoque res etiam naturam dedicat eius,
quam tenui constet textura quamque loco se
contineat paruo, si possit conglomerari, 210
quod simul atque hominem leti secura quies est
indepta atque animi natura animaeque recessit,
nil ibi libatum de toto corpore cernas
ad speciem, nil ad pondus: mors omnia praestat
uitalem praeter sensum calidumque uaporem. 215
ergo animam totam perparuis esse necessest

194 leuibu' constat *Heinze*   198 conlectum *Muretus*: coniectum *OQV*
203 est *Vatic. Barb. Lat. 154*: om. *OQV*   210 si *L*: se *OQV*

seminibus nexam per uenas uiscera neruos,
quatenus, omnis ubi e toto iam corpore cessit,
extima membrorum circumcaesura tamen se
incolumem praestat nec defit ponderis hilum.   220
quod genus est Bacchi cum flos euanuit aut cum
spiritus unguenti suauis diffugit in auras
aut aliquo cum iam sucus de corpore cessit:
nil oculis tamen esse minor res ipsa uidetur
propterea neque detractum de pondere quicquam,   225
nimirum quia multa minutaque semina sucos
efficiunt et odorem in toto corpore rerum.
quare etiam atque etiam mentis naturam animaeque
scire licet perquam pauxillis esse creatam
seminibus, quoniam fugiens nil ponderis aufert.   230
      Nec tamen haec simplex nobis natura putanda est.
tenuis enim quaedam moribundos deserit aura
mixta uapore, uapor porro trahit aera secum.
nec calor est quisquam, cui non sit mixtus et aer:
rara quod eius enim constat natura, necessest   235
aeris inter eum primordia multa moueri.
iam triplex animi est igitur natura reperta,
nec tamen haec sat sunt ad sensum cuncta creandum,
nil horum quoniam recipit mens posse creare
sensiferos motus et mens quaecumque uolutat.   240
quarta quoque his igitur quaedam natura necessest
attribuatur. east omnino nominis expers,
qua neque mobilius quicquam neque tenuius exstat,
nec magis e paruis et leuibus est elementis,
sensiferos motus quae didit prima per artus.   245
prima cietur enim paruis perfecta figuris;
inde calor motus et uenti caeca potestas

222 unguenti *Itali*: unguente *O*: unguentes *Q*: unguentis *Q¹*   224 nil
Itali: nihil *OQ*: nilo *Heinsius*   236 multa moueri *O¹*: multam quaeri *O*:
multam queri *Q*   239 mens] res *Bernays*   240 et mens quaecumque
Frerichs: quaedam quae mente *O*: quedamque mente *Q*   244 e] est *Itali*
est *Wakefield*: ex *OQV*

accipit, inde aer; inde omnia mobilitantur,
concutitur sanguis, tum uiscera persentiscunt
omnia, postremis datur ossibus atque medullis   250
siue uoluptas est siue est contrarius ardor.
nec temere huc dolor usque potest penetrare neque acre
permanare malum, quin omnia perturbentur
usque adeo ut uitae desit locus atque animai
diffugiant partes per caulas corporis omnis.   255
sed plerumque fit in summo quasi corpore finis
motibus: hanc ob rem uitam retinere ualemus.

   Nunc ea quo pacto inter sese mixta quibusque
compta modis uigeant rationem reddere auentem
abstrahit inuitum patrii sermonis egestas;   260
sed tamen, ut potero summatim attingere, tangam.
inter enim cursant primordia principiorum
motibus inter se, nil ut secernier unum
possit nec spatio fieri diuisa potestas,
sed quasi multae uis unius corporis exstant.   265
quod genus in quouis animantum uiscere uulgo
est odor et quidam color et sapor, et tamen ex his
omnibus est unum perfectum corporis augmen:
sic calor atque aer et uenti caeca potestas
mixta creant unam naturam et mobilis illa   270
uis, initum motus ab se quae diuidit ollis,
sensifer unde oritur primum per uiscera motus.
nam penitus prorsum latet haec natura subestque,
nec magis hac infra quicquam est in corpore nostro,
atque anima est animae proporro totius ipsa.   275
quod genus in nostris membris et corpore toto
mixta latens animi uis est animaeque potestas,
corporibus quia de paruis paucisque creatast:
sic tibi nominis haec expers uis facta minutis

249 sanguis tum *Pontanus*: tum sanguis *OQV*   254 ut *add. Lambinus*:
om. *OQV*   257 retinere *O*: retinemus *OQV*   261 ut *Q*: ui *OV*
267 color *Lambinus*: calor *OQV*

corporibus latet atque animae quasi totius ipsa   280
proporrost anima et dominatur corpore toto.
consimili ratione necessest uentus et aer
et calor inter se uigeant commixta per artus
atque aliis aliud subsit magis emineatque
ut quiddam fieri uideatur ab omnibus unum,   285
ni calor ac uentus sorsum sorsumque potestas
aeris interimant sensum diductaque soluant.
est etiam calor ille animo, quem sumit in ira,
cum feruescit et ex oculis micat acribus ardor.
est et frigida multa comes formidinis aura,   290
quae ciet horrorem membris et concitat artus.
est etiam quoque pacati status aeris ille,
pectore tranquillo qui fit uultuque sereno.
sed calidi plus est illis quibus acria corda
iracundaque mens facile efferuescit in iram.   295
quo genere in primis uis est uiolenta leonum,
pectora qui fremitu rumpunt plerumque gementes
nec capere irarum fluctus in pectore possunt.
at uentosa magis ceruorum frigida mens est
et gelidas citius per uiscera concitat auras,   300
quae tremulum faciunt membris exsistere motum.
at natura boum placido magis aere uiuit,
nec nimis irai fax umquam subdita percit
fumida, suffundens caecae caliginis umbra,
nec gelidis torpet telis perfixa pauoris: 305
interutrasque sitast, ceruos saeuosque leones.
sic hominum genus est: quamuis doctrina politos
constituat pariter quosdam, tamen illa relinquit

280 animae quasi] animai *Lambinus*   284 aliis] alias *Brieger* (*cf.* 288 *sqq.*)
288 etiam] etenim *Faber* (*cf. adn. ad* 284)   289 feruescit *Laur. xxxv 31*:
feruescat *O*: feruescet *QV*   acribus *Lambinus*: acrius *OQV*   293 qui fit
Marullus: fit qui *OQV*   295 iram *Bentley*: ira *OQV*   298 *post* 295 *transp.*
Lachmann   303 nimis *Laur. xxxv 31*: minus *OQV*   304 umbra *Q*:
umbram *OV*   305 pauoris *O*[2]: uaporis *OQV* (-i)   306 inter utrosque
Auancius: interutraque *Lachmann*   sitast *Auancius*: sitas *OQV*: secus *Lachmann*

naturae cuiusque animi uestigia prima,
nec radicitus euelli mala posse putandumst, 310
quin procliuius hic iras decurrat ad acris,
ille metu citius paulo temptetur, at ille
tertius accipiat quaedam clementius aequo.
inque aliis rebus multis differre necessest
naturas hominum uarias moresque sequaces, 315
quorum ego nunc nequeo caecas exponere causas
nec reperire figurarum tot nomina quot sunt
principiis, unde haec oritur uariantia rerum.
illud in his rebus uideo firmare potesse,
usque adeo naturarum uestigia linqui 320
paruula quae nequeat ratio depellere nobis,
ut nil impediat dignam dis degere uitam.

Haec igitur natura tenetur corpore ab omni
ipsaque corporis est custos et causa salutis:
nam communibus inter se radicibus haerent 325
nec sine pernicie diuelli posse uidentur.
quod genus e turis glaebis euellere odorem
haud facile est quin intereat natura quoque eius:
sic animi atque animae naturam corpore toto
extrahere haud facile est quin omnia dissoluantur. 330
implexis ita principiis ab origine prima
inter se fiunt consorti praedita uita.
nec sibi quaeque sine alterius ui posse uidetur
corporis atque animi sorsum sentire potestas,
sed communibus inter eas conflatur utrimque 335
motibus accensus nobis per uiscera sensus.
praeterea corpus per se nec gignitur umquam
nec crescit neque post mortem durare uidetur.
non enim, ut umor aquae dimittit saepe uaporem

309 naturae *Marullus*: natura *OQV*   317 quot *O*[1]: quod *OQV*   319
uideor *Faber*   firmare *O*[2]: formare *OQV*   321 nobis *Lachmann*: noctis
O: noctes *QV*: mentis *Meurig Davies*   325 = v 554   332 fiunt consorti
Marullus: consorti fiunt *OQV*   uita *Q*[1]: uitae *OQV*   *post hunc u. uett. edd.
secutus grauiter distinxi*   335 eas *Lachmann*: eos *OQV*: se *Merrill*

qui datus est neque ea causa conuellitur ipse,   340
sed manet incolumis, non, inquam, sic animai
discidium possunt artus perferre relicti,
sed penitus pereunt conuulsi conque putrescunt.
ex ineunte aeuo sic corporis atque animai
mutua uitalis discunt contagia motus   345
maternis etiam membris aluoque reposta,
discidium ut nequeat fieri sine peste maloque:
ut uideas, quoniam coniunctast causa salutis,
coniunctam quoque naturam consistere eorum.

Quod superest, si quis corpus sentire refutat   350
atque animam credit permixtam corpore toto
suscipere hunc motum quem sensum nominitamus,
uel manifestas res contra uerasque repugnat.
quid sit enim corpus sentire quis adferet umquam,
si non ipsa palam quod res dedit ac docuit nos?   355
'at dimissa anima corpus caret undique sensu':
perdit enim quod non proprium fuit eius in aeuo,
multaque praeterea perdit cum expellitur aeuo.
dicere porro oculos nullam rem cernere posse,
sed per eos animum ut foribus spectare reclusis,   360
difficilest, contra cum sensus ducat eorum:
sensus enim trahit atque acies detrudit ad ipsas,
fulgida praesertim cum cernere saepe nequimus,
lumina luminibus quia nobis praepediuntur.
quod foribus non fit; neque enim, qua cernimus ipsi,   365
ostia suscipiunt ullum reclusa laborem.
praeterea si pro foribus sunt lumina nostra,
iam magis exemptis oculis debere uidetur
cernere res animus sublatis postibus ipsis.

Illud in his rebus nequaquam sumere possis,   370

---

346 reposta *Vatic. Barb. Lat. 154*: reposto *OQV*   347 ut *add. Marullus*: om. *OQV*   350 renutat *Lambinus, fortasse recte*   358 *sic Vatic. 3276, Vatic. Barb. Lat. 154*: perditum expellitur aeuo quam *OQV*: perdit quam expellitur ante *Munro*

Democriti quod sancta uiri sententia ponit,
corporis atque animi primordia singula priuis
apposita alternis uariare ac nectere membra.
nam cum multo sunt animae elementa minora
quam quibus e corpus nobis et uiscera constant,   375
tum numero quoque concedunt et rara per artus
dissita sunt dumtaxat ut hoc promittere possis,
quantula prima queant nobis iniecta ciere
corpora sensiferos motus in corpore, tanta
interualla tenere exordia prima animai.   380
nam neque pulueris interdum sentimus adhaesum
corpore nec membris incussam sidere cretam,
nec nebulam noctu neque aranei tenuia fila
obuia sentimus, quando obretimur euntes,
nec supera caput eiusdem cecidisse uietam   385
uestem nec plumas auium papposque uolantis,
qui nimia leuitate cadunt plerumque grauatim,
nec repentis itum cuiusuiscumque animantis
sentimus nec priua pedum uestigia quaeque,
corpore quae in nostro culices et cetera ponunt.   390
usque adeo prius est in nobis multa ciendum
semina corporibus nostris immixta per artus,   393
quam primordia sentiscant concussa animai   392
et tantis interuallis tuditantia possint
concursare coire et dissultare uicissim.   395

   Et magis est animus uitai claustra coercens
et dominantior ad uitam quam uis animai.
nam sine mente animoque nequit residere per artus
temporis exiguam partem pars ulla animai,
sed comes insequitur facile et discedit in auras   400
et gelidos artus in leti frigore linquit.

371 = v 622   372 priuis *Bentley*: primis *OQV*   374 elementa minora
animai *Lachmann*   383 aranei *Marullus*: arani *OQ*   391 ciendum *V*:
ciendo *OQ*   393 *ante* 392 *transp. Marullus*   394 tantis *Wakefield*: quantis
OQV: quam in his *Lachmann*: quam sis *Turnebus*   400 et *Q*[1]: e *OQV*

at manet in uita cui mens animusque remansit:
quamuis est circum caesis lacer undique membris
truncus, adempta anima circum membrisque remota
uiuit et aetherias uitalis suscipit auras. 405
si non omnimodis, at magna parte animai
priuatus, tamen in uita cunctatur et haeret:
ut, lacerato oculo circum si pupula mansit
incolumis, stat cernundi uiuata potestas,
dummodo ne totum corrumpas luminis orbem 410
et circum caedas aciem solamque relinquas;
id quoque enim sine pernicie non fiet eorum.
at si tantula pars oculi media illa peresa est,
occidit extemplo lumen tenebraeque sequuntur,
incolumis quamuis alioqui splendidus orbis. 415
hoc anima atque animus uincti sunt foedere semper.

Nvnc age, natiuos animantibus et mortalis
esse animos animasque leuis ut noscere possis,
conquisita diu dulcique reperta labore
digna tua pergam disponere carmina uita. 420
tu fac utrumque uno sub iungas nomine eorum,
atque animam uerbi causa cum dicere pergam,
mortalem esse docens, animum quoque dicere credas,
quatenus est unum inter se coniunctaque res est.
    Principio quoniam tenuem constare minutis 425
corporibus docui multoque minoribus esse
principiis factam quam liquidus umor aquai
aut nebula aut fumus (nam longe mobilitate
praestat et a tenui causa magis icta mouetur:
quippe ubi imaginibus fumi nebulaeque mouetur, 430
quod genus in somnis sopiti ubi cernimus alte

---

403 circum *Laur. xxxv 31* : cretum *OQV*   404 remota Q^1: remot Q: remotus
OV: remotis *Itali*   405 aerias *Lachmann*   415 alioquist *Kannengiesser*
417 mortalis *Laur. xxxv 31* : mortalibus *OQV*   428 iam *Lachmann*
430 mouetur *Marullus*: mouentur *OQV*   431 alte *Lachmann*: alta *OQV*

exhalare uaporem altaria ferreque fumum;
nam procul haec dubio nobis simulacra feruntur) –
nunc igitur quoniam quassatis undique uasis
diffluere umorem et laticem discedere cernis   435
et nebula ac fumus quoniam discedit in auras,
crede animam quoque diffundi multoque perire
ocius et citius dissolui in corpora prima,
cum semel ex hominis membris ablata recessit.
quippe etenim corpus, quod uas quasi constitit eius,   440
cum cohibere nequit conquassatum ex aliqua re
ac rarefactum detracto sanguine uenis,
aere qui credas posse hanc cohiberier ullo,
corpore qui nostro rarus magis †incohibescit?

Praeterea gigni pariter cum corpore et una   445
crescere sentimus pariterque senescere mentem.
nam uelut infirmo pueri teneroque uagantur
corpore, sic animi sequitur sententia tenuis.
inde ubi robustis adoleuit uiribus aetas,
consilium quoque maius et auctior est animi uis.   450
post ubi iam ualidis quassatum est uiribus aeui
corpus et obtusis ceciderunt uiribus artus,
claudicat ingenium, delirat lingua, labat mens,
omnia deficiunt atque uno tempore desunt.
ergo dissolui quoque conuenit omnem animai   455
naturam, ceu fumus, in altas aeris auras:
quandoquidem gigni pariter pariterque uidemus
crescere et, ut docui, simul aeuo fessa fatisci.

Huc accedit uti uideamus, corpus ut ipsum
suscipere immanis morbos durumque dolorem,   460
sic animum curas acris luctumque metumque:

---

432 uaporem O^1: uapore OQV 433 hinc *Bentley*   feruntur *Creech*:
geruntur OQV: genuntur *Lambinus*   438 in *add.* Q^1: *om.* OQV 444 is
cohibessit? *Lachmann*: incohibensquest *Bergk*   450 auctior Q^1: auctor
OQV 453 labat *add. Lachmann*: *om.* OQV: madet Q^1, *nimirum ex u.* 479
456 aeris *Vatic. Barb. Lat. 154*: acris OQV 458 ut *add.* Q^1: *om.* OQV
fatisci (P): fatiscit Q^1: faetis OQ: fetis V

quare participem leti quoque conuenit esse.
quin etiam morbis in corporis auius errat
saepe animus: dementit enim deliraque fatur
interdumque graui lethargo fertur in altum   465
aeternumque soporem oculis nutuque cadenti,
unde neque exaudit uoces nec noscere uultus
illorum potis est, ad uitam qui reuocantes
circumstant lacrimis rorantes ora genasque.
quare animum quoque dissolui fateare necessest,   470
quandoquidem penetrant in eum contagia morbi.
nam dolor ac morbus leti fabricator uterquest,
multorum exitio perdocti quod sumus ante.   473
denique cur, hominem cum uini uis penetrauit   476
acris et in uenas discessit diditus ardor,
consequitur grauitas membrorum, praepediuntur
crura uacillanti, tardescit lingua, madet mens,
nant oculi, clamor singultus iurgia gliscunt,   480
et iam cetera de genere hoc quaecumque sequuntur,
cur ea sunt, nisi quod uemens uiolentia uini
conturbare animam consueuit corpore in ipso?
at quaecumque queunt conturbari inque pediri,
significant, paulo si durior insinuarit   485
causa, fore ut pereant aeuo priuata futuro.
quin etiam subito ui morbi saepe coactus
ante oculos aliquis nostros, ut fulminis ictu,
concidit et spumas agit, ingemit et tremit artus,
desipit, extentat neruos, torquetur, anhelat   490
inconstanter, et in iactando membra fatigat.
nimirum quia uis morbi distracta per artus
turbat agens animam spumas, ut in aequore salso

---

470 fateare *Laur. xxxv 31*: fatere *OQV*   474–5 et quoniam mentem
sanari corpus ut aegrum (= 510) | et pariter mentem sanari corpus inani
del. Naugerius, Lambinus   482 cur ea *Laur. xxxv 31*: curba *OQV*   492 quia
(*P*): qua *OQV* districta *L. A. MacKay*   493 spumas *Tohte* (*qui tamen*
animă spumas *uoluit*): spumans *OQV* ut *add. Itali*: quasi *Lachmann*: om.
OQV

uentorum ualidis feruescunt uiribus undae.
exprimitur porro gemitus, quia membra dolore 495
adficiuntur et omnino quod semina uocis
eiciuntur et ore foras glomerata feruntur
qua quasi consuerunt et sunt munita uiai.
desipientia fit, quia uis animi atque animai
conturbatur et, ut docui, diuisa seorsum 500
disiectatur eodem illo distracta ueneno.
inde ubi iam morbi reflexit causa reditque
in latebras acer corrupti corporis umor,
tum quasi uaccillans primum consurgit et omnis
paulatim redit in sensus animamque receptat. 505
haec igitur tantis ubi morbis corpore in ipso
iactentur miserisque modis distracta laborent,
cur eadem credis sine corpore in aere aperto
cum ualidis uentis aetatem degere posse?
et quoniam mentem sanari, corpus ut aegrum, 510
cernimus et flecti medicina posse uidemus,
id quoque praesagit mortalem uiuere mentem.
addere enim partis aut ordine traiecere aequumst
aut aliquid prorsum de summa detrahere hilum,
commutare animum quicumque adoritur et infit 515
aut aliam quamuis naturam flectere quaerit.
at neque transferri sibi partis nec tribui uult
immortale quod est quicquam neque defluere hilum.
nam quodcumque suis mutatum finibus exit,
continuo hoc mors est illius quod fuit ante. 520
ergo animus siue aegrescit, mortalia signa
mittit, uti docui, seu flectitur a medicina:
usque adeo falsae rationi uera uidetur
res occurrere et effugium praecludere eunti
ancipitique refutatu conuincere falsum. 525

---

497 eiiciuntur *Lambinus*: eliciuntur *OQV*   498 uiai *Itali*: uia *OQV*
510 = 474   519–20 = i 670–71, 792–3, ii 753–4   523 rationi *O¹* (?)
sicut coni. Marullus: rationis *OQV*   525 refutatu *Q¹*: refutatur *OQV*

Denique saepe hominem paulatim cernimus ire
et membratim uitalem deperdere sensum,
in pedibus primum digitos liuescere et unguis,
inde pedes et crura mori, post inde per artus
ire alios tractim gelidi uestigia leti.   530
scinditur †atque animo haec† quoniam natura nec uno
tempore sincera exsistit, mortalis habendast.
quod si forte putas ipsam se posse per artus
introrsum trahere et partis conducere in unum
atque ideo cunctis sensum deducere membris,   535
at locus ille tamen, quo copia tanta animai
cogitur, in sensu debet maiore uideri:
qui quoniam nusquamst, nimirum, ut diximus ante,
dilaniata foras dispargitur, interit ergo.
quin etiam si iam libeat concedere falsum   540
et dare posse animam glomerari in corpore eorum,
lumina qui linquunt moribundi particulatim,
mortalem tamen esse animam fateare necesse,
nec refert utrum pereat dispersa per auras
an contracta suis e partibus obbrutescat,   545
quando hominem totum magis ac magis undique sensus
deficit et uitae minus et minus undique restat.

Et quoniam mens est hominis pars una, loco quae
fixa manet certo, uelut aures atque oculi sunt
atque alii sensus qui uitam cumque gubernant,   550
et ueluti manus atque oculus naresue seorsum
secreta ab nobis nequeunt sentire neque esse,
sed tamen in paruo liquuntur tempore tabe:
sic animus per se non quit sine corpore et ipso

526–47 *post* 669 *transp. Giussani*   531 itque animae hoc *Munro*: itque
animae haec *Bailey*: aeque animi haec *Bernays*: atque animo *Büchner*:
fortasse ergo [= *Heinze*] animae   535 deducere *Vatic. 3276, Vatic.
Barb. Lat. 154*: diducere *OQV*   538 ante *add.* (*P*): *om. OQV*
544 artus *J. D. Duff*   548 quae *Lachmann*: que *OQV*   553 liquuntur
I. Vossius (licuntur *Creech*): linguntur *OQV*   tabe *Creech*: tale *V*: tali
OQ

esse homine, illius quasi quod uas esse uidetur 555
siue aliud quid uis potius coniunctius ei
fingere, quandoquidem conexu corpus adhaeret.
　Denique corporis atque animi uiuata potestas
inter se coniuncta ualent uitaque fruuntur:
nec sine corpore enim uitalis edere motus 560
sola potest animi per se natura nec autem
cassum anima corpus durare et sensibus uti.
scilicet auulsus radicibus ut nequit ullam
dispicere ipse oculus rem sorsum corpore toto,
sic anima atque animus per se nil posse uidetur. 565
nimirum quia per uenas et uiscera mixtim,
per neruos atque ossa, tenentur corpore ab omni
nec magnis interuallis primordia possunt
libera dissultare, ideo conclusa mouentur
sensiferos motus quos extra corpus in auras 570
aeris haud possunt post mortem eiecta moueri
propterea quia non simili ratione tenentur.
corpus enim atque animans erit aer, si cohibere
in se animam atque in eos poterit concludere motus
quos ante in neruis et in ipso corpore agebat. 575
quare etiam atque etiam resoluto corporis omni
tegmine et eiectis extra uitalibus auris
dissolui sensus animi fateare necessest
atque animam, quoniam coniunctast causa duobus.
　Denique cum corpus nequeat perferre animai 580
discidium quin in taetro tabescat odore,
quid dubitas quin ex imo penitusque coorta
emanarit uti fumus diffusa animae uis,
atque ideo tanta mutatum putre ruina

555 uas esse *L*: uasse *O*: uase *QV*　564 ipse oculus *Laur. xxxv 31*: oculus ipse *OQV*　566 per *L*: *om. OQV*　mixtim *L*: mixti *OV*: mixta *Q* 571 moueri *Lambinus*: mouere *OQV*　573 animans erit *Lambinus*: animam serit *OQV*　574 in se animam *Wakefield*: sese anima *O*: esse anima *Q*: esse animam *V*　576 quare *Q¹*: quae *O*: que *Q*　582 ex *Q¹*: ea *OQ*　583 animae uis *Laur. xxxv 31*: anima eius *OQ*: animaei *V*

conciderit corpus, penitus quia mota loco sunt   585
fundamenta, foras anima emanante per artus
perque uiarum omnis flexus, in corpore qui sunt,
atque foramina? multimodis ut noscere possis
dispertitam animae naturam exisse per artus
et prius esse sibi distractam corpore in ipso   590
quam prolapsa foras enaret in aeris auras.
quin etiam finis dum uitae uertitur intra,
saepe aliqua tamen e causa labefacta uidetur
ire anima ac toto solui de corpore uelle
et quasi supremo languescere tempore uultus   595
molliaque exsangui cadere omnia corpore membra.
quod genus est, animo male factum cum perhibetur
aut animam liquisse, ubi iam trepidatur et omnes
extremum cupiunt uitae reprehendere uinclum.
conquassatur enim tum mens animaeque potestas   600
omnis et haec ipso cum corpore collabefiunt,
ut grauior paulo possit dissoluere causa.
quid dubitas tandem quin extra prodita corpus
imbecilla foras, in aperto, tegmine dempto,
non modo non omnem possit durare per aeuum   605
sed minimum quoduis nequeat consistere tempus?
nec sibi enim quisquam moriens sentire uidetur
ire foras animam incolumem de corpore toto
nec prius ad iugulum et supera succedere fauces,
uerum deficere in certa regione locatam,   610
ut sensus alios in parti quemque sua scit
dissolui: quod si immortalis nostra foret mens,
non tam se moriens dissolui conquereretur,
sed magis ire foras uestemque relinquere, ut anguis.

---

586 anima emanante *Wakefield*: manant animaeque *OQV*: manante anima
usque *Lachmann*   594 uelle *Lachmann*: omnia membra *OQV, nimirum ex u.*
596 *antequam corruptus est et ille*   596 cadere omnia corpore *Laur. xxxv 31*:
cadere omnia *OQV*: trunco cadere omnia *Lachmann*   597 peribetur *Q¹*:
peribet *QV*: periberet *O*   609 supera *OQ*: superas *Q*: superac *V*
611 alios *O*: alius *QV*

Denique cur animi numquam mens consiliumque 615
gignitur in capite aut pedibus manibusue, sed unis
sedibus et certis regionibus omnibus haeret,
si non certa loca ad nascendum reddita cuique
sunt et ubi quicquid possit durare creatum
atque ita multimodis partitis artubus esse, 620
membrorum ut numquam exsistat praeposterus ordo?
usque adeo sequitur res rem neque flamma creari
fluminibus solitast neque in igni gignier algor.

Praeterea si immortalis natura animaist
et sentire potest secreta a corpore nostro, 625
quinque, ut opinor, eam faciundum est sensibus auctam.
nec ratione alia nosmet proponere nobis
possumus infernas animas Acherunte uagari.
pictores itaque et scriptorum saecla priora
sic animas introduxerunt sensibus auctas. 630
at neque sorsum oculi neque nares nec manus ipsa
esse potest animae neque sorsum lingua neque aures:
haud igitur per se possunt sentire neque esse.

Et quoniam toto sentimus corpore inesse
uitalem sensum et totum esse animale uidemus, 635
si subito medium celeri praeciderit ictu
uis aliqua ut sorsum partem secernat utramque,
dispertita procul dubio quoque uis animai
et discissa simul cum corpore dissicietur.
at quod scinditur et partis discedit in ullas, 640
scilicet aeternam sibi naturam abnuit esse.
falciferos memorant currus abscidere membra
saepe ita de subito permixta caede calentis,
ut tremere in terra uideatur ab artubus id quod

post u. 619 *lacunam statuit Munro*   620 ita (*P*): ta *OQV* partitis *Bernays*: pertotis *OQV*: perfectis *Lachmann*   621 ut *O*: *om. QV*   623 solitast *Laur. xxxv 31*: solita *OQ*   in igni *Q¹*: insigni *OQ*   624 (= 670) immortalis *Q¹*: mortalis *OQ* animaist *Q¹*: animaest *OQ*   628 uagari *Lachmann*: uagare *Q¹*: uacare *OQ*   632 animae *Pius*: anima *OQ*   633 haud igitur *Lachmann*: auditum *OQ*   644 ab *O¹*: ad *OQ*

decidit abscisum, cum mens tamen atque hominis uis   645
mobilitate mali non quit sentire dolorem
et simul in pugnae studio quod dedita mens est;
corpore relicuo pugnam caedesque petessit,
nec tenet amissam laeuam cum tegmine saepe
inter equos abstraxe rotas falcesque rapaces,   650
nec cecidisse alius dextram, cum scandit et instat.
inde alius conatur adempto surgere crure,
cum digitos agitat propter moribundus humi pes,
et caput abscisum calido uiuenteque trunco
seruat humi uultum uitalem oculosque patentis,   655
donec reliquias animai reddidit omnis.
quin etiam tibi si lingua uibrante, minanti
serpentem cauda, procero corpore, †utrumque
sit libitum in multas partis discidere ferro,
omnia iam sorsum cernes ancisa recenti   660
uulnere tortari et terram conspargere tabo,
ipsam seque retro partem petere ore priorem
uulneris ardenti ut morsu premat icta dolore.
omnibus esse igitur totas dicemus in illis
particulis animas? at ea ratione sequetur   665
unam animantem animas habuisse in corpore multas.
ergo diuisast ea quae fuit una simul cum
corpore: quapropter mortale utrumque putandumst,
in multas quoniam partis disciditur aeque.

Praeterea si immortalis natura animai   670
constat et in corpus nascentibus insinuatur,
cur super anteactam aetatem meminisse nequimus
nec uestigia gestarum rerum ulla tenemus?
nam si tanto operest animi mutata potestas

post u. 646 *dist. edd. nonnulli*   650 rotas *L*: rote *OQ*   657 minanti *O*:
om. Q: micanti *Lachmann*   658 serpentem *Marullus*: serpentis *OQ*   cauda
*O*¹: caude *OQ*   utrimque *Marullus*: truncum *Giussani*   662 seque *L*:
sequere *OQ*   663 ardentem *Brieger*   dolorem *Lachmann*   670 = 624
post u. 672 interiisse et quae [*hactenus litteris uncialibus*] nunc est nunc
esse creatam (= 678) *habet O*: *spatium ii uu. reliquit Q*   674 operest animi

omnis ut actarum exciderit retinentia rerum, 675
non, ut opinor, id ab leto iam longius errat:
quapropter fateare necessest quae fuit ante
interiisse et quae nunc est nunc esse creatam.
    Praeterea si iam perfecto corpore nobis
inferri solitast animi uiuata potestas 680
tum cum gignimur et uitae cum limen inimus,
haud ita conueniebat uti cum corpore et una
cum membris uideatur in ipso sanguine cresse,
sed uelut in cauea per se sibi uiuere solam
conuenit, ut sensu corpus tamen affluat omne. 685
quare etiam atque etiam neque originis esse putandumst
expertis animas nec leti lege solutas.
nam neque tanto opere adnecti potuisse putandumst
corporibus nostris extrinsecus insinuatas,
quod fieri totum contra manifesta docet res: 690
namque ita conexa est per uenas uiscera neruos
ossaque, uti dentes quoque sensu participentur,
morbus ut indicat et gelidai stringor aquai
et lapis oppressus subsit si frugibus asper;
nec, tam contextae cum sint, exire uidentur 695
incolumes posse et saluas exsoluere sese
omnibus e neruis atque ossibus articulisque.
quod si forte putas extrinsecus insinuatam
permanare animam nobis per membra solere,
tanto quique magis cum corpore fusa peribit: 700
quod permanat enim dissoluitur, interit ergo.
dispertitus enim per caulas corporis omnis
ut cibus, in membra atque artus cum diditur omnis,

Marullus: opere animist *OQ*   676 a...longiter *Charisius GL i 204. 14 K.*,
Nonius Marcellus p. 828 L.   680 solitast animi *Vatic. 3276, Vatic. Barb.
Lat. 154*: solita animist *OQ*   685 affluat *O*: afluat *Q*   690–94 *post*
685 *transp. Lachmann*   691 per uenas uiscera *Q¹*: uiscera per uenas *OQ*
694 subsit si *A. C. Clark*: subitis e *OQ*: subiit si e *Bernays*: subito sub
L. A. MacKay   702 dispertitus *Pius*: dispertitur *OQ*: dispertita *Laur.
xxxv 31*   enim *Vatic. 3276, Vatic. Barb. Lat. 154*: ergo *OQ*

disperit atque aliam naturam sufficit ex se,
sic anima atque animus quamuis integra recens in   705
corpus eunt, tamen in manando dissoluuntur,
dum quasi per caulas omnis diduntur in artus
particulae quibus haec animi natura creatur,
quae nunc in nostro dominatur corpore nata
ex illa quae tunc periit partita per artus.   710
quapropter neque natali priuata uidetur
esse die natura animae nec funeris expers.
   Semina praeterea linquuntur necne animai
corpore in exanimo? quod si linquuntur et insunt,
haud erit ut merito immortalis possit haberi,   715
partibus amissis quoniam libata recessit.
sin ita sinceris membris ablata profugit
ut nullas partis in corpore liquerit ex se,
unde cadauera rancenti iam uiscere uermis
exspirant atque unde animantum copia tanta   720
exos et exsanguis tumidos perfluctuat artus?
quod si forte animas extrinsecus insinuari
uermibus et priuas in corpora posse uenire
credis nec reputas cur milia multa animarum
conueniant unde una recesserit, hoc tamen est ut   725
quaerendum uideatur et in discrimen agendum,
utrum tandem animae uenentur semina quaeque
uermiculorum ipsaeque sibi fabricentur ubi sint,
an quasi corporibus perfectis insinuentur.
at neque cur faciant ipsae quareue laborent   730
dicere suppeditat. neque enim, sine corpore cum sunt,
sollicitae uolitant morbis alguque fameque.
corpus enim magis his uitiis adfine laborat
et mala multa animus contage fungitur eius.

---

705 integra recens in *Marullus*: est integra reces *OQ*   710 tum *ed.*
Brixiensis 1473   718 ut *ed. Veronensis 1486*: et *OQ*   723 priuas in *Laur.*
xxxv 31: priua si *OQ*   727 utrum *O*: uerum *Q*   732 alguque *Nonius*
Marcellus p. 100 L.: algoque *OQ*   733 atfine *Q*: affine *Q¹*: ecfine *O¹*

sed tamen his esto quamuis facere utile corpus   735
cui subeant: at qua possint uia nulla uidetur.
haud igitur faciunt animae sibi corpora et artus.
nec tamen est utqui perfectis insinuentur
corporibus: neque enim poterunt subtiliter esse
conexae neque consensus contagia fient.   740
  Denique cur acris uiolentia triste leonum
seminium sequitur, uulpes dolus, et fuga ceruis
a patribus datur et patrius pauor incitat artus,
et iam cetera de genere hoc cur omnia membris
ex ineunte aeuo generascunt ingenioque,   745
si non certa suo quia semine seminioque
uis animi pariter crescit cum corpore quoque?
quod si immortalis foret et mutare soleret
corpora, permixtis animantes moribus essent,
effugeret canis Hyrcano de semine saepe   750
cornigeri incursum cerui tremeretque per auras
aeris accipiter fugiens ueniente columba,
desiperent homines, saperent fera saecla ferarum.
illud enim falsa fertur ratione, quod aiunt
immortalem animam mutato corpore flecti: 755
quod mutatur enim dissoluitur, interit ergo.
traiciuntur enim partes atque ordine migrant:
quare dissolui quoque debent posse per artus,
denique ut intereant una cum corpore cunctae.
sin animas hominum dicent in corpora semper   760
ire humana, tamen quaeram cur e sapienti
stulta queat fieri, nec prudens sit puer ullus   762
nec tam doctus equae pullus quam fortis equi uis.   764
scilicet in tenero tenerascere corpore mentem   765

---

736 cui *Bernays*: cum *OQ*: cur *Q¹*   qua *Marullus*: que *OQ*   738 utqui
Munro: ut   quicum *OQ*   740 consensus *Lachmann*: consensu *OQ*
742 ceruis *ed. Veneta 1495*: ceruos *OQ*   743 *u. secl.* 'doctus quidam' *ap. Lam-
binum*   patrius *O¹*: a patrius *OQ*   746 = 763   747 quoque *O*: toto *Q*
756 ~ 701   759 *om. Q*   760 sin *Pontanus*: sic *OQ*   corpora *Q¹*: corpore
OQ   763 = 746 *del. Lachmann*   764 pullus *L*: paulus *OQ*

confugient; quod si iam fit, fateare necessest
mortalem esse animam, quoniam mutata per artus
tanto opere amittit uitam sensumque priorem.
quoue modo poterit pariter cum corpore quoque
confirmata cupitum aetatis tangere florem   770
uis animi, nisi erit consors in origine prima?
quidue foras sibi uult membris exire senectis?
an metuit conclusa manere in corpore putri
et domus aetatis spatio ne fessa uetusto
obruat? at non sunt immortali ulla pericla.   775
    Denique conubia ad Veneris partusque ferarum
esse animas praesto deridiculum esse uidetur,
exspectare immortalis mortalia membra
innumero numero certareque praeproperanter
inter se quae prima potissimaque insinuetur;   780
si non forte ita sunt animarum foedera pacta
ut quae prima uolans aduenerit insinuetur
prima neque inter se contendant uiribus hilum.
    Denique in aethere non arbor, non aequore in alto
nubes esse queunt nec pisces uiuere in aruis   785
nec cruor in lignis neque saxis sucus inesse:
certum ac dispositumst ubi quicquid crescat et insit.
sic animi natura nequit sine corpore oriri
sola neque a neruis et sanguine longius esse.
quod si posset enim, multo prius ipsa animi uis   790
in capite aut umeris aut imis calcibus esse
posset et innasci quauis in parte soleret,
tandem in eodem homine atque in eodem uase manere.
quod quoniam nostro quoque constat corpore certum
dispositumque uidetur ubi esse et crescere possit   795
sorsum anima atque animus, tanto magis infitiandum

---

770 ~ v 847   775 immortali O^1: iam mortali OQ 784–96 = v 128–40
784 in alto] salso Lachmann coll. v 128   789 longiter Lambinus: cf. adn. ad
676   790 quod] hoc Marullus u. sic dist. Wakefield: quid si posset enim?
multo... Lachmann   792 et innasci O: enim nasci Q

totum posse extra corpus durare genique.
quare, corpus ubi interiit, periisse necessest
confiteare animam distractam in corpore toto.
quippe etenim mortale aeterno iungere et una   800
consentire putare et fungi mutua posse
desiperest. quid enim diuersius esse putandumst
aut magis inter se disiunctum discrepitansque,
quam mortale quod est immortali atque perenni
iunctum in concilio saeuas tolerare procellas?   805
praeterea quaecumque manent aeterna necessest
aut quia sunt solido cum corpore respuere ictus
nec penetrare pati sibi quicquam quod queat artas
dissociare intus partis, ut materiai
corpora sunt quorum naturam ostendimus ante;   810
aut ideo durare aetatem posse per omnem,
plagarum quia sunt expertia, sicut inanest
quod manet intactum neque ab ictu fungitur hilum;
aut etiam quia nulla loci fit copia circum,
quo quasi res possint discedere dissoluique,   815
sicut summarum summast aeterna, neque extra
quis locus est quo diffugiant neque corpora sunt quae
possint incidere et ualida dissoluere plaga.
quod si forte ideo magis immortalis habendast,
quod uitalibus ab rebus munita tenetur,   820
aut quia non ueniunt omnino aliena salutis
aut quia quae ueniunt aliqua ratione recedunt
pulsa prius quam quid noceant sentire queamus,

.   .   .   .   .

praeter enim quam quod morbis cum corporis aegret,

800 mortale O^1: mortalem OQ 805 u. om. Q saeuas Marullus: saluas O
806–18 = v 351–63 del. Lachmann   806 necessust v 351   809 partis ut
corr. ex v 354 edd.: partus et O: partusset Q 814 fit Lachmann: sit OQ
816 sicut corr. ex v 361 edd.: sicuti OQ extra Q^1: exire O: ex ira Q
817 quis] qui v 362   dissiliant v 362   post u. 818 lacunam suspicati sunt
edd. nonnulli   820 letalibus Lambinus   post u. 823 lacunam statuit Lambinus   824 morbis Auancius: morbist OQ aegret Gifanius: aegrit OQ

aduenit id quod eam de rebus saepe futuris 825
macerat inque metu male habet curisque fatigat,
praeteritisque male admissis peccata remordent.
adde furorem animi proprium atque obliuia rerum,
adde quod in nigras lethargi mergitur undas.

Nil igitvr mors est ad nos neque pertinet hilum, 830
quandoquidem natura animi mortalis habetur.
et, uelut anteacto nil tempore sensimus aegri
ad confligendum uenientibus undique Poenis,
omnia cum belli trepido concussa tumultu
horrida contremuere sub altis aetheris oris 835
in dubioque fuere utrorum ad regna cadendum
omnibus humanis esset terraque marique,
sic, ubi non erimus, cum corporis atque animai
discidium fuerit quibus e sumus uniter apti,
scilicet haud nobis quicquam, qui non erimus tum, 840
accidere omnino poterit sensumque mouere,
non si terra mari miscebitur et mare caelo.
et, si iam nostro sentit de corpore postquam
distractast animi natura animaeque potestas,
nil tamen est ad nos qui comptu coniugioque 845
corporis atque animae consistimus uniter apti.
nec, si materiem nostram collegerit aetas
post obitum rursumque redegerit ut sita nunc est
atque iterum nobis fuerint data lumina uitae,
pertineat quicquam tamen ad nos id quoque factum, 850
interrupta semel cum sit repetentia nostri.
et nunc nil ad nos de nobis attinet, ante
qui fuimus, neque iam de illis nos adficit angor.

826 macerat *Laur. xxxv 31*: maceret *OQ*   835 oris *Gifanius*: auris *O*:
auras *Q*   844 distracta est *Q¹*: distractas *OQ*   847 materiem *Q*:
materiam *O*   851 repetentia *Q*: repentia *O*: retinentia *Auancius coll.* 675
nostri *Pius*: nostris *OQ*   852 et (&) *O*: te *Q*: ut *Susemihl, Heinze*
853 fuimus *Laur. xxxv 31*: fumus *OQ*   neque *Lachmann* (nec iam *Marullus*):
om. *OQ*: nil *Merrill*   afficit *Laur. xxxv 31*: adfigit *OQ*

nam cum respicias immensi temporis omne
praeteritum spatium, tum motus materiai   855
multimodis quam sint, facile hoc adcredere possis,
semina saepe in eodem, ut nunc sunt, ordine posta
haec eadem, quibus e nunc nos sumus, ante fuisse.   [865]
nec memori tamen id quimus reprehendere mente: [858]
inter enim iectast uitai pausa, uageque   860 [859]
deerrarunt passim motus ab sensibus omnes.   [860]
debet enim, misere si forte aegreque futurumst,   [861]
ipse quoque esse in eo tum tempore, cui male possit   [862]
accidere. id quoniam mors eximit esseque probet   [863]
illum cui possint incommoda conciliari,   865 [864]
scire licet nobis nil esse in morte timendum
nec miserum fieri, qui non est, posse neque hilum
differre an nullo fuerit iam tempore natus,
mortalem uitam mors cum immortalis ademit.

Proinde ubi se uideas hominem indignarier ipsum,   870
post mortem fore ut aut putescat corpore posto
aut flammis interfiat malisue ferarum,
scire licet non sincerum sonere atque subesse
caecum aliquem cordi stimulum, quamuis neget ipse
credere se quemquam sibi sensum in morte futurum.   875
non, ut opinor, enim dat quod promittit et unde
nec radicitus e uita se tollit et eicit,
sed facit esse sui quiddam super inscius ipse.
uiuus enim sibi cum proponit quisque futurum,
corpus uti uolucres lacerent in morte feraeque,   880
ipse sui miseret: neque enim se diuidit illim
nec remouet satis a proiecto corpore et illum
se fingit sensuque suo contaminat adstans.

856 multimodis *Vatic. Barb. Lat. 154*: multimodi *OQ*   858 [865] *post* 857
transp. Lachmann   862 misere si *Pontanus*: miserest *OQ*   864 mors *Q¹*:
mos *Q*: mox *O*   probet *Lachmann* (prohibet *iam Turnebus*): prohibe *OQ*
868 an nullo *Pontanus*: annullo anullo *O*: anullo anullo *Q*   871 putescat
Auancius: putes *OQ*: putrescat *Laur. xxxv 31*   873 non *Q¹*: no *O*: nos *Q*
880 lacerent *L*: iacerent *OQ*   881 diuidit illim *O*: uidit illum *Q*

hinc indignatur se mortalem esse creatum
nec uidet in uera nullum fore morte alium se   885
qui possit uiuus sibi se lugere peremptum
stansque iacentem se lacerari uriue dolere.
nam si in morte malumst malis morsuque ferarum
tractari, non inuenio qui non sit acerbum
ignibus impositum calidis torrescere flammis   890
aut in melle situm suffocari atque rigere
frigore, cum summo gelidi cubat aequore saxi,
urgeriue superne obtritum pondere terrae.
    'Iam iam non domus accipiet te laeta neque uxor
optima, nec dulces occurrent oscula nati   895
praeripere et tacita pectus dulcedine tangent.
non poteris factis florentibus esse tuisque
praesidium. misero misere' aiunt 'omnia ademit
una dies infesta tibi tot praemia uitae.'
illud in his rebus non addunt 'nec tibi earum   900
iam desiderium rerum super insidet una.'
quod bene si uideant animo dictisque sequantur,
dissoluant animi magno se angore metuque.
'tu quidem ut es leto sopitus, sic eris aeui
quod superest cunctis priuatu' doloribus aegris.   905
at nos horrifico cinefactum te prope busto
insatiabiliter defleuimus aeternumque
nulla dies nobis maerorem e pectore demet.'
illud ab hoc igitur quaerendum est, quid sit amari
tanto opere, ad somnum si res redit atque quietem,   910
cur quisquam aeterno possit tabescere luctu.
    Hoc etiam faciunt ubi discubuere tenentque

886 qui *Laur. xxxv 31*: cui *OQ*   uiuus *O¹*: uibus *OQ*   887 se *Laur. xxxv 31*:
om. *OQ*   dolore *Monacensis 8162*: dolore *O*: dolorem *Q*   893 obtritum
Marullus: obrutum *OQ*   894 iam iam *Laur. xxxv 31*: amiam *O*: uimiam *Q*
896 tangent *O*: tangunt *Q*   897 factis *Q¹*: facti *OQ*   901 una]
ullum *Giussani coll.* 922   902 quod *L*: quo *OQ*   905 *om. Q*
906 cinefactum *Nonius Marcellus p. 133 L.*: cinem factum *OQ*   907 deflebimus *uett. edd.*   908 e *Q¹*: et *OQ*

pocula saepe homines et inumbrant ora coronis,
ex animo ut dicant 'breuis hic est fructus homullis;
iam fuerit neque post umquam reuocare licebit.' 915
tamquam in morte mali cum primis hoc sit eorum,
quod sitis exurat miseros atque arida torrat,
aut aliae cuius desiderium insideat rei.
nec sibi enim quisquam tum se uitamque requirit,
cum pariter mens et corpus sopita quiescunt: 920
nam licet aeternum per nos sic esse soporem,
nec desiderium nostri nos adficit ullum.
et tamen haudquaquam nostros tunc illa per artus
longe ab sensiferis primordia motibus errant,
cum correptus homo ex somno se colligit ipse. 925
multo igitur mortem minus ad nos esse putandumst,
si minus esse potest quam quod nil esse uidemus:
maior enim turba et disiectus materiai
consequitur leto, nec quisquam expergitus exstat
frigida quem semel est uitai pausa secuta. 930
    Denique si uocem rerum natura repente
mittat et hoc alicui nostrum sic increpet ipsa
'quid tibi tanto operest, mortalis, quod nimis aegris
luctibus indulges? quid mortem congemis ac fles?
nam si grata fuit tibi uita anteacta priorque 935
et non omnia pertusum congesta quasi in uas
commoda perfluxere atque ingrata interiere,
cur non ut plenus uitae conuiua recedis
aequo animoque capis securam, stulte, quietem?
sin ea quae fructus cumque es periere profusa 940
uitaque in offensast, cur amplius addere quaeris,
rursum quod pereat male et ingratum occidat omne,

---

914 fructus *Laur. xxxv 31*: fluctus *OQ*   917 torrat *O*^{8}*Q*: torret *O*: torres *Lachmann*: (aridu') torror *Housman*: tortet *M.L. West*: *an* torreat *?*   919 requirit *Naugerius*: requiret *OQ*   921 soporem *O*: praemo *Q*   922 adficit *Lambinus*: adigit *OQ*   925 colligat *Winkelmann*   928 turba et *Goebel*: turbae *OQ*   935 si grata *Naugerius*: gratis *OQ*   gratis fuit haec *Lachmann* 941 offensast *Itali*: offensost *O*^{8}*Q*: offensust *Lambinus*   942 male *Q*: mali *O*

non potius uitae finem facis atque laboris?
nam tibi praeterea quod machiner inueniamque,
quod placeat, nil est; eadem sunt omnia semper.   945
si tibi non annis corpus iam marcet et artus
confecti languent, eadem tamen omnia restant,
omnia si perges uiuendo uincere saecla,
atque etiam potius, si numquam sis moriturus:'
quid respondemus, nisi iustam intendere litem   950
naturam et ueram uerbis exponere causam?
grandior hic uero si iam seniorque queratur   [955]
atque obitum lamentetur miser amplius aequo,   [952]
non merito inclamet magis et uoce increpet acri?   [953]
'aufer abhinc lacrimas, baratre, et compesce
                                        querellas.   955 [954]
omnia perfunctus uitai praemia marces;
sed quia semper aues quod abest, praesentia temnis,
imperfecta tibi elapsast ingrataque uita
et nec opinanti mors ad caput adstitit ante
quam satur ac plenus possis discedere rerum.   960
nunc aliena tua tamen aetate omnia mitte
aequo animoque agedum †magnis† concede: necessest.'
iure, ut opinor, agat, iure increpet inciletque.
cedit enim rerum nouitate extrusa uetustas
semper, et ex aliis aliud reparare necessest,   965
nec quisquam in barathrum nec Tartara deditur atra;
materies opus est ut crescant postera saecla,
quae tamen omnia te uita perfuncta sequentur:
nec minus ergo ante haec quam tu cecidere cadentque.

943 facis *Auancius*: iacis *OQ*   945 placeat *L*: placet *OQ*   948 pergas
Lambinus   950 nisi *Marullus*: si *OQ*   952 [955] *post* 951 *transp. Lachmann*   955 baratro *Bailey dubitanter*: balatro *Turnebi amicus*: blatero *Merrill*
958 imperfecta *Laur. xxxv 31*: imperfecte *OQ*   960 discedere *L*: discere
Q: dicere *O*   962 agedum *L*: agendum *OQ*   magnis] iam aliis *Marullus*:
gnatis *Bernays*: iam annis *Traina* (age nunc annis *iam Merrill*): mage dignis
(cede) *M. L. Clarke* (dignis *iam Lachmann*)   966 deditur *O*: dedit *Q*:
decidit *Q¹*   969 antehac *Heinze*

sic alid ex alio numquam desistet oriri 970
uitaque mancipio nulli datur, omnibus usu.
respice item quam nil ad nos anteacta uetustas
temporis aeterni fuerit quam nascimur ante:
hoc igitur speculum nobis natura futuri
temporis exponit post mortem denique nostram; 975
numquid ibi horribile apparet, num triste uidetur
quicquam, non omni somno securius exstat?
    Atque ea nimirum quaecumque Acherunte profundo
prodita sunt esse, in uita sunt omnia nobis.
nec miser impendens magnum timet aere saxum 980
Tantalus, ut famast, cassa formidine torpens,
sed magis in uita diuum metus urget inanis
mortalis, casumque timent quem cuique ferat fors.
nec Tityon uolucres ineunt Acherunte iacentem
nec quod sub magno scrutentur pectore quicquam 985
perpetuam aetatem possunt reperire profecto:
quamlibet immani proiectu corporis exstet,
qui non sola nouem dispessis iugera membris
obtineat, sed qui terrai totius orbem,
non tamen aeternum poterit perferre dolorem 990
nec praebere cibum proprio de corpore semper.
sed Tityos nobis hic est, in amore iacentem
quem uolucres lacerant atque exest anxius angor
aut alia quauis scindunt cuppedine curae.
Sisyphus in uita quoque nobis ante oculos est 995
qui petere a populo fascis saeuasque securis
imbibit et semper uictus tristisque recedit.
nam petere imperium quod inanest nec datur umquam
atque in eo semper durum sufferre laborem,
hoc est aduerso nixantem trudere monte 1000

983 cuique *O*: cumque *Q*   985 quod *Laur. xxxv 31*: quid *OQ*   988 dispessis *Turnebus*: dispersis *OQ*   992 est *Q¹*: es *OQ*   994 cuppedine *Pontanus*: curpedine *OQ*: cupedine *Q¹*: turpedine *O¹*   995 quoque *O*: om. *Q*   997 tristisque *Q¹*: tristique *OQ*

saxum, quod tamen e summo iam uertice rursum
uoluitur et plani raptim petit aequora campi.
deinde animi ingratam naturam pascere semper
atque explere bonis rebus satiareque numquam,
quod faciunt nobis annorum tempora, circum   1005
cum redeunt fetusque ferunt uariosque lepores,
nec tamen explemur uitai fructibus umquam,
hoc, ut opinor, id est, aeuo florente puellas
quod memorant laticem pertusum congerere in uas,
quod tamen expleri nulla ratione potestur.   1010
Cerberus et Furiae iam uero et lucis egestas,
Tartarus horriferos eructans faucibus aestus,
qui neque sunt usquam nec possunt esse profecto.
sed metus in uita poenarum pro male factis
est insignibus insignis scelerisque luella,   1015
carcer et horribilis de saxo iactu' deorsum,
uerbera carnifices robur pix lammina taedae;
quae tamen etsi absunt, at mens sibi conscia facti
praemetuens adhibet stimulos torretque flagellis
nec uidet interea qui terminus esse malorum   1020
possit nec quae sit poenarum denique finis
atque eadem metuit magis haec ne in morte grauescant.
hic Acherusia fit stultorum denique uita.

   Hoc etiam tibi tute interdum dicere possis:
'lumina sis oculis etiam bonus Ancu' reliquit,   1025
qui melior multis quam tu fuit, improbe, rebus.
inde alii multi reges rerumque potentes
occiderunt, magnis qui gentibus imperitarunt.

1001 e *Vatic. 3276, Vatic. Barb. Lat. 154*: om. *OQ*   1007 uitai fructibus
Itali: uita fructibus *O*: uitae runtibus *Q*   1008 ut *Q*: om. *O*   1009 congerere *Q*¹: congere *Q*: cogere *O*   1010 nulla *L*: ulla *OQ*   *post hunc u. sunt
qui Ixionis mentionem desiderauerunt*   1011 egenus *Itali*   *post u.* 1011 *lacunam
statuit Munro*: *post* 1012   *olim Bailey*   1013 qui] haec *Marullus*
1016 iactu' deorsum *Lambinus*: iactus eorum *OQ*: iactu' reorum *Heinsius*
1017 lammina *Q*¹: iam mina *OQ*   1018 facti *Itali*: factis *OQ*   1019 ter-
retque *Lachmann*: torquetque *Heinsius*

ille quoque ipse, uiam qui quondam per mare magnum
strauit iterque dedit legionibus ire per altum   1030
ac pedibus salsas docuit super ire lacunas
et contempsit equis insultans murmura ponti,
lumine adempto animam moribundo corpore fudit.
Scipiadas, belli fulmen, Carthaginis horror,
ossa dedit terrae proinde ac famul infimus esset.   1035
adde repertores doctrinarum atque leporum,
adde Heliconiadum comites, quorum unus Homerus
sceptra potitus eadem aliis sopitu' quietest.
denique Democritum postquam matura uetustas
admonuit memores motus languescere mentis,   1040
sponte sua leto caput obuius obtulit ipse.
ipse Epicurus obit decurso lumine uitae,
qui genus humanum ingenio superauit et omnis
restinxit, stellas exortus ut aetherius sol.
tu uero dubitabis et indignabere obire,   1045
mortua cui uita est prope iam uiuo atque uidenti,
qui somno partem maiorem conteris aeui
et uigilans stertis nec somnia cernere cessas
sollicitamque geris cassa formidine mentem
nec reperire potes tibi quid sit saepe mali, cum   1050
ebrius urgeris multis miser undique curis
atque animi incerto fluitans errore uagaris?'
    Si possent homines, proinde ac sentire uidentur
pondus inesse animo quod se grauitate fatiget,
e quibus id fiat causis quoque noscere et unde   1055
tanta mali tamquam moles in pectore constet,
haud ita uitam agerent ut nunc plerumque uidemus
quid sibi quisque uelit nescire et quaerere semper

1031 superare L lacunas Q¹ : lucunas OQ,rec. Lachmann, Munro   1033 fudit
Pontanus: fugit OQ   1038 potitus Laur. xxxv 31 : potius OQ   1039 ma-
tura Q : natura O   1042 obit Laur. xxxv 31 : obiit OQ   1044 aetherius
Lactantius Inst. III xvii 28 : aerius O¹Q : haerius O   1050 potes tibi quid
Lachmann (sed quid iam Laur. xxxv 31 teste Büchnero): potest ibi quod OQ
1051 multis O : om. Q   1052 animi Lambinus : animo OQ   incertus Bentley

commutare locum quasi onus deponere possit.
exit saepe foras magnis ex aedibus ille,   1060
esse domi quem pertaesumst, subitoque reuertit
quippe foris nilo melius qui sentiat esse.
currit agens mannos ad uillam praecipitanter,
auxilium tectis quasi ferre ardentibus instans;
oscitat extemplo, tetigit cum limina uillae,   1065
aut abit in somnum grauis atque obliuia quaerit
aut etiam properans urbem petit atque reuisit.
hoc se quisque modo fugit, at quem scilicet, ut fit,
effugere haud potis est, ingratis haeret et odit
propterea, morbi quia causam non tenet aeger;   1070
quam bene si uideat, iam rebus quisque relictis
naturam primum studeat cognoscere rerum,
temporis aeterni quoniam, non unius horae,
ambigitur status, in quo sit mortalibus omnis
aetas, post mortem quae restat cumque manenda.   1075
     Denique tanto opere in dubiis trepidare periclis
quae mala nos subigit uitai tanta cupido?
certa quidem finis uitae mortalibus adstat,
nec deuitari letum pote quin obeamus.
praeterea uersamur ibidem atque insumus usque   1080
nec noua uiuendo procuditur ulla uoluptas.
sed dum abest quod auemus, id exsuperare uidetur
cetera; post aliud, cum contigit illud, auemus,
et sitis aequa tenet uitai semper hiantis.
posteraque in dubiost fortunam quam uehat aetas,   1085
quidue ferat nobis casus quiue exitus instet.

1061 reuertit *Politianus*: reuisit *Proll*: remigrat *Merrill*: *om. OQ*
1063 praecipitanter *L*: praecipiter *O*: praecepiter *Q*   1068 fugit at *O*,
legit *Seneca Tranq. an. 2. 14*: fugit ad *Q*: fugitat *Madvig*   1069 ingratis
Lambinus: ingratius *OQ*: ingratus *Q*[1]: ingratiis *Itali*   1073 temporis aeterni
Vatic. 3276, Vatic. Barb. Lat. 154: aeterni temporis *Q*: aeternitatem corporis *O*
1075 manenda *Lambinus*: manendo *OQ*   1078 certa quidem *Auancius*:
certe equidem *OQ*   1082, 1083 auemus *Q*: abemus *O*: habemus *O*[1]
1084 hiantis *L*: hientis *O*: hientes *Q*   1085 fortunam *Vatic. 3276, Vatic.
Barb. Lat. 154*: fortuna *OQ*

nec prorsum uitam ducendo demimus hilum
tempore de mortis nec delibare ualemus
quo minus esse diu possimus forte perempti.
proinde licet quot uis uiuendo condere saecla: 1090
mors aeterna tamen nilo minus illa manebit,
nec minus ille diu iam non erit, ex hodierno
lumine qui finem uitai fecit, et ille
mensibus atque annis qui multis occidit ante.

1088 delibare *Vatic. 3276, Vatic. Barb. Lat. 154*: deliberare *OQ*   1089 possimus *O¹*: possumus *OQ*   sorte *ed. Aldina 1500*: morte *Lambinus*   1090 quot
Laur. xxxv 31, Vatic. 3276 teste Büchnero: quod *OQ*   condere *O*: ducere *Q*

COMMENTARY

I. INTRODUCTION

1–30

Prooemium. Lucretius begins each book of the poem with a prooemium in the high 'pathetic' style; in Books I, III, V and VI this takes the form of a panegyric on Epicurus (see Introd. 12–13).

1–4 The opening lines are carefully structured to create and then satisfy expectation. The apostrophe announced by *o* (see next n.) is deferred by the intervening *qui*-clause and so gains in weight; the grammatical and rhetorical structure is defined by the sequence of monosyllables *o > qui > te*, each beginning a verse. This simple articulation is complicated and enriched by 'anticipation' and enjambment (*extollere...potuisti, tuis...signis*), by the enclosure of the vocative phrase between *te* and *tuis*, and by 'theme and variation', *sequor* being expanded in the following clause *inque...signis*. As throughout the Prooemium and indeed throughout the poem the emotional effect is reinforced by alliteration. The style and feeling of the address to Epicurus are hymnic; later in the poem he is actually called a god: 5. 8 *deus ille fuit, deus.* Cf. 9–10 nn.

1 o: this, the reading of the MSS, and not the Renaissance correction *e*, is certainly what L. wrote (Timpanaro, *Ph.* 104 (1960) 147–9). 'The preposition is not worthy of the precise and vivid imagination of this poet' (West 80). L. uses *o* very sparingly, for emotional effect: the only other instances in the poem are 2. 14, 3. 3, 5. 1194. *o bone* at 3. 206 is rather different: see n.

tenebris may be local abl. 'in the midst of darkness' or dat. of disadvantage 'so as to put the darkness to flight': for the sense given by the first cf. Cic. *Sull.* 40 *in tantis tenebris erroris et inscientiae clarissimum lumen menti meae praetulistis.* Opposition between light and darkness is a common enough idea in Epicurean and other philosophical literature, but L. uses it with a special emphasis: note the chiastic structure *tenebris tantis...clarum...lumen.* If men could only be brought to think clearly, they would *see* how irrational are their fears and hopes: cf. 2 n., 18, 25–30.

2 primus: Democritus and Leucippus are ignored: so far as L. was concerned Epicurus was the founder of the system. Cf. 9 *rerum inuentor*, 1. 66–7 *primum Graius homo mortalis tollere contra | est oculos ausus primusque obsistere contra*. See Introd. 1–3.

inlustrans commoda uitae: until Epicurus opened their eyes men did not know what was good for them.

3 Graiae gentis decus: only once in the poem (3. 1042, see n.) does L. name Epicurus: the periphrasis is appropriate to his divine status. *Graius* not *Graecus* is the usual poetic form of the adj.

4 'I plant my own footsteps firmly in the prints that you have made'; the phrases *ficta uestigia* and *pressa signa* hardly differ in meaning, and this emphasizes the fidelity with which L. follows the tracks of his master.

ficta: the original (and correct) form of *fixa*.

5 non ita 'less'. The construction is *quam quod te propter amorem imitari aueo*.

6–8 The first of these comparisons would be recognized by L.'s readers as coming from the literary tradition: Pindar, *Ol.* 2. 87–8, compares rival poets to ravens screaming ineffectually at an eagle; and Theocritus' goatherd taunts a shepherd with the words 'it is not right for jays to strive with nightingales or hoopoes with swans' (5. 136–7). Elsewhere in the poem (4. 181) L. uses a similar comparison, between the swan and the crane, to his own advantage (Kenney 371–2). Here he chooses the swallow in self-disparagement, possibly because for the Greeks the speech of barbarians seemed to resemble its twittering: χελιδονίʒω = talk gibberish. The second comparison appears to be an original stroke of invention. Each comparison is differently emphasized: the first by juxtaposing the words *hirundo | cycnis* (note the spondaic word occupying the first foot of the verse), the second by placing the words *haedi, equi uis* at the ends of their verses.

8 fortis equi uis 'a mighty horse', as at 764: on the model of Greek epic and tragic periphrases with βία ('strength') + genitive. Cf. 296, 645, 764, 790 nn.

9–10 tu...tu...tuisque: the repetition is characteristic of a hymn. Cf. the invocation to Venus at 1. 6–9 *te, dea, te fugiunt uenti, te*

nubila caeli | aduentumque tuum, tibi suauis daedala tellus | summittit flores,
tibi rident aequora ponti...; Callim. *Hymn* 1. 6–7 (to Zeus). See Nisbet
and Hubbard on Hor. *C.* 1. 10. 9.

10 tuis...ex, inclute, chartis: the word-order adj.–prep.–noun
is common in poetry, but the separation by the vocative is unusual.
Cf. 421 n.

inclute: applied at 5. 8 to Memmius, but more frequently used of
gods: at 1. 40 Venus is called *incluta*.

chartis: the writings of Epicurus possessed for his disciples the
character of sacred books (Introd. 1–2): cf. 12 *aurea dicta*. Most have
been lost. The groundwork of his system was contained in his great
Περὶ Φύσεως (On Nature): opinions are divided as to whether L. based
himself directly on it or relied principally on an epitome. There is
ample evidence throughout the *D.R.N.* that his studies were far from
superficial.

11–13 The comparison of the poet to a bee was a commonplace,
here dignified by the substitution of the doctrines of Epicurus for the
conventional sources of inspiration, such as the gardens of the Muses
(Plato, *Ion* 534 a). The repetitions *omnia...omnia...aurea...aurea*
occur in identical places in the verse and contribute to the hymnic
feeling of the passage. Syntactically and functionally, however, they
are not identical. The first repetition makes the factual point that L.
has neglected no part of the master's doctrines; the second is emphatic
in a way that recalls the pathetic repetitions of proper names in epic
(e.g. Hom. *Il.* 2. 870–71, Virg. *A.* 7. 649–51, 10. 180–81). The
repetition of *aurea* has the effect of creating a pause after the first foot
of 13, thus lending weight to what follows, which is further dignified
by the enclosing word-order *perpetua...uita* (Pearce 162–4). Cf.
4. 789–90, 5. 950–51. For the sound of 13 cf. 420.

14 uociferari: the challenge to superstition is uttered loudly and
fearlessly.

15 coorta: Orelli's correction, referring to *ratio* 'the philosophy to
which your superhuman intellect gave birth', with an implicit
reference to the birth of Athena, goddess of Wisdom, from the head
of Zeus, chief of the gods: the allusive application of divine mythology
to Epicurus (which in a different context might be polemical) is

appropriate in the hymnic setting (1-4n.). The *coortam* of the MSS (*coartam* QV being merely a secondary corruption) has been explained in two ways: (i) 'Your book on the true nature of the universe, born of your divine intellect', i.e. *naturam rerum* interpreted as a translation of Epicurus' Περὶ Φύσεως. This strains the language and spoils the imagery, converting Epicurus into a huckster of his book. (ii) 'The true nature of the universe arising from (i.e. revealed by) your divine intellect.' This, Giussani's interpretation, essentially reaffirmed in a more sophisticated guise by Waszink (*Mnem.* Ser. 4. 2 (1949) 68-9), seems to strain *coortam*. The corruption *coorta > coortam* would be very easy after *naturam*: scribes were apt to copy a line at a time, paying little or no attention to the context.

16-17 The vision of Epicurean *ratio* pierces the surface of what is visible to the human eye and sees (*uideo*) the workings of the universe. The image seems to be that of clouds parting: cf. Juv. 10. 3-4 *remota | erroris nebula*; Val. Max. 7. 2 *ext.* 1 (the sentiment is attributed to Socrates) *etenim densissimis tenebris inuoluta mortalium mens, in quam late patentem errorem caecas precationes tuas spargis!* The idea is as old as Plato (*Alcib.* 2. 150 d-e). Once again alliteration lends emphasis.

16 **animi terrores:** (i) *religio*, groundless fear of the gods, disposed of in 18-24; (ii) fear of punishment after death, 25-8.

 moenia mundi: the limits of our world, stormed and conquered by Epicurus in a magnificently aggressive series of images at 1. 72-7 *ergo uiuida uis animi peruicit et extra | processit longe flammantia moenia mundi | atque omne immensum peragrauit mente animoque, | unde refert nobis uictor quid possit oriri, | quid nequeat, finita potestas denique cuique | quanam sit ratione atque alte terminus haerens.* Cf. Sykes Davies 34.

17-18 **diffugiunt...discedunt:** L. loves to emphasize his points by such reiteration of prefixes. *di(s)*- is a particular favourite: see 435-7, 539, 638-9, 702-4, 802-3, 815; and for other prefixes see e.g. 70-71, 179-80, 253, 335, 343, 454, 502, 600-1, 740, 845-6, 925, 929, 958, 963.

17 **inane** = τὸ κενόν, the void. 'It is this knowledge that the universe depends on the eternal working of the atomic laws which refutes the belief in divine interference' (Bailey).

18-22 According to the Epicurean view the gods live in spaces between the different worlds (*mundi*, κόσμοι), the *intermundia* (μετα-κόσμια). There, in complete detachment (24), they exist beautifully and peacefully: they do not and cannot influence the affairs of men. These self-sufficient gods were much derided by rival schools. L. chooses to depict their existence in a picture modelled on Homer's account of Olympus, *Od.* 6. 42–6 ὅθι φασὶ θεῶν ἕδος ἀσφαλὲς αἰεὶ | ἔμμεναι· οὔτ' ἀνέμοισι τινάσσεται οὔτε ποτ' ὄμβρῳ | δεύεται οὔτε χιὼν ἐπιπίλναται, ἀλλὰ μάλ' αἴθρη | πέπταται ἀνέφελος, λευκὴ δ' ἐπιδέδρομεν αἴγλη. | τῷ ἔνι τέρπονται μάκαρες θεοὶ ἤματα πάντα, 'where evermore they say the seat of the gods stays sure: for the winds shake it not, nor is it wetted by rain, nor approached by any snow. All around stretches the cloudless firmament, and a white glory of sunlight is diffused about its walls. There the blessed gods are happy all their days' (T. E. Lawrence). It is not quite true that L. follows Homer 'closely' (Bailey): some important differences will be pointed out in the following notes. Here, as at 15 (see n.), L. uses traditional religious mythology to make an Epicurean point, and so prepares the reader for the carefully designed paradox at 28–30 (see n.).

18   apparet marks the culmination of the vision: 'l'apparition a quelque chose de miraculeux' (Ernout–Robin). Possibly L.'s language is deliberately paradoxical, for *numen* (from **nuo* 'nod') = 'divine power' is an abstract conception; it was only in post-Republican Latin that it came to be used simply = 'god'.

quietae: more pointed than Homer's ἀσφαλές; cf. 21 *uidet.*

19–21   The Homeric list of wind, hail and snow is expanded and particularized by vivid descriptive strokes, heightened by alliteration. This strongly physical presentation throws into relief the security of the gods from all such assaults (a good analysis at West 31–3).

21–2 The Homeric λευκή...αἴγλη, 'white splendour', is expanded, with a characteristic insistence on *light*: with the phrase *large diffuso lumine ridet* we return to the idea, now in a much enriched form, of *apparet.*

21   innubilus: unique in Latin and no doubt coined by L. to render Homer's ἀνέφελος.

22   ridet: sc. *aether.* Lachmann emended to *rident*, arguing that it is rather the *sedes* of the gods that should be said to smile: '*ridere*...

dicuntur quae illustrantur, non quae illustrant.' But (i) for the expression with *ridet* compare 1. 8–9 *tibi rident aequora ponti* | *placatum-que nitet diffuso lumine caelum*; (ii) it is in L.'s manner to string together the elements of a description in a 'linear' sequence (see Introd. 24–6), whereas a sudden return to a plural verb governed by *sedes* would be uncharacteristic; (iii) *integit* in first place followed by *et* raises expecta-tions of another verb in the singular: cf. 996–7. Lines of this kind framed by two verbs may be seen as a special case of 'enclosing' word-order (cf. Pearce 160).

23–4 An expression in Epicurean terms of the Homeric τέρπονται κτλ.: the gods need nothing and are untouched by what happens in the *mundi*, which they do not inhabit or frequent.

25–7 Epicurean *ratio* pierces downwards as well as upwards and shows that there is no underworld, only the regular workings of nature as explained by the atomic theory.

25 Acherusia templa 'the place of Acheron'. L. uses *templum* in a variety of ways (Bailey 620, on 1. 120): here he probably borrowed from Ennius' *Andromacha, Sc.* 107–8 V.[2] (98 Jocelyn) *Acherusia templa alta Orci saluete infera*. Acheron, familiar from Plautus onwards in the old Latin form *Acheruns*, was one of the rivers in the traditional underworld geography.

28–30 L. contemplates the Epicurean vision of the universe with an awe that can only be called religious. *uoluptas*, unmixed pleasure, was the end of the system (cf. 38–40n.); the combination with the peculiarly Roman *horror* is most remarkable (cf. Boyancé 294).

28 his...rebus 'because of these things'.
  ibi 'then', when I listen to the voice of *ratio*.

30 manifesta patens...retecta: this emphasis on revelation and illumination returns the reader to the point of departure in 1. This type of cyclic movement, called 'ring-composition', is common in ancient literature from Homer onwards, and L. habitually rounds off his paragraphs in this way: see e.g. 96 *hominis partem* ~ 131 *pars hominis*, 136 ~ 159, 161 ~ 175, etc. It is a technique particularly suitable for literature designed to be read aloud, and it is not confined to poetry: cf. (e.g.) R. M. Ogilvie, *A commentary on Livy Books 1–5*

(1965) 769; G. Williams, *Tradition and originality in Roman poetry* (1968) 808.

31–93

The subject of Book III is now announced: the fear of death and the need to conquer it. This is the second of the *animi terrores* (16n.); the first, *religio*, has been dealt with in Books I and II (Introd. 12), the argument of which is summed up in 31–4.

31   cunctarum exordia rerum: the atoms, more frequently called *primordia rerum*; cf. 121 n.

33   sponte sua: i.e. without divine intervention.

34   quoue = *quoque*, as at 1. 57. Commonly in early Latin and not infrequently in classical and post-Augustan Latin *-ue* means 'and' rather than 'or' (Hofmann–Szantyr 503). Cf. 551 n. and contrast 150 n.

35   hasce secundum res 'next'.

35–6   animi...animae 'the mind...the vital principle': the distinction will be developed at 94–116.

36   claranda: again the persistent emphasis on illumination.

37   foras praeceps...agendus 'bundled out neck and crop', a vivid and unceremonious phrase. L.'s imagery is consistently physical: see the wonderful personification of *religio* at 1. 62–79 (West 57–63), and cf. 38–40, 362, 525 nn.

38–40   Fear of death disturbs human life and corrupts its pleasures. These are fundamental Epicurean ideas, which L. expresses in a most remarkable image. Death is conventionally called 'black' in both Greek and Latin poetry: L. visualizes the blackness of death in physical terms as a noxious cloud of mud stirred up from the bottom of a spring of clear water, making it undrinkable. Cf. West 3.

40   liquidam puramque: the same collocation at Cic. *Caec.* 78 *ita probata fides ut quicquid inde haurias purum te liquidumque haurire sentias*; cf. *De Fin.* 1. 58 *quo minus animus a se ipse dissidens secumque discordans gustare partem ullam liquidae uoluptatis et liberae potest.* Epicurus taught that without a true understanding of nature unalloyed enjoyment was impossible: Κ.Δ. 12 οὐκ ἦν ἄνευ φυσιολογίας ἀκεραίους [*liquidam puramque*] τὰς ἡδονὰς ἀπολαμβάνειν (74 Us.).

41–7   Some deny that they fear death, appealing to 'commonsense' theories of the nature of the *animus*, but they deceive themselves. Here and at 91–3 L. insists on a fundamental Epicurean tenet, that salvation was only to be found within the 'faith' (cf. Introd. 1–2).

41   **quod** 'although', literally 'as to the fact that'. *quod* commonly takes its semantic colouring from its apodosis, which here begins grammatically at 46, logically at 48 (see n.).

42   **ferunt** 'proclaim', more pompous than *aiunt*.
   Tartara leti 'the infernal regions which belong to death'.

43–4   Such theories were held by other schools, but *si fert ita forte uoluntas* shows that L. is referring to materialistic views of the *animus* casually held by those who pride themselves on their independence of any particular sect. For the word-play in *fert. . .forte* cf. 983 n.
   sanguinis . . .uenti: genitives of material.

45   **quicquam** 'at all', adverbial acc.

46   **hinc:** from what follows in 47 ff.; cf. 180–81, 208 nn.
   aduertas animum: for the more usual *anim(um) aduertas*; cf. 54.

46–7   **laudis . . .causa** 'merely to show off': the enjambment helps to emphasize *laudis*.

48–86   The appeal to contemporary experience. Bailey (993) speaks of 'the vehemence and strangeness' of L.'s treatment and remarks (994) that he 'elaborates and magnifies this theme in a very surprising manner'. Before assenting to this verdict we should remember that L. lived at a time when freebooting political ambition was bringing the Roman commonwealth to its knees, and exile, disgrace and death were part of the common experience of the upper classes of Rome (Introd. 8–9). It is precisely the fact that his vivid imagination had these experiences to work upon that turns a string of philosophical commonplaces into moving poetry. It is worth remembering also that Epicurus had endured exile: 'Nul n'a souffert plus que lui des bouleversements politiques de l'époque' (Festugière 63).

6   KLU

48–9 The *infamis uita* to which, according to their previous protestations, they ought to prefer death.

48 idem: used here as a connective and taking its colour from the context, so practically = 'however' (Kühner–Stegmann 1 627–8); cf. 121, 41 n.

50 denique: best taken with what precedes: 'though in short beset with every kind of tribulation they go on living'.

51–4 Just when, according to their professed principles, they should embrace extinction, they devote themselves most fervently to attempting, by propitiatory sacrifices to the gods of the underworld, to mitigate the rigours of the afterlife. L.'s scorn is accentuated by the alliteration in the verses and by the climactic position of *religionem*.

51 tamen: with *parentant*; to whatever straits they are reduced, they still sacrifice.

parentant: properly used of sacrifice to the *di parentes*, the departed ancestors.

52 nigras...pecudes: the correct offering to the infernal deities.

manibu' diuis: a metrical variation of the phrase common in sepulchral inscriptions, *dis manibus*. For the treatment of the *s* of *manibus* cf. 905, 1016, 1025, 1038 and see Introd. 22. *manes* generally signified 'the beneficent and worshipful rather than the maleficent and dangerous spirits of the dead' (J. G. Frazer on Ov. *Fast.* 5. 421); but for the need to appease them see Nisbet and Hubbard on Hor. *C.* 1. 4. 16.

55–6 This has a proverbial ring: cf. Cato *ap.* Gell. 6. 3. 14 *aduorsae res edomant et docent quid opus siet facto*; Ov. *Tr.* 1. 5. 25–6 *scilicet ut flauum spectatur in ignibus aurum,* | *tempore sic duro est inspicienda fides,* 5. 5. 49–50 *scilicet aduersis probitas exercita rebus* | *tristi materiam tempore laudis habet*; and perhaps Eur. fr. 237 N.² ἀλλ' οἱ πόνοι τίκτουσι τὴν εὐδοξίαν, 'it is trouble that makes it possible to achieve reputation'. It is allied to the commonplace (Nisbet and Hubbard on Hor. *C.* 1. 35. 26) that misfortune is the true test of friendship. However, L. gives an original turn to the idea in 57–8.

55 in dubiis...periclis 'in time of trouble and trial': *peric(u)lum*

retains much of its original sense of 'attempt', 'experiment', cf. the
classical phrase *periculum facere*.

56 qui 'what sort of man'.

57 For thought and phrasing cf. Catull. 64. 198 *quae quoniam uerae
nascuntur pectore ab imo*, possibly an imitation (but Norden on Virg. *A.*
6. 55 postulates a common source in Ennius).

58 eliciuntur: this, the reading of the MSS, should stand. The
correction *eiciuntur*, adopted by Lachmann and Munro, may seem to
be supported by *nascuntur* in the Catullan passage quoted in the
preceding n., but in this context *elicio* is the more appropriate word:
the 'true utterance' is *brought* out by *external* circumstances, the
aduersae res. The commentators quote Cic. *Deiot.* 3 *in qua quaestione
dolor elicere ueram uocem possit etiam ab inuito*. Contrast 497 n.

persona is usually interpreted as 'mask', but Farrington (*Hermath.*
85 (1955) 3–12) argues for the sense 'civic dignity', 'social position';
this does not suit *eripitur*.

manet res 'the reality remains'. This early correction has become
the received text. It has been questioned because it does not complete
the striking image of the torn-off mask as might have been expected,
but none of the other attempts at emendation has produced anything
like so telling and forceful a conclusion to the verse.

59–86 The idea that avarice and ambition, with all their attendant
crimes, are motivated by the fear of death seems to be L.'s own
extension of the Epicurean thesis that it was a desire for security
(ἀσφάλεια = *stabilis uita* 66) that drove men to seek fame and status
(K.Δ. 7, 73 Us.; cf. Cic. *De Fin.* 1. 59–61). See also 65–73 n. What
lends L.'s exposition of the idea its peculiarly urgent flavour is of
course its contemporary relevance: Heinze quotes a most apposite
passage from Sallust's *Catiline*: *igitur primo pecuniae, deinde imperi
cupido creuit; ea quasi materies omnium malorum fuere. namque auaritia fidem
probitatem ceterasque artis bonas subuortit; pro his superbiam crudelitatem deos
neglegere omnia uenalia habere edocuit. ambitio multos mortalis falsos fieri
subegit, aliud clausum in pectore, aliud in lingua promptum habere, amicitias
inimicitiasque non ex re sed ex commodo aestumare, magisque uoltum quam
ingenium bonum habere* (10. 3–5). Whatever its historical truth, this
picture of a decline in morals during the late Republic, which we

meet also in Virgil and Horace, forms the essential background to the understanding of the *D.R.N.* as a tract for the times.

59   auarities: avarice, one of the Seven Deadly Sins of the Middle Ages, has tended in modern times to be generalized under references to 'the acquisitive society': ancient moralists, especially the Stoics, took it more personally. A century and a half later Juvenal begins his denunciation of the vices of contemporary Rome with *auaritia.* That it played a prominent part in current political analysis can be seen from the passage of Sallust quoted in the preceding n.; for its role in philosophy and satire cf. N. Rudd, *The Satires of Horace* (1966), 314 s.v. 'Greed'.

61   socios...ministros '*as* companions and accomplices', predicative.

63   uulnera uitae 'running sores' (Latham). A similar use of the image at 5. 1196–7.

65–73   The real *dulcis stabilisque uita* is the life of modest obscurity recommended in the famous precept λάθε βιώσας, 'live so that no one will ever know that you have lived'. However, L.'s argument runs, most men (*ferme*) are blind to this truth, seeing the lack of wealth and fame as equivalent to disgrace and poverty, next door to death. But *cunctarier* (67) implies hesitation and uncertainty and hence a contrast with *stabili*: thus the career of criminal acquisition = flight from uncertainty to security (58–86n.) = revulsion from the idea of death. If this, as suggested by Perret (*Mélanges...offerts à A. Ernout* (1940) 279–83) and Desmouliez (*Latomus* 17 (1958) 318–21) is L.'s logic, it is not above criticism, as turning on a rather strained play of words and ideas, but that is often true of the logic of preachers and moralists.

66   uidetur: it is normal in Latin for the verb of a compound subject to agree only with the nearest element of it: cf. 295, 436 nn. Lambinus' *uidentur* would entail taking *semota* as n. pl. (cf. 136 n.), which here is awkward and unnecessary.

67   This idea is further developed by Virgil: in the anteroom of his Hades (*A.* 6. 273–81) live Grief, Cares, Sickness, Old Age, Fear, Hunger, Poverty, etc.

cunctarier: the archaic form of the inf. pass., retained even in Augustan poetry for metrical convenience.

68–9 se must be taken as the subject of *effugisse*; for this redundant construction with *uolo* there is an analogy if not a precise parallel at 5. 1120 *at claros homines uoluerunt se atque potentis.* For *remosse* a reflexive object *se* may be understood from the preceding *se*; or the verb may be used intransitively as is *mouere* at 6. 595.

68 falso terrore has a double reference, to men's fear of death and to their abhorrence of poverty and obscurity.

69 effugisse...remosse (= *remouisse*) : genuine perfects: 'they wish to have escaped and to have got well clear'. Contrast 683 n.

70–71 The words *sanguine ciuili* show that L. had Rome's present troubles in mind (Sellar 290), and the weight and positioning of the two long words *conduplicant...accumulantes* point a sardonic equation between the amassing of wealth and the amassing of murders: ambition = death. *conflant* 'rake together' also has a pejorative ring.

72 fratris: Macrobius' citation is 'non-specific', i.e. this is not the word that he is concerned to illustrate (cf. 94 n.), but his reading is obviously more pointed than *fratres* and is supported by the Virgilian adaptation quoted in the next note. *fratris* became *fratres* after *crudeles*: cf. 15 n.

72–3 'C'est du Salluste en vers' (Martha 188). Nothing in the Civil Wars seared the Roman conscience more than their effect on the ties of family and kinship. It is a favourite theme of Horace's (see Nisbet and Hubbard on *C*. 1. 35. 34) and a century later was to obsess Lucan. Virgil clearly had the present passage in mind when he wrote the lines *hic petit excidiis urbem miserosque penatis,* | *ut gemma bibat et Sarrano dormiat ostro;* | *condit opes alius defossoque incubat auro;* | *hic stupet attonitus rostris, hunc plausus hiantem* | *per cuneos geminatus enim plebisque patrumque* | *corripuit; gaudent perfusi sanguine fratrum,* | *exsilioque domos et dulcia limina mutant* | *atque alio patriam quaerunt sub sole iacentem* (*G*. 2. 505–12). Behind such sentiments may be detected the echo of a favourite commonplace on the decline of conventional morality: cf. Catull. 64. 397–404.

73 mensas: they are afraid of being poisoned.

74 ab 'as a result of'.

75–7 L.'s 'linear' style of writing (Introd. 24–6) dictates that the acc. and inf. construction in 75–6 depends on *macerat inuidia*, which is syntactically equivalent to *inuident*, 'they are envious that...'; cf. Plaut. *Bacch.* 543 *nullus est quoi non inuideant rem secundam optingere*, *Truc.* 745 *nam inuidere alii bene esse, tibi male esse, miseria est.* Lachmann, followed by several later editors, punctuated after *inuidia* and referred all the indirect statements to *queruntur* in 77; but L. was writing for readers of an *unpunctuated* text, who in the absence of specific guidance would not pause after *inuidia* and who would be expecting an object after *macerat inuidia*, which is supplied by the acc. and inf. clause.

75–6 illum...illum: not 'this man...that man', ἄλλον μέν... ἄλλον δέ, but anaphora to convey the ambitious man's obsession with the success of his rival: '*he...he...*not I'.

77 caeno: a common metaphor; as we say, 'in the gutter'.

78 intereunt partim 'some die'.
statuarum et nominis ergo: an almost Juvenalian phrase. The archaic preposition *ergo* = *causā* lends weight and dignity. Epicurus relegated garlands and statues to the class of unnecessary and unnatural pleasures (Schol. K.Δ. 29, 78 Us.), but scorn of such trappings is not specifically Epicurean.

79–84 The paradox that men will kill themselves through fear of death goes back to Democritus, who observed that in avoiding death men pursued it, ἄνθρωποι τὸν θάνατον φεύγοντες διώκουσιν (68 B 203 DK). Seneca ascribes the sentiment to Epicurus: *obiurgat Epicurus non minus eos qui mortem concupiscunt quam eos qui timent, et ait:* '*ridiculum est currere ad mortem taedio uitae, cum genere uitae ut currendum ad mortem esset effeceris*'. *item alio loco dicit:* '*quid tam ridiculum quam adpetere mortem, cum uitam inquietam tibi feceris metu mortis?*' (*Ep.* 24. 22–3); cf. Cic. *De Fin.* 1. 49.

80 humanos = *homines*, as at 837.

81 maerenti pectore 'mourning'.

82–4 The effect of the anaphora *hunc...hunc...hunc* is both connective and emphatic. The reader who interprets the text by ear (cf. 75–7 n.)

is constrained to take all the infinitives *esse...uexare...rumpere...
euertere* as parallel, with the last limb of the utterance as climax and
summary. Hence *euertere* depends on *obliti*, and the *suadet* given by the
MSS in 84 must be corrupt. None of the suggested corrections is wholly
convincing. Lambinus' *fundo* is printed *exempli gratia*; Bailey's *e
summa...sede*, though subsequently rejected by its author, also
deserves consideration.

Love of friends, family and country was practised and commended
by Epicurus (D.L. 10. 10); for a Roman these were the primary
loyalties. The catalogue of sinners in Virgil's Hell culminates in the
traitors and the incestuous (*A.* 6. 621–4). L. wishes to show the lengths
to which men may be driven by the fear of death.

83 Apart from the weak caesura in the second foot, a non-caesural line,
strictly speaking, since the elided final syllable of *pudorem* is nevertheless felt (Soubiran 528–33). Such lines are rare even in L.; there is
another at 770. Cf. 773 n. and contrast 174, 976 nn.

pudorem 'honour'.
amicitiai: the archaic genitive form, freely used by L. for metrical
convenience and euphonic effect.

84   in summa: apparently 'in short' = *denique*, but the text cannot
be regarded as certain; elsewhere in L. the phrase = 'in the universe'.
fundo 'utterly' = *funditus*: the only other recorded instance of this
absolute use is at Virg. *A.* 10. 88–9 *nosne tibi fluxas Phrygiae res uertere
fundo | conamur?*, which lends support to Lambinus' correction.

85   iam: almost 'in fact'; these things are not hypothesized, they
have already happened.

86   prodidĕrunt: the original quantity: the form in *-ērunt* probably
represents a contamination between *-ēre* and *-ĕrunt* (L. R. Palmer, *The
Latin language* (1954) 275). Cf. 134, 1028.
Acherusia templa: 25 n.
petentes: i.e. *dum petunt*.

87–93 A transitional formula to introduce the argument proper:
L. uses it in whole or part more than once in the poem (see app. crit.).
The repetition of *nam* in 87 so soon after *nam* in 85 seems to indicate
that these verses have been inserted here *en bloc*.

88   in tenebris...in luce: that that these fears were childish was a philosophical commonplace, to which L. imparts a new twist by his favourite opposition between darkness and light. Our bodies may be in daylight, but our minds are in darkness: cf. 91.

91   animi: take with both *terrorem* and *tenebras*: cf. 189 n.

92   lucida tela diei 'the bright shafts of day', a characteristic image to provide a transition to the idea that these fears must be attacked with the arms provided by the Epicurean philosophy: metaphorical darkness will be assailed with metaphorical weapons.

93   naturae species ratioque 'the outer view and the inner law of nature' (Bailey). *species* = the phenomena, *ratio* = the atomic system which produces the phenomena. On the various meanings of *ratio* Bailey's note on 1. 51 (605–6) should be consulted.

II. ARGUMENT

A. THE SOUL IS MATERIAL

94–135

The *animus* is part of the body, not an abstract relationship, a 'harmony'.

94   primum 'in the first place' = *principio*.

animum: 'mind' may be used for the sake of convenience to render *animus*, but no English term is entirely satisfactory. L. distinguishes *animus*, the rational part of the soul, from *anima*, the irrational part (see 117 n.). In this he is following Epicurus, who considered the common Greek distinction between 'mind' (νοῦς) and 'soul' (ψυχή) unsatisfactory, preferring to distinguish between two parts of the ψυχή, a rational part (τὸ λογικὸν μέρος) and an irrational (τὸ ἄλογον μέρος). L. confuses his terminology, however, by also using *anima* (= ψυχή) for the whole soul: cf. 143 n.

quam: Charisius' citation is 'non-specific', since he is illustrating the adverbial use of *primum* (cf. 72 n.); however, L. regularly allows attraction of the relative pronoun to the gender of its predicate, and the correction of *quem* to *quam* was made independently by the Italian scholars of the fifteenth century on that ground: cf. 99–100, 1. 834, 4. 132.

saepe 'commonly', but, strictly speaking, inaccurately, for *animus* (= θυμός) embraces the emotions, whereas *mens* is purely intellectual. L. seems to recognize this fact implicitly in phrases like *mens animi* (4. 758) or *animi…mens consiliumque* (3. 615) or *mens animusque* (3. 139, 142, 398, 402); occasionally he uses *mens* alone = *animus* (3. 228).

95 consilium…regimen: the rational and the guiding principle, probably renderings of the Greek terms τὸ λογικόν and τὸ ἡγεμονικόν.

96–7 This fundamental doctrine is reinforced by the emphasis on the physical: hands, feet, eyes can all be *seen* and *felt*, and the *animus*, though it cannot be seen, is every bit as corporeal as they are.

96 ac 'than'; cf. 1093 n.

97 exstant: here, as commonly in L. (but cf. 194 n.), *exstare* means little more than *esse*.

After this verse one or more lines have fallen out; the sense must have been 'but there are some who hold that…'.

98 sensum 'the power to feel'.
certa 'defined', 'particular'; cf. 104.

99 habitum…uitalem corporis 'a condition of the body that maintains life' (Smith): *uitalem* is explained in 100–1 *quod faciat nos | uiuere cum sensu*.

100 harmoniam: L. uses the Greek technical term in addition to his periphrasis, so that there shall be no misunderstanding and the doctrine that he is attacking shall be clearly identified. Cf. 1. 830–32, where he apologizes for the necessity, forced on him by the deficiencies of the Latin language, of using the term *homoeomeria*. The view that the soul was nothing more than a harmonious relationship of the parts of the body is discussed in Plato's *Phaedo* (86 ff.).
quam: 94 n.
quod 'the thing which', 'something which'.

101 uiuere cum sensu 'live and feel'. The construction with acc. and inf. after *faciat* is unknown to classical prose and is probably colloquial (Hofmann–Szantyr 354); cf. 301.

nulla...in parte 'in no defined part'; cf. 98, 104.
cum 'although'; cf. 107 n.
siet: archaic for *sit*.

102–3   To explain the doctrine of *harmonia* recourse was usually had
to analogies; here to that of health, but more commonly to the musical
analogy alluded to in 131–5.

102   The rhythm of the verse, with weak caesura in the second foot
and strong caesura in the fourth only, is unusual, but no special effect
seems to be intended: cf. 317 n.
bona: *ualetudo*, in spite of its derivation from *ualere*, is commonly
neutral in sense.

103   corporis...ualentis: L. is almost playing with language:
good health is 'of' the body in the sense that it belongs to and is
inseparable from it, but it is not a part of the healthy man.
ualentis: usually in L. *ualere* = *esse*; here the sense 'be healthy'
is imposed by *ualetudo* preceding.

104   sic: it is impossible to be sure whether this picks up the *ut*-
clause of 102–3 (which in that case has a double reference, both
forward and back), or whether it refers to 98–103 in general, 'on the
basis of this belief'.

105   diuersi 'in the wrong direction': they are completely at sea.

106–11   The reasoning is: different parts of the body feel pain and
pleasure independently from each other; so also do the body and the
mind: (therefore the mind is a part of the body). The argument is
syllogistic, with the premisses presented in reverse order and the
conclusion left to be inferred by the reader.

106   itaque refers back to 97.
aegret: the verb occurs in Latin only here and at 824, where
aegret is an easy correction of the *aegrit* of the MSS. In this case the
grammarian's citation is specific (contrast 72, 94 nn.). The *aegrum*
offered here by the MSS is in itself unobjectionable, but would need
the addition of *est* to conform to Lucretian usage.

107   cum 'although', here with indic. instead of the usual subjunctive
(contrast 101): cf. 146, 150, 645, 653. The usage is archaic: see

W. M. Lindsay, *Syntax of Plautus* (1907) 69–71; Bennett 1 141–2. Cf. also 112, 363, 847nn.

parte latenti: the *animus*, contrasted with those parts of the body which can be seen *in promptu* 'obviously'.

108   retro...contra...uicissim 'vice versa', a striking tautology.

109   ex animo 'in the mind', not as at 914 'from the heart', the common meaning of the phrase.

111   in nullo...dolore: the phrase *in dolore esse* seems to be unique in literary Latin.

112–16   In sleep the mind is active while the body is not. The full discussion of the mechanism of sleep that is to follow at 4. 907–1036 is here taken for granted.

112   cum 'when', but in view of *tamen* at 114 it has a concessive flavour, almost = 'although'. Cf. 41, 107, 218nn.

113   onustum 'heavy' (Bailey), i.e. weighed down with sleep, rather than 'replete' (Latham): cf. 4. 956 *sopor ille grauissimus*.

114   aliud: the *animus*.

116   curas cordis = *animi curas* (4. 908): for the alliteration cf. (e.g.) 994, 6. 645 *cernentes pauida complebant pectora cura*.
   inanis: acc. pl. with *curas*.

117–29   The *anima* too is corporeal, consisting of particles of air and heat.

117   animam 'vital principle'; for convenience in translating 'soul' may be used, but cf. 94n. The distinction between *animus* and *anima* was implied early in the poem, at 1. 131 *unde anima atque animi constet natura uidendum*, and the *uitalis animae nodos* are referred to at 2. 950; but only now are the two expressly differentiated.

117–18   in membris...esse: it has a physical existence all over the body (being in this unlike the *animus*); it is not a condition or a relationship.

118   'And it is not in virtue of any *harmonia* that the body possesses sensation.'

119   detracto corpore multo 'even when we lose one or more limbs': *tamen* in 120 shows that the participle has a concessive force. Cf. 171, 441–2 nn.

121   eadem rursum 'again on the other hand', a somewhat tautologous expression, since *eadem* (sc. *uita*) has an adversative colouring: cf. 48 n.

   corpora pauca 'a few atoms'; they are called *corpora* again at 125, *semina* at 127: cf. 31, 180 nn. *pauca* contrasts with *multo* at 119: these atoms of heat and air are few in comparison with those of the visible body, but their presence or absence is a matter of life and death.

121–2   caloris...aer 'heat...air', varied below (126) as *uapor* and *uentus*. The Greek *aer* is fully naturalized by the time of Cicero: contrast Ennius, *Ann.* 148 V.[2] *uento quem perhibent Graium genus aera lingua*. When L. comes to discuss these phenomena more scientifically he distinguishes *uentus* and *aer*: 232–6 n.

122   per os: L. is not speaking scientifically: it was (and is) a popular belief that the soul escapes through the mouth. The Epicurean position is accurately stated at 254–5.

124–5   If the *anima* were a *harmonia* its existence would depend equally on all parts of the body and their constituent atoms, but this we have just seen is not the case.

125   salutem 'life', 'existence'.

126–9   L. speaks as if at 121–2 he had demonstrated that the *anima* consists of atoms of heat and air, whereas what was said in those verses amounted merely to 'when the body grows cold in death and the breath leaves it'; the idea of soul-atoms was insinuated into the description *via* the phrase *corpora pauca*, and their existence is now taken as proved. The *igitur* of 128 thus verges on the fraudulent.

128   est 'there exists', emphatic.

128–9   in ipso corpore 'there, in the body'; for this use of *ipse* cf. 459, 483, 506, 575, 590 and see the other examples collected by Munro in his note on 4. 736. The effect here is enhanced by enjambment.

130–35 Aristoxenus, a pupil of Aristotle's, explained the soul as a harmony in musical terms (Cic. *Tusc.* 1. 19), and the same analogy was used by Plato in the *Phaedo* (86 b). L. no doubt has this explanation in mind when he says sarcastically that the musicians may have the term back.

130 quapropter quoniam: an effective use of essentially prosaic words to enforce and dignify the argument. Compare Propertius' use of *quandocumque igitur* (2. 1. 71, 2. 13. 17), both times with reference to the inevitable approach of death.

130–31 animi natura...atque animae: periphrases of this kind with *natura* are common in L., but they are not purely formal: L. means the *animus* and the *anima* as we – as instructed Epicureans – actually know them to be; cf. 161 n.

131 quasi 'almost', 'as it were'. This qualification, after the emphatic statement at 94–7, is a little odd; but L. has a habit of unexpectedly apologizing in this way: cf. 280, 707 nn.

harmoniai: the archaic Latin termination (83 n.) is here grafted on to a Greek word, and one which was never naturalized in Latin, as (e.g.) *aer* was (121–2 n.). It is possible that L. intended a slightly grotesque effect in keeping with the sneering tone of the whole passage (see following nn.).

132 organicos 'musicians'. The sarcastic tone of the verse is unmistakable. Harmonia in Greek mythology was a child of the Muses (Eur. *Med.* 834) or of Aphrodite (Eur. *Phoen.* 7); L. tells the musicians that, however lofty her origins may be (*alto delatum Heliconi*), they may keep her. Cicero is similarly scornful in rejecting the theory and the term, which he likewise restores to music, where it belongs (*Tusc.* 1. 41; cf. Boyancé 151 n. 1).

Heliconi is abl.; cf. 611 *parti*.

133–4 '...(whether they received it straight from Helicon) or appropriated it from some other source as being in want of a term for this thing.' *siue* picks up an unexpressed *siue* from the preceding verse. This sarcastic afterthought is not gratuitous. Epicurus insisted on the use of simple and appropriate language: D.L. 10. 13; Cic. *De Fin.* 2. 6. L. implies that the use of second-hand metaphor (*transferre* = μεταφέρειν) does not advance our understanding.

133   aliunde: from medicine (102–3) or perhaps, as suggested by Duff, carpentry.

   illam: sc. *rem*, attracted into the relative clause.

134   transtulĕrunt: 86n.

135   quidquid id est 'be that as it may', 'however that may be'.
   habeant 'they can keep it'; the more usual form of the phrase is *sibi habere*. In contrast with the tone of 132 (see n.) the diction is brusque and unceremonious.
   tu: Memmius or the reader? One cannot be sure.

136–160

The relationship of the *animus* and the *anima*; the *animus* as the dominant partner.

136–7   On the *animus* and *anima* as parts of the 'soul' (ψυχή) see 94n.

136   coniuncta: n. pl., referring to nouns of different gender. This construction is relatively rare in Cicero, commoner in post-Augustan prose and verse (Hofmann–Szantyr 435), frequent in L.: see 283, 287, 349, 412, 421, 458, 506, 552, 559, 601, 705, 920. Cf. 66, 335nn.

137   inter se: with *coniuncta*; the enjambment confers emphasis (cf. 6–8n.).

138   caput...quasi 'what we may call the head', i.e. the dominant part, a common figurative sense of the word. L. goes out of his way to qualify *caput* since he is about to affirm that the chest and *not* the head is the seat of reason. On the metre see 174n.

139   Cf. 94n.

140   situm...haeret 'is lodged in and does not move from', in contrast to the *anima*, which is distributed throughout the body (143); cf. 548–50, 615–17. The idea that the *animus* was situated in the chest was traditional long before it was adopted by Epicurus; it was familiar to Homer, and generally 'the heart had more advocates than the brain' (Munro).

141–2   L.'s argument confuses the distinction between the *mens* and the rest of the *animus* (cf. 94n.): his examples are all of emotions and do not support the location of the *mens* proper in the chest (cf. 145n.).

hic...haec...hic: the anaphora (cf. 82–4n.) lends impetus and so helps to gloss over the logical inconsequence.

141 circum: the preposition, here placed after its noun, as not infrequently in poetry.

142 laetitiae 'feelings of pleasure'; for the pl., nowhere else used by L., cf. Cat. 76. 22 *expulit ex omni pectore laetitias*.

143 animae: used here and at 150 = ψυχή, the whole soul, *animus* + *anima*. This terminological shift was perhaps forced on L. by the *patrii sermonis egestas*. It is undeniably awkward, but there is no real danger of misunderstanding his meaning. The alternative explanation that *animae* is a defining (Ernout–Robin) or 'appositional' (Smith) genitive and that the phrase = 'the other part, that is the *anima*' is strained. Cf. 175n.

144 paret: sc. *menti*.

ad numen...momenque 'at its direction and impulse'; L. is translating the Greek terms νεῦσις and ῥοπή, but *momen* is a favourite word of his in any case. The combination in this verse of alliteration and 'figura etymologica' (*momen...mouetur*) lends a characteristically Lucretian emphasis: cf. 188n. As is sometimes the case in Latin, 'only' must be added to the English rendering to bring out the full sense (cf. 145 *solum*): see Shackleton Bailey, *C.Q.* 41 (1947) 91. Cf. 351, 589nn.

145 idque looks back to 140, the intervening verses being parenthetic to the main argument. Emphasis is imparted by alliteration and anaphora, the latter with variation of metrical ictus and vowel quantity: *ĭdque sibĭ...ĭd sibĭ* (on this type of variation cf. 427n.; Munro on 4. 1259; Nisbet and Hubbard on Hor. *C.* 1. 32. 11).

sapit: the only reference to the rational activity of the *animus*, whose operation here as above (141–2n.) is otherwise discussed in terms of the emotions.

146 cum: 107n.

unā 'together', sc. with the *animus*. However, the text of the MSS entails taking *neque res* = *nihil*, which is distinctly awkward; and there is something to be said for the old and easy emendation *ulla*: 'when no single thing affects either the body or the mind'. For the phrase *res...ulla* cf. 184.

147 **quasi** 'just as', not 'as if'.

148 **concruciamur** is unique in Latin and is probably a coinage of L.'s own (note the alliteration with *corpore* in 149). Cf. 153n.

150 **-que** 'or': for this sense of *-que* cf. 198, 284, 333–4, 797, 841 nn., 2. 825 and the notes of the commentators; also Fordyce on Catull. 45. 6. Copulative particles, like conjunctions (41n.) or participles (119n.) take their precise meaning from the context. It may be, as here, disjunctive; or adversative, as at Ov. *Met.* 1. 15, 18 (cf. E. Fraenkel, *Horace* (1957) 219n. 4); or even inferential, as at Ov. *Met.* 6. 459 (see F. Bömer on Ov. *Met.* 3. 260). Cf. 164, 340, 442, 816, 900nn.; and contrast *-ue* = 'and' at 34, 551 (see nn.).
  cum: 107n.
  cetera pars animai: 143n.

151 **nulla nouitate** 'by no new sensation'.

152 **uerum** 'however'. In 147–51 L. has enlarged on the point made in 145 (note *solum*), the capacity of the *animus* to act and be acted upon independently of the *anima*. He now returns to the fundamental point from which the argument started (136–7), that the two are nevertheless intimately connected, as is shown by what happens when a stimulus of sufficient strength is applied. Once more alliteration (note also position of *mens*) lends emphasis.
  magis: take with *uementi*.
  mens must here stand for *animus* or *mens animusque*.

153 **consentire** 'is equally affected', a translation of συμπάσχειν: cf. Cic. *De Nat. Deor.* 3. 28 *consensus, quam* συμπάθειαν *Graeci uocant*. Cf. 148, 740nn.

153–8 **uidemus...uidemus...quiuis:** the usual Epicurean and Lucretian insistence on the evidence of our senses, from which even the man in the street (*quiuis*) can, if properly instructed, draw the correct conclusions. Cf. 165 *uidemus*.

154–6 This catalogue of symptoms recalls the famous poem of Sappho

(31 L.-P.) adapted by Catullus (51). L. was well read in the poets (Kenney, passim), and it is perhaps more probable than not that he knew the Sappho poem; but the resemblances do not seem so striking as to impose the conclusion that he had it in mind here. Exact observation of such phenomena is a marked feature of his method, as is shown by the description of drunkenness at 476-80.

155 'The utterance becomes disconnected and the voice dies away.' *infringi* need not be explained as a rendering of Sappho's Greek, which, it may be remarked, Lobel–Page regard as corrupt.

156 **sonere:** the archaic form of *sonare*, also at 873. Cf. *lauare*, *lauere*. L. uses such variant forms freely (Bailey 85–6), no doubt for metrical convenience. Increased discretion in the use of such devices is one of the hallmarks of Augustan classicism (Introd. 22–3). Cf. 184 n.

159-60 The sequence of action is *animus* > *anima* > *corpus*.

159 **c(um) animo:** the only instance, according to Soubiran (404), of the elision of the preposition *cum* in the entire corpus of epic from Cicero to Silius. Cf. 853 n. The elision of the conjunction in *c(um) animi*, on the other hand, is relatively frequent (Soubiran 405), but it is curious that L. should elide this monosyllable twice in the same verse.

160 **percussast:** Nonius' citation is to illustrate *icit* and cannot be pressed in support of *perculsa est*: cf. 72, 94 nn. For *percussa* cf. 4. 887–8, for *perculsa* 1. 13; but *perculsa* is too strong a word here (not too weak, as Bailey suggests).
  exim 'immediately' = *exinde*.
  icit: L. uses the simple verb only here and at 4. 1050 *icimur*. In classical Latin forms other than the pf. part. *ictus* are rare except in the technical phrase *foedus icere* 'make a treaty'.

161-176

The *animus* and the *anima* are corporeal. This has so far been taken for granted; it is now explicitly demonstrated.

161 **naturam animi atque animai:** a cumbersome periphrasis for

7

ψυχή, but it serves as a reminder of the fundamental points already established; cf. 130–31 n.

163   mutareque: L. is less reluctant than Cicero or the Augustans to attach -*que* to a short *e*, but his usage can hardly be called 'frequent' (Bailey 129). If we accept the figures in J. Paulson's *Index Lucretianus*[2] (1926) 126, -*que* occurs 1288 times in the *D.R.N.*, and the instances of -*ĕque* noticed by Bailey number 25.

164   regere ac uersare 'cause to move in a straight line or change direction'; cf. 150, 333, 442 nn.

  uidetur 'is seen to' not 'seems': cf. 153–8 n. This sense of *uideri* is normal throughout L.'s argument.

165–6 A fundamental premiss of the system: cf. 1. 304 *tangere enim et tangi nisi corpus nulla potest res*; 434–44, esp. 443 *at facere et fungi sine corpore nulla potest res*; 2. 434–5 *tactus enim, tactus, pro diuum numina sancta,* | *corporis est sensus.*

168   fungi 'is acted upon', πάσχειν. In 161–7 it was shown that the *animus* acts on the body, now that the reverse is also true.

169   consentire: 153 n.

170   si minus = *si non. minus*, originally a colloquial and slightly milder variant for *non*, is standard Latin in the phrases *si minus* and *quo minus* (Hofmann–Szantyr 454–5).

171 'Driven in and so laying bare the bones and sinews': the participle is causal, taking its colour from the context (cf. 119, 441–2 nn.). The aspect of the pf. part. is often, as here, felt as contemporaneous rather than past; indeed the pf. part. passive may originally have been a verbal adj. without implications of past time (E. Laughton, *The participle in Cicero* (1964) 2–3).

172–4 *languor terraeque petitus* describes the effects of the swoon on the *anima*, *aestus mentis* and *exsurgendi uoluntas* the effects on the *animus*.

173   suauis: the idea that a swoon may be 'pleasant' has troubled many interpreters, and various emendations of the text have been proposed, of which Munro's *segnis* is perhaps the best. But (i) all the corrections are at best commonplace when compared with the transmitted text; (ii) Seneca is clearly appealing to what he conceives to be common experience when he writes (of the death of Marcellinus) *defecit, ut aiebat, non sine quadam uoluptate, quam adferre solet lenis dissolutio non inexperta nobis, quos aliquando liquit animus* (*Ep.* 77. 9). Heinze also quotes an interesting passage from Montaigne which bears out the idea. L., as has been seen (154–6 n.), is precise in such descriptions, and *suauis* looks more like accurate (if laconically communicated) observation than scribal error.

174 The lumpy and heaving rhythm reflects the spasmodic efforts of the wounded man to rise. The main caesura of the verse is what may be called a 'quasi-caesura', associated with elision (here, as chance would have it, of *quasi*). Generally elision of the first *longum* of the third foot of the hexameter occurs only before a monosyllable, usually a conjunction or preposition; in such cases what is in question is aphaeresis rather than true elision, that is to say at (e.g.) 138 we should read *sed caput esse quasi (e)t dominari in corpore toto* rather than *quas(i)'et*: cf. Soubiran 181, 527–8. The formulation may be extended to cover monosyllabic prefixes deemed to be etymologically separable from the word of which they form part: cf. (e.g.) 612 *...dissolui: quod s(i) im|mortalis nostra foret mens*, 715, 958, 1043, 2. 1059 *sponte sua fort(e) of|fensando semina rerum*; (two instances in a single line) Prop. 2. 17. 11 *quem modo felic(em) in|uidi(a) ad|mirante ferebant* (the commentators continue to repeat from M. Platnauer, *Latin elegiac verse* (1951) 8, the erroneous opinion that the verse has no caesura). Cf. 258, 630 nn. For examples of genuinely non-caesural lines see 83 n.

175–6 These verses do not summarize the preceding argument, as *ergo* might seem to imply, so much as introduce an additional point, the corporeal nature of the weapons which inflict damage on the mind.

175 animi: here and at 177, 237, for ψυχή, *animus + anima*. The motive for this further variation in terminology (cf. 143 n.), if it is not to be attributed to pure negligence, may be metrical. At 177 *anima* would not scan at all, and here the elision *anim(ae) esse* would probably have been felt as objectionable (374 n.).

176 laborat 'is in trouble', 'suffers'.

177–230

The structure of the *animus* and the *anima*: (*a*) the soul-particles. L. demonstrates that the soul is composed of groups of atoms (180n.) which are exceedingly small, smooth and light.

177   animus: 175n. However, down to 207 at all events, L. seems to be thinking primarily of the *animus* proper.

   unde = *ex quibus*.

178   constiterit 'consists' = *constet*; cf. 180 *constare*.

179–80   persubtilem...minutis perquam (for *perminutis*, ruled out by metre): cf. 187. L. is fond of compounds with *per* = 'very' (cf. 473n., 216, 249). They seem to have been generally regarded as too colloquial for literary use; Cicero is the only writer of artistic prose who makes much use of them, and outside L. they are rare in the 'high' genres of poetry (B. Axelson, *Unpoetische Wörter* (1945) 37–8; Hofmann–Szantyr 164). The phrase translates the Epicurean technical term λεπτομερές (*Ep. ad Hdt.* 63, 19 Us.). Cf. also 253n.

180   corporibus: strictly speaking not 'atoms' but 'particles', compounded of atoms of four different constituents, as explained in 231–57. These atoms are themselves of course very light, round and smooth, and however they are figured as being grouped, the *animus* is certainly made up out of them; but the arguments drawn by L. from the speed of the thought-process at 180–85 entail that he is thinking in terms of *animus*-particles and not of individual atoms. Again a terminological imprecision, but we need not suppose any confusion in L.'s mind: in this context it could be taken for granted that *corpora* or *semina* (187) or *figurae* (190) or *elementa* (374) or *primordia* (392), all words elsewhere used of atoms, meant 'the atoms as grouped in *animus*-particles'. Cf. 374, 708nn.

180–81   A more 'logical' order would be 'licet animum aduertas ut hinc pernoscere possis id ita esse'; but the emphasis is thereby destroyed. *hinc* 'from what follows', as at 46 (see n.).

182   adeo...celeri ratione: a periphrasis for *tam celeriter*. The speed of thought was proverbial from Homer onwards.

183   'As what the mind pictures to itself as happening and then itself sets in motion' or, more abstractly, 'the reception of the image and its translation into the beginnings of action'. The stages of the process are reserved for full description at 4. 877–906.

quam: understand *quod* from *nil* in 182. This type of ellipse, of *ut, cum, si, qui,* etc., after *quam,* is common, and appears to be colloquial: 'it is as old as the language itself' (E. Löfstedt, *Vermischte Studien* (1936) 26). Cf. Catull. 10. 32 *utor tam bene quam* [sc. *si*] *mihi pararim* and Fordyce's note; Hofmann–Szantyr 594–5, 826.

184   perciet: contrast 303 *percit* and cf. 156n.

185   quorum...natura = *quae.* The periphrasis with *natura* is here quite colourless. For the treatment of *res* as if it were neuter L. himself offers analogies rather than exact parallels: cf. 1. 449–50 *nam quaecumque cluent, aut his coniuncta duabus | rebus ea inuenies aut horum euenta uidebis.* Munro compares *inter al.* Sall. *Jug.* 41. 1 *abundantia earum rerum quae prima mortales ducunt.* See Hofmann–Szantyr 431–2.

186 The unusual rhythm, with the second foot consisting of a dactylic word, is probably descriptive; cf. 190. Since the elided syllable of *tanto* is felt (83n.) there is, strictly speaking, a caesura only in the fourth foot.

rutundis is the usual spelling in L.'s MSS. The Latin orthography now in use was normalized in late antiquity and cannot be taken to reflect the usage of the ancient authors at all closely. Where the consensus of the MS tradition offers old spellings it is customary editorial practice to accept them. See A. E. Housman's edition of Juvenal (1938) xxi n. 1.

187   seminibus 'particles': see 180n.

debet 'must', 'is bound to'; cf. 2. 451–2 *illa quidem debent e leuibus atque rutundis | esse magis, fluuido quae corpore liquida constant.*

188   momine...moueri: the 'figura etymologica' (cf. 144n.) contributes to and encloses a symmetrical alliterative scheme: *m–p–p–p* [im-*p*ulsa: see 174n.]–*m.*

189   tantillo momine is to be taken with both verbs, an example of the figure called ἀπὸ κοινοῦ: see Hofmann–Szantyr 834–6; Kenney, *C.Q.* n.s. 8 (1958) 55; F. Leo, *Ausgew. kl. Schriften* 1 (1960) 71 ff. (= *Analecta Plautina* 3 ff.); and cf. 264, 267, 288, 424, 623nn. L. nowhere else uses *tantillus*, but *pauxillus* occurs at 3. 229 and elsewhere. Diminutives were generally avoided by the Augustans as colloquial (Gow, *C.Q.* 26 (1932) 150–57), but L.'s contemporary Catullus used them freely for emotional effect (not however in his epigrams): see Fordyce on Catull. 3. 18; D. O. Ross, *Style and tradition in Catullus* (1969) 22–5. Cf. 914 *homullis*, 1015 *luella*.

flutat for *fluitat*; this contracted form has also been restored by conjecture at 4. 77. Only in these two places is it required by the metre; elsewhere L. uses the normal form. The analogies of *probet* = *prohibet* at 864 (also a conjectural restoration) and (apparently) *torrat* = *torreat* at 917 (see nn.) suggest that L.'s attitude to language occasionally verged on the arbitrary. Cf. Introd. 22–3.

190   quippe 'as being'.
   figuris 'particles': see 180 n. and contrast 246 n.

191   The rhythm, with only one dactyl in the verse and that not in the fifth foot, is obviously descriptive. The spondaic fifth foot was one of the hallmarks of the neoteric style: Catullus has 30 instances in the 408 verses of *C.* 64 (see Fordyce on 64. 2), not all of which are obviously onomatopoeic or descriptive. L. uses the device relatively more sparingly for special effects: cf. 198, 249, 417, 545, 907.
   constantior 'more closely composed': L. somewhat stretches the sense of *consto*.

192   magis: take with *pigri*.
   actus 'movement'; the word is relatively uncommon in this literal sense.

194   nimirum 'obviously'.
   exstat must here = *constat*; cf. 244 n. Heinze's conjecture *leuibu' constat* supposes a deliberate alteration of the text by a corrector who wished to eliminate what he took to be a metrical anomaly.

196–8   papaueris…aceruus…lapidum: the words are positioned in the verse to bring out the emphasis: 'of *poppy-seed* a light breath will disperse a tall *heap*, but of *stones*…'.

196   suspensa 'checked', i.e. very light: cf. 5. 1069 *suspensis… dentibus* 'not closing her teeth', and the phrase *suspenso gradu* 'on tiptoe'.

197   tibi 'before your eyes', 'as you can see for yourself': cf. 153–8 n. **diffluat** 'is dispersed'.

198   conlectum 'heap'; Muretus' correction of the *coniectum* of the MSS must be accepted. Elsewhere in Latin, including L., *coniectus* = the act of throwing, not its result. The same corruption at 4. 414 *conlectus aquae* (Lambinus: *coniectus* MSS).

spicarumque: L. nowhere else ends a verse with four spondees (cf. 191 n.), but that in itself is no reason for attempting to emend *spicarumque* away. -*que* = 'or' (see 150 n.); stones and corn-ears are chosen for different reasons, on account of their weight and their spikiness respectively: in these characteristics they contrast with both the poppy-seeds and the light, smooth particles of the *animus*; cf. 201–2 *pondere magno* | *asperaque*, and note 198 *at contra* ~ 201 *at contra*.

199   noenu potest: sc. *aura* (196); 'a light breeze may blow away poppy-seeds...it is by no means the case that it can do the same with stones or corn-ears'. *noenu* is an archaic form of *non*, which was formed from *ne* (the ancient Latin negative) + *oinom* (the ancient form of *unum*); here it is used for emphasis. Cf. 220 n.

paruissima: the form is found in Varro (*Sat. Men.* 375) and Festus (pp. 442–3 L.); it is unknown in classical Latin but relatively frequent in later authors. L. appears to distinguish between *paruissimus* 'very small' and *minimus* 'the least possible'.

proquam 'according as' = *prout*, peculiar to L.

200   The unusual rhythm, dactylic with diaereses after the second and third feet, is descriptive.

201   magis: take with both *magno* and *aspera*.

204   egregie 'if anything ever was', *par excellence*. **perquam:** take with the adjj. in the next verse.

206–7   The admonitory tone and the insistence on usefulness are both characteristically Epicurean: *Ep. ad Hdt.* 52, 47 (13. 10 Us.); Lucret. 1. 331 *quod tibi cognosse in multis erit utile rebus.*

206   o bone 'my dear fellow', 'my good sir', like ὠγαθέ, but occurring mostly in satire and clearly felt as colloquial; perhaps therefore addressed rather to the general reader than to Memmius.

207   cluebit = *erit*, as at e.g. 1. 449 *quaecumque cluent* 'whatever exists'; cf. Greek καλοῦμαι = εἰμί.

208–9   The 'proleptic' type of indirect question, familiar from the 'I know thee who thou art', οἶδά σε τίς εἶ, of the Gospels (Mk 1. 24, Lk 4. 34). In Latin, however, it is predominantly a colloquial construction: Hofmann–Szantyr 471–2; Bennett II 222–4.

208   haec quoque res refers forward to *quod* at 211; cf. 46n.
   quoque...etiam: the same pleonasm at 292.
   dedicat = *declarat*, the original sense of the word.
   eius: the *animus*, but it soon appears from 216 that L. is now thinking of the *anima*.

211   secura quies: L. anticipates the comparison with sleep that is to come at 919–30.

213   cernas 'one can see', the generalizing 2nd pers. subj. pres., as at e.g. 370 *possis*, 854 *respicias*, etc.

214   ad 'as regards'.
   praestat 'keeps safe'. *praesto* = 'guarantee', 'undertake', 'execute', 'show', 'prove', etc., must be distinguished from *praesto* (*prae-sto*) = 'excel'; the ancient authorities connected it with *praes* 'surety'. Death, so to speak, keeps faith; the commercial/legal metaphor would come naturally to a Roman. Cf. 332, 971 nn.

216   animam: the first unambiguous indication that L. now has in mind the *anima* rather than the *animus*.
   perparuis: 179n.

216–17   It is best not to punctuate, as most editors do, after *seminibus*, but to read the two verses as a whole: we may paraphrase 'the tiny particles of which the *anima* is formed are distributed continuously through every part of the body' (cf. 691). There is an apparent syntactical ambiguity: are we to construe 'that it consists of very small particles [for the unaccompanied abl. cf. 194, where *exstat* = *est*], and is bound together...' or 'that it is bound together with (in) very small particles [taking *nexam* with *esse*]'? The question, when put in this form, is misleading: the reader of an unpunctuated text would have no warning that he was to pause at *seminibus* (contrast 230, where *quoniam* is a clear sign-post) and would have no difficulty, reading the two verses as a single utterance, in understanding the abl. as expressing the ideas *both* of composition *and* of connexion; and this may indeed have been L.'s intention. It is the modern use of syntactical, as opposed to rhetorical, punctuation that tends to create problems where an ancient reader would have seen none.

218 quatenus 'since', the invariable sense in L. and not uncommonly in Augustan poetry.

ubi '*even* when': *tamen* in 219 imparts a concessive flavour. Cf. 112 n.

219 extima = *extrema*; cf. *intimus, infimus*.

circumcaesura 'outline', formed on the model of περικοπή. The word occurs in classical Latin only here and at 4. 647.

220 praestat: 214 n.

nec defit ponderis hilum 'and there is not the slightest loss of weight'. *hilum* is a word of uncertain origin and sense, used (like *floccus, naucus*, etc.) to mean 'very little indeed'; generally it follows a negative, as here (but see 514 n.), and represents a more emphatic variant of the usual *nec...quicquam* (see e.g. 225). Of the twelve occurrences of the word in L. eight are in this book (220, 514, 518, 783, 813, 830, 867, 1087). For this type of compound negative expression one may compare French *ne...pas, ne...point*, etc. (Hofmann–Szantyr 84*); and cf. 199 n. on the etymology of *non*.

221 quod genus est 'just as'.

Bacchi...flos 'the bouquet of wine'. At 2. 656 L. speaks of 'misusing the name of Bacchus', *Bacchi nomine abuti*; but here and at e.g. 2. 472 (Neptune = the sea) he seems to use metonymy as one of the conventional poetic devices without evident embarrassment.

223 aliquo 'any other'.

sucus 'flavour'; cf. 226–7.

224 nil 'not at all', to be taken with *minor*. L. regularly uses the abl. of *nihil* with comparatives (cf. e.g. 89, 96), and Heinsius' *nilo*, a very small alteration which supposes merely the loss of one letter *o* in the sequence *nilooculis* ('haplography'), is attractive. However, L. nowhere else elides *nilo*, and *nil* = *non* is perfectly normal Latin, though verging on the colloquial: Hofmann–Szantyr 454.

226   nimirum: 194n.

multa: L. argues, and ends by stressing the point (229), that it is because the soul-particles are exceedingly small and light that there is no apparent diminution in the weight of the body when the *anima* leaves it. It is also implied by 209–10, though not actually stated until 278, that they are few in number. *multa* here is therefore odd. In spite of the tempting antithesis with *in toto corpore* the word should not, however, be emended to *pauca*; it seems rather that L. has momentarily lost sight of the main thread of his argument in developing his analogy. It is possible indeed that his predilection for alliteration betrayed him into writing *multa minutaque* without regard to its implications for the context as a whole.

227   rerum 'these things', i.e. those mentioned in 221–3 and their like.

228–30   These verses return us to the point of departure at 177–80; cf. 30n.

228   etiam atque etiam 'without a shadow of doubt', a favourite formula of L.'s.

mentis...animaeque: yet another variation; cf. 94n.

229   pauxillis: 189n.

231–257

The structure of the *animus* and the *anima*: (*b*) the soul-elements. So far as the main argument is concerned this section and the next are parenthetic, and a reader who is anxious not to lose the thread might do well to turn straight to 323. It has been suggested that L. now begins to draw on a source distinct from his main sources (cf. 10n.); for some of these doctrines he is our only authority.

232–6   The soul consists of *aura*, *uapor* and *aer*. *aura* 'wind' and *uapor* 'heat' we have already met at 126–9 as *uentus* and *calor*. *aer*, which at 122 was merely a variant for *uentus*, is now a soul-element in its own right, 'air' as distinct from 'wind'. It appears that this distinction was Epicurean, but it cannot be said that L.'s brief explanation is very enlightening: that all heat must have some air mixed with it because of the nature of heat. There may be some connexion with the doctrine that wind is air in motion (6. 685 *uentus enim fit ubi est agitando percitus aer*: cf. 292 n.), but if so it is obscure (Boyancé 155).

232 tenuis: scanned as a disyllable, the *u* being treated as a consonant, as at 243, 383, 448. Contrast 330 n.

233–4 uapore...cui: the variation in construction with *mixtus* is odd and apparently unmotivated, unless by metrical convenience; but that with the abl. is normal, with dat. unusual and poetic.

234 quisquam 'any at all' = *ullus*, emphatic.
  et 'as well'.

235 enim: for its position cf. 560, 790, 876.

237 animi for *animi atque animae*, the ψυχή; cf. 175 n.

238 sat: the only certain example in L. against a dozen of *satis*, though *sat* is restored by conjecture at 5. 881.
  cuncta 'all together', the proper sense of the word.

239–40 The required sense is clear, but the text is garbled past redemption. With some hesitation the solution of Bailey is followed: to accept the text of the MSS in 239 and Frerichs's correction in 240: '...since the mind does not admit that any of these things can bring about the motions that cause sensation and the thoughts which the mind turns over'. Bernays's *res* 'the facts of the case' eliminates the repetition of *mens*, but (i) the repetition is not necessarily objectionable from a stylistic point of view, (ii) it may conceivably embody a point: the mind rejects an explanation which does not satisfactorily account for its own activities.

241–5 This hypothesis of a 'fourth nature' which had no name not unnaturally earned the Epicureans a certain amount of ridicule. (There is a similar vagueness in L.'s discussion of the nature of the gods at 5. 148–54: like the *quarta natura* it is *tenuis*.) An even more fundamental application of this type of reasoning, in which recourse is had to some unknown principle as the only way of explaining the apparent facts, is seen in the doctrine of the atomic 'swerve', the *clinamen*, described by Cicero as *tertius quidam motus...extra pondus et plagam* (*De Fato* 22). In the history of modern science phlogiston and ether (Leonard 46) offer analogies for this type of argument.

243   tenuius: to be scanned as a dactyl: 232 n.

exstat: 'exists'; but see next n.

244   est: the correction eliminates two difficulties, (i) the pointless repetition *e...ex*, which is not paralleled by 6. 353–4 *e paruis quia facta minute | corporibus uis est et leuibus ex elementis*, where the two prepositions have a noun apiece; (ii) the necessity of understanding *exstat* as now equivalent to *constat* (cf. 194 n.). Wakefield's conjecture is supported against that of the Itali by 6. 330 *adde quod e paruis et leuibus est elementis*.

245   didit prima 'initiates and distributes'.

246   perfecta 'as being formed': the context confers a causal colouring on the participle. Cf. 171 n.

figuris 'atoms': contrast 190 n.

247–50 The *sensiferi motus* are transmitted through a chain of substances which grow less and less rarefied and culminate in the core (*medullae*) of the most massive bodily structures, the bones.

247   motus: acc. pl.

249   uiscera 'flesh' not 'entrails'.

persentiscunt 'begin to feel throughout'. The verb, and the idea which it expresses, gains weight from its position and rhythm (191 n.), and from its composition (179–80 n.), but the reader is carried on by the enjambment of *omnia* in the next verse.

250   postremis 'last of all'. Adjectives are commonly used with adverbial force in expressions involving direction or sequence, whether spatial or, as here, temporal: Hofmann–Szantyr 171–2.

medullis: generally used in the pl.: each bone has its own *medulla*.

251 'The resulting sensation, be it pleasure or the opposite passion': the subject of *datur*, which embraces both *uoluptas* and *contrarius ardor*, must be inferred from the *siue*-clauses.

ardor 'heat', here much the same as *affectus*, 'emotion' or 'passion'.

252–3 'It does not get so far for nothing, without catastrophic disorder following.' *temere* almost = *impune*: such extreme penetration does not often occur (cf. 256–7) but when it does there is no escaping the consequences.

252 huc...usque: as far as the bones and marrow.

253 permanare...perturbentur: the completeness of the upset answers to the completeness of the penetration: the point is made by placing (249 n.) and composition (179–80 n.) of the verbs and by the rhythm (191 n.).

255 partes: the particles of the *anima*, distributed throughout the body: cf. 216–17, 691.

per caulas corporis omnis: the same phrase at 702. *caulae* are 'pores', πόροι; this is the scientific, as opposed to the popular, account of the process of dying (contrast 122 n.).

256 quasi 'almost', qualifying *summo*: the disturbances in fact rarely reach far below the surface of the body.

258–322

The structure of the *animus* and the *anima*: (c) the interrelationships of the soul-elements and their effects on behaviour. Cf. 231–57 n.

258–60 A careful piece of writing in the style of L.'s prooemia (cf. 1–4 n.), with the syntax designed to lead up to the subject of the sentence, on which the weight of the apology thus falls.

258 On the metre cf. 174 n. Here and at 6. 1067 *quae memorare que(am) in|ter se singlariter apta* L. treats *inter* as divisible for metrical purposes, just as Virgil does at *A.* 1. 180 *Aeneas scopul(um) in|terea conscendit*: cf. L. Müller, *De re metrica*[2] (1894) 461–2; E. Norden, *P. Vergilius Maro Aeneis Buch VI*[3] (1934) 429–31. Strictly speaking there is no caesura in the fourth foot, since *inter sese* cohere very closely, but the combination of anomalies is not such as to invite suspicion. No special emphasis or descriptive effect seems to be intended.

259 compta 'united': the primitive sense of *emo* (*como* < *coemo*) is 'take'.

uigeant 'function', 'act'.

260   patrii sermonis egestas: a complaint that occurs more than once, at 1. 832 (in the same words) and at 1. 136–9. Here L. seems to be referring to the lack of a technical vocabulary in which to describe the interaction and intermingling of the soul-atoms (262–5 n.); cf. 273–4 n. In general of course the idiom of literary Latin was still poverty-stricken in comparison with Greek, which enjoyed the advantages of a much longer and richer tradition, a proliferation of genres and dialects, a facility in forming compounds which Latin never possessed, and so on.

261   tangam = *attingam*, as at Catull. 89. 5 *qui ut nihil attingat nisi quod fas tangere non est.* A compound verb is not infrequently followed in Greek and Latin by its simple form, in which the force of the compound persists: cf. 1. 941 *deceptaque non capiatur*, 2. 566 *et res progigni et genitas procrescere posse* (and see Bell 338–9). The usage is as old as the Twelve Tables: 8. 12 *si im* [= *eum*] *occisit, iure caesus esto*; it may have been Indo-European, as argued by Watkins, *H.S.C.P.* 71 (1966) 115–19 (with useful list of earlier discussions); see also for additional Greek examples R. Renahan, *Greek textual criticism* (1969) 78–85. Cf. 287, 382, 431, 437, 662–3, 1006 nn.

262–5   The atoms of the four soul-elements are so thoroughly inter-mingled that neither the elements nor their properties can be assigned to particular parts of the body. *enim* refers to the preceding apology (260 n.).

262   inter...cursant: the type of separation technically called 'tmesis' (cutting): cf. 343 n., 484, 860. It was a Greek licence, generously copied by Ennius, sparingly by Virgil; L.'s usage lies between these extremes.

principiorum = *suis*, that is the motion proper to atoms. *primordiorum* of course would not scan.

263   unum is best taken predicatively, 'nothing can be separated so as to stand on its own': the reference is to the soul-elements, not to the individual atoms, as is shown by *potestas* in the next verse.

264 'And their individual functions cannot be separated either': *spatio* modifies both infinitives (189 n.) and *fieri diuisa* (a periphrasis for the unmetrical *diuidi*) is a variation of *secernier*. The idea is expressed positively in the next verse.

265 This is equivalent to saying that the *animus* is a single entity (*corpus*) with diverse properties. *quasi* shows that L. is aware that his terminology is not entirely adequate (260 n.): the reader needs to be put on his guard against taking *corporis* = the human body. The rhythm, with a spondaic word occupying the second foot and providing the verse with a false ending at that place, is dictated by the antithetical phrasing: *multae uis*)(*unius corporis.*

uis = *uires*, an old form used once or twice elsewhere by L.

266 quod genus: 221 n.

uiscere: 249 n.

uulgo 'as we commonly see', the usual appeal to observation.

267 quidam 'a distinct', sc. in each case, qualifying all three nouns (cf. 189 n.): L. is drawing the same contrast as he did with *multae...unius* at 264.

color: Lambinus' correction for the *calor* of the MSS; the two words were frequently confused by copyists. The same list of properties at 2. 680–81 *denique multa uides quibus et color et sapor una | reddita sunt cum odore. calor* spoils the argument by analogy, for which a totally different set of properties is essential.

268 'And yet from all these things [sc. together] there is, completed, a single mass of body.' *augmen* 'the result of increase' seems to express the contribution made by each element to the whole; the word is not found in classical Latin outside L. and is probably one of his coinages.

270–71 mobilis illa uis: the *quarta natura* (241–5 n.).

271–2 Cf. 245–6.

271 ab se 'starting from itself'.

diuidit 'distributes', like *didit* at 245.

ollis = *illis*, i.e. the other three elements. This old form of *ille* occurs with some frequency in L.; by Virgil it is used very sparingly as a conscious archaism.

272 The verse restates and amplifies 271: *unde = ex qua* and refers, like *quae* in 271, to *mobilis illa uis. motus* is repeated in the interests of clarity: L. does not set out to cultivate variation purely for its own sake.

273–4 penitus...latet...subestque...infra: L. refers, not to the distance of the *quarta natura* from the surface of the body, but to its 'remoteness from perception by the senses' (Bailey): cf. 2. 312–13 *omnis enim longe nostris ab sensibus infra | primorum natura iacet*, 4. 111–12 *primordia tantum | sunt infra nostros sensus*. The *patrii sermonis egestas* constrains him to use the terminology of spatial relationships, but a reader who remembers 262–5 and attends to the argument at 276–8 is in no danger of misunderstanding him. Cf. 284n.

275 The *quarta natura* is to the *anima* as the *anima* is to the body: it initiates sensation in the *anima*, the *anima* in the body. In what follows this point is developed.

proporro 'in turn', as at 281. The word is peculiar to L.

276 membris et corpore toto: both the parts and the whole are pervaded by the power of the *anima*: cf. 375, 682–3, 737 for similar expressions, which are not purely tautologous. See also 346n.

277 latens...est = *latet*; for the sense cf. 273–4n.
animi uis...animaeque potestas 'the force and power of the soul': *animus + anima* = ψυχή.

278 paucisque: it was implied by 209–10, and might have been assumed, that the soul-atoms are few in number, but this is the first time that L. says so: cf. 226n.

279 nominis haec expers uis: another variation for the *quarta natura*.

280 quasi: it is difficult to explain why L. should now feel impelled to apologize for his metaphor (contrast 275), and Lambinus' *animai* is tempting. But see 131, 707nn.

281 dominatur corpore toto recalls the statement made at 138, which is now corrected and refined.

282–7 So far L. has been dealing with the relationship of the *quarta natura* to the other three elements; he now considers their relationships among themselves.

282 consimili ratione looks back to the beginning of the section, 258–65: the phrase *uigeant commixta* in the next verse is clearly intended to take up *mixta...uigeant* at 258–9.

283 commixta: 136n.

284 'And one is lower or higher than another.' L. again uses, *faute de mieux*, the language of spatial relationships, as at 273–4 (see n.). The meaning must be that the three elements differ from each other, according to the size of their atoms, in 'perceptibility'. *-que* = 'or' (150n.). A quite different interpretation is entailed by accepting Brieger's *alias*: in that case the meaning is 'now this element is prominent, now that', and the reference is to what follows at 288–306. However, the reference forward seems on the whole unlikely and necessitates the further correction of *etiam* to *etenim* (Faber) at 288; and the resemblance of the language here to that of 273–4 suggests that L. is making a point of the same type rather than quite a new one.

285 ut: either (i) final, referring to *commixta* in 283, in which case 284 must be taken as parenthetical to the run of the argument; or, better, (ii) restrictive = *ita tamen ut* (Hofmann–Szantyr 641; cf. 620–21 n.), qualifying what has preceded; 'only to the extent that there is still seen to be a single whole composed of all'. The three elements, that is to say, are different, but they must form a single entity (*quiddam unum* ~ 265 *unius corporis*; cf. 270), otherwise the *anima* would not have its characteristic properties.

286 ni: for *nei*, the ancient form of *ne*. To say 'lest so-and-so should occur' is equivalent to saying 'otherwise it will occur'.

sorsum sorsumque: the emphasis is on the idea of separation in general, not on the separation of the third element in particular from the other two.

287 diductaque soluant: for the gender of *diducta* cf. 136n. The idea is the same as that expressed by *diuisa potestas* at 264; *soluant* should probably be read as = *dissoluant* after *diducta*: cf. 261 n.

288–306 The three elements and the emotions. The idea that the emotions and the behaviour were motivated by the mixture of *bodily* constituents was ancient; the idea that the decisive factor was the temperament of the *mind* appears to have been Epicurus'. L. is in fact the only source for this particular doctrine, which is introduced very abruptly. For the case against mitigating this abruptness by accepting Faber's correction *etenim* and referring 284 to what follows see 284n.;

8

Heinze further observes that, except in the formula *quippe etenim*, L. consistently places *etenim* first word in the sentence. The single exception (6. 912) hardly justifies infringing the rule in the face of the other objections. So far as there is a connexion of thought it is implicit: L. has just said that the elements cannot function independently, but he goes on to remark that one or the other may predominate, temporarily or permanently, in the soul. The passage is very carefully constructed: *calor* (2 vv.) + *uentus* (2) + *aer* (2) ~ *leones* (3) + *cerui* (3) + *boues* (4) + *cerui et leones* (1). Lachmann's insensitive proposal to transfer 298 to follow 295 lends weight to the criticism of Mommsen that he did not read the texts he emended.

288 The common punctuation, with a comma after *sumit*, imposes a phrasing that could never have been intended by L. or dreamed of by an ancient reader relying on his ear. *in ira* must be construed, according to the natural movement of the verse, with *sumit*; and then, retrospectively, with *cum feruescit* as well (cf. 189n.); this is easy even without *efferuescit in ira* at 295 (where however see n.). (On punctuation in ancient MSS see Pearce 145; Reynolds and Wilson 4.)

ille 'that we know'; cf. 292, 308.

289   acribus: Lambinus' correction is supported by the evident imitation by Virg. *A*. 12. 102 *oculis micat acribus ignis*; for the sense of *acer* cf. 294. The *acrius* of the MSS, which can only mean 'more fiercely than usual', is illogical.

290   frigida...aura: i.e. *uentus*; cf. 299–301.

292   etiam quoque: 208n.

pacati is equivalent to *placidi*; cf. 302. Air is, by definition, always at rest: cf. 232–6n.

293   pectore tranquillo...uultuque sereno 'when the heart etc. is at peace'. This sort of abl. is variously described as 'comitative', 'sociative', 'descriptive', 'of attendant circumstances', etc.; in origin it is instrumental: cf. Hofmann–Szantyr 114–19; L. R. Palmer, *The Latin language* (1954) 300–3. Cf. 302 *placido aere*.

294   calidi plus 'more heat', partitive gen. This seems to imply that it is the *quantity* of the elements, rather than their *action*, that conditions behaviour.

295 efferuescit refers to both *corda* and *mens* but agrees, as usual, with the nearer subject: 66 n.

iram: Bentley's conjecture, unregarded by modern editors, gives the appropriate sense. *iracunda* 'prone to anger' shows that the point being made is the ease with which this temperament breaks out *into* (displays of) anger; the point is emphasized by the 'framing' position of *iracunda...iram* (for the care with which the passage is written cf. 288–306 n.): the anger which is latent at the beginning of the verse is overt by the end. For L.'s propensity to make points in this way cf. 364 n. With the *ira* of the MSS the verse can only mean 'the mind that is prone to anger easily boils over when it is angry' – a pointless statement. The MSS reading is not supported by *ira* at 288, which is rather the source of the corruption (cf. Reynolds and Wilson 159–60).

296 quo genere in primis 'first in this category'; the phrase recurs at 5. 59.

uis...uiolenta is equivalent to *uiolentia*; cf. 741 *uiolentia*. For the periphrasis cf. 8 n.

297–8 The alliteration is, by Lucretian standards, discreet, but none the less effective: note particularly the sequence of intervocalic *r*s in *caper' irarum.*

297 gementes 'groaning': the word is exactly descriptive and is imitated by Virgil, *A.* 7. 15 *gemitus iraeque leonum.*

298 capere 'have room for', 'contain'.

irarum fluctus 'their swelling anger', the same image of boiling or bubbling water as at 295.

299 mens must, strictly speaking, mean *animus* here, since the Epicureans held that the lower animals were lacking in reasoning power, ἄλογα.

300 The dactylic rhythm is descriptive.

300–1 For the sequence of events cf. 246–51.

301 exsistere: 101 n.

302 placido magis aere uiuit 'has more of calm air in its composition'; *uiuit* is colourless = *est* or *constat*. For the abl. cf. 293 n.

303–4 A vividly pictorial image in L.'s manner: cf. 38–40 n. *subdita*, which is *vox propria* of setting fire to something, lends a touch of concreteness with *fax*. Cf. 305 n.

303   nimis...percit are to be taken together. For the form of *percit* cf. 184 n.

304   suffundens caecae caliginis umbra 'clouding it [sc. *naturam*] with the shadow of murky gloom'. *umbra* should be preferred to *umbram* in spite of its inferior MS authority. Latin admits two constructions with verbs like *suffundo* (the type is that of *circumdo*): one may say *suffundo naturam umbra* (abl.) or *suffundo naturae* (dat.) *umbram*. With *suffundo* the first construction is in general commoner and is preferred by L.; and the sentence here reads more easily if *naturam*, which must be understood as the obj. of *percit*, is also the obj. of *suffundens*, which agrees with the subject of *percit*.

305   An abrupt change of image to emphasize the contrast between the two emotional extremes of anger and fear; the effect, as usual, reinforced by alliteration.

306   interutrasque 'in between'; this adverb is peculiar to L. (five times elsewhere in *D.R.N.*). If the text is sound, *inter* must be felt as having sufficient prepositional force to govern the following accusatives. This is very unusual Latin, but L. is a daring writer, and an editor should hesitate before accepting Avancius' easy correction to *inter utrosque*.

307   doctrina is ordinary, 'non-sectarian', education as opposed to the Epicurean *ratio* (321) which is the only avenue to real mastery of the passions.

308   pariter: take with *politos* in 307.
    illa 'those first traces', sc. that we have just been discussing in animals, referring to *uestigia prima*, rather than fem. sing. referring to *doctrina*.
    relinquit 'leaves unchanged', i.e. does not eradicate; cf. 320 *linqui*. The connexion of thought becomes clearer if a comma, rather than the usual full stop, is printed after 309, as in the old editions: this allows the opposition between 307–9 and 310–13 to emerge more clearly.

311–13 L.'s analogy between animals and men is a little strained: *clementia* does not correspond very closely to the *natura boum*. Moreover *metus* does not consort very happily with *ira* and *clementia* in the human context. Anger might on occasion be counted as a virtue, forbearance a vice: Epicurean and indeed pagan ethics generally knew nothing of turning the other cheek. Fear, on the other hand, was a *malum* pure and simple, which it was the object of the system to banish from the life of mankind. Strictly speaking, *citius paulo* in 312 represents an inconsistency.

311 procliuius: sc. *aequo*; cf. 313.

decurrat: the word is normally used by L. of motion in a straight line rather than downwards, and this is probably the case here, in spite of the literal meaning of *procliuis* 'downhill': the point is the speed and directness of such a man's arousal to anger.

313 Cf. Cic. *De Leg.* 1. 21 (referring to the Epicureans) *solent enim, id quod bonorum uirorum est, admodum irasci.*

314–18 L. has discussed only three types of character, representing the three simple predominances; if combinations are taken into account, many other possibilities arise. It has been suggested that L.'s source, whatever it was (231–57 n.), here went into detail which L. refrained from reproducing, either because of the technical difficulties of rendering it into Latin (260 n.) or because he shrank from extending what is essentially a digression. It is possible, however, that we have here a purely literary motif. This type of *recusatio* occurs in poetry from Homer onwards: *Il.* 2. 488–90; Aratus, *Phaen.* 456–61; Enn. *Ann.* 561–2 V.², Virg. *G.* 2. 42–4, 103–8; Hostius, fr. 3 (Morel 33); Serv. *ad. A.* 6. 625 (ascribed to L.). Closer than any of these is Cic. *Arat.* 234 *quarum ego nunc nequeo tortos euoluere cursus*; this translation was an early, almost a juvenile, work, and in view of the close resemblance we may reasonably guess that L. was borrowing from Cicero.

315 sequaces: either *qui naturas sequuntur* or *qui homines sequuntur*; probably the latter in view of 2. 48 *metus hominum curaeque sequaces*, where *metus* and *curae* are too like each other for one to be said to follow the other. Translate 'the varying temperaments and characters that never forsake a man'.

317–18 'To find a name for every possible combination of atoms', equivalent to *tot nomina figurarum quot habent principia figuras.*

317 The rhythm of the verse is identical with that of 102, where see n.

318 unde = *ex quibus*, sc. *figuris.*

  uariantia = *uarietas*, which would not scan; cf. 675 *retinentia*, 851 *repetentia.*

  rerum: not things in general, but those with which the argument is here concerned, i.e. *morum.*

319–22 L. now continues his transition back to the main argument. *potesse* picks up *nequeo* in 316: L. cannot, he says, pursue these doctrines into all their details, but one great principle he *can* affirm, that in no man is the natural imbalance of elements and characteristics so strong, after education (319–20 ∼ 308–9), that it cannot be corrected by Epicurean *ratio.* His statement marks a climax and a strong break, which helps to facilitate the transition.

319 illud in his rebus 'this fact', a formula peculiar to L.

  uideo firmare potesse: sc. *me*, a not uncommon type of ellipse in L. and many other writers (Hofmann–Szantyr 362). *firmare* 'state', for *affirmare* or *confirmare*: the use of the simple for the compound verb is common in poetry and poetical prose (Hofmann–Szantyr 298–300; on the metrical convenience of the shorter forms cf. Pearce 318). Cf. 261 n.

  potesse = *posse*, an archaic form; cf. 1010, 1079 nn.

320–21 The construction is ⟨*ea*⟩ *naturarum uestigia quae nobis ratio depellere nequeat usque adeo paruula linqui, ut* eqs.: *paruula* is predicative (note its placing at the beginning of the verse). A little remains that *ratio* cannot dislodge, but it is negligible.

322 The Epicurean gods did not intervene in the affairs of men (18–22 n.) but they were not purely ornamental. By contemplating images and ideas of the gods men could help themselves to achieve the same state of security, ἀταραξία, freedom from disturbance, and hence become like them: cf. 6. 68–78. Epicurus had promised one of his disciples (*Ep. ad Men.* 135, 66 Us.) that he should live like a god among men, and Diogenes of Oenoanda wrote of influences that 'make our disposition godlike' (52 IV 2–3 Chilton). Cf. Introd. 1–2.

dignam dis degere: the alliteration lends special emphasis to the verse and helps to mark a climax and a break. We now return to the sequence of argument that was interrupted at 231.

323–349

The relationship of soul and body: (*a*) they are indissolubly linked, and life can only continue while they are linked. L. here, as Boyancé remarks (159), states rather than demonstrates. (See the stylistic analysis of this section, Introd. 26–7.)

323–6 The relationship is one of mutual protection: the idea is the same as that succinctly expressed by Diogenes of Oenoanda, 'the soul is bound and binds in return', ἀντέδησε δεσμουμένη (37 I 10 Chilton). In this section L. demonstrates only that the existence of the living body depends on that of the soul (324); the converse proposition (323) is reserved for the discussion of the mortality of the soul at 417–829.

323 haec...natura: the soul; the phrase picks up *mentis naturam animaeque* from 228.

tenetur 'is protected': L. has in mind Epicurean terms such as στεγάζειν 'shelter', συνέχειν 'hold together', περιέχειν 'enclose', used of the role of the body as protector of the soul.

corpore ab omni: because, as we have seen (216–17), the *anima* is distributed over the whole body. For the unnecessary *ab* cf. 820n.

324 est custos = *tenet* 'protects'; cf. 396 *uitai claustra coercens*.
salutis: 125n.

326 pernicie: sc. of both.
uidentur 'clearly cannot'; cf. 164n.

327 turis: this, and not *thuris*, is the spelling that is consistently found in Virgil's capital MSS, which rank among our best guides to the ancient orthography.

328, 330 haud facile 'impossible'; cf. 361 *difficilest*.
quin intereat natura quoque eius (i.e. *turis*): without its ceasing to be frankincense.

330   dissoluantur: the *u* is treated as a vowel to give a dactyl in the fifth foot, as at 706, 815. Where the word occurs elsewhere in the verse (e.g. 455, 470, al.) this scansion is probable though the metre does not require it. Contrast 232 n.

331–2 These verses resume (*ita*) the argument so far, and should be followed by a strong stop, as in the older editions.

331   implexis...principiis: the participle is to be taken with *inter se* in the next verse. For the abl. cf. 293 n. The sense repeats 325, but what was there expressed metaphorically is now expressed scientifically, in terms of the atomic theory.

332   consorti...uita: 'they are coheirs or copartners of a life, which is a *sors*, a patrimony or capital, which cannot be divided, but must be used by them in common' (Munro). For *consortium* see A. Berger, *Encyclopedic dictionary of Roman law* (1953), s.v. Legal metaphors are much commoner in Roman poetry than in Greek; cf. 214, 971 nn. The idea is enlarged and embroidered upon in 333–6.

333–4 'The power of body or [*atque* is disjunctive: 150 n.] mind cannot feel separately, each for itself without the other.' *quaeque*, in 'partial apposition' to *potestas*, strictly speaking = 'each of three or more', so that one would expect *utra* or *altera*; but *quisque* has an affinity for *sibi*, and Latin writers often wrote more informally than standard grammar books sometimes allow to appear.

335   eas: the two *potestates*. The *eos* of the MSS would have to refer to *corporis atque animi*, but in that case L.'s usage would demand a neuter pronoun (136 n.).

335–6   conflatur...accensus 'kindled and blown into flame'; the same image at 4. 925–8, where however it is contained in a simile. For *accendere* of sensation cf. 2. 943, 959. L. is here not dealing with the genesis of sensation, which was shown at 246–51 to lie with the *quarta natura*, but emphasizing the fact that the process depends for its fulfilment on the existence of the body: note that the words conveying ideas of cooperation and reciprocity are all crowded into 335.

337–43 Common experience shows that the body cannot exist apart from the soul. This topic is developed more fully at 445–525.

337 **praeterea** might be expected to introduce a second argument, but 325–36 are less an argument than an amplification and illustration of the main thesis stated at 323–4. However, L. does not always distinguish between statement and proof.

338 **uidetur** has its usual sense of 'is seen to' (164n.); but after the indicatives *gignitur* and *crescit* it is difficult to resist the suspicion that L. uses a convenient metrical cliché to round out the verse (Ernout–Robin). Cf. Introd. 24–6.

339 **enim:** for the elision cf. *quidem* at 904. Elision of the final syllable of a cretic sequence ($-\cup-$) is comparatively rare in Latin poetry (Soubiran 207–38). L. never elides a long vowel or diphthong in this position, only syllables in *-m* (ibid. 219).
umor aquae = *aqua*, a common Lucretian periphrasis.

339–40 **dimittit…qui datus est:** the heat is not a property of the water as scent is of frankincense (327–8) but something added from outside which can be surrendered without any change in the 'nature' of the water.

340 **neque** 'although…not'; cf. 150, 900nn.
conuellitur 'torn apart', i.e. it does not suffer a *discidium* (342); cf. 343 *conuulsi*.

342 **discidium** refers to the separation of the atoms of the *anima* from each other rather than the separation of the *anima* from the body, though the second of course follows on the first.

343 **penitus:** take with *conuulsi*.
conque putrescunt: for the tmesis cf. 262n. Here, as at 484, the device serves to introduce a word which would otherwise be excluded by metre.

344–7 These verses substantially restate what was said at 325–36.

344 **ex ineunte aeuo** ∼ 331 *ab origine prima*.

344–5 'The reciprocal contacts of body and soul learn the motions of life', i.e. the body and soul through their contacts with each other acquire sensation. There is a slight awkwardness in making *contagia* the grammatical subject of the sentence.

345 Formally a 'golden' line, with two pairs of epithet–noun phrases framing a verb. Possibly the effect is deliberate, to reflect the mutuality of the body–soul contact, but it is Virgil and Ovid in particular who can be seen making conscious artistic use of the device: see S. E. Winbolt, *Latin hexameter verse* (1903) 219–23; L. P. Wilkinson, *Golden Latin artistry* (1963) 215–17; F. Bömer on Ov. *Met.* 2. 163.

contagia: the form may have been invented by L.; *contagio*, the ordinary word, will not scan.

346 **maternis . . . membris aluoque** 'in the body and womb of the mother'; *aluo* particularizes *membris*: cf. 1. 348 *in saxis ac speluncis* 'in caves among the rocks'; Cic. *Pro Sull.* 82 *his temporibus et periculis* 'in these dangerous times'. Some grammarians classify this type of phrase as an example of the 'explicative' use of conjunctions: *-que, ac, et* = 'i.e.', 'that is' (so Ernout–Robin). They can also be regarded as a special instance of 'hendiadys' ('the resolution of a complex expression into its parts': Moore, *A.J.P.* 12 (1891) 273; cf. Serv. *ad* Virg. *A.* 1. 61); see Bell 258–61. Latin, though less flexible than Greek, is not a language in which usages can always be rigidly defined and pigeonholed; for the difficulty of classifying this particular type cf. Hofmann–Szantyr 782–3. Cf. 554–5, 793 nn.

reposta = *reposita*; the word agrees grammatically with *contagia* but refers in sense to *corpus atque anima*.

347 **sine peste maloque** 'without wrack and ruin' (Bailey), a curious phrase, possibly a metrical variation on *sine mala peste*: cf. Enn. *Sc.* 162 V.[2] (323 Jocelyn) *malam pestem*.

348 **causa salutis:** the usual reference back to the beginning of the paragraph (324).

349 **eorum:** n. pl., referring to *corpus atque anima* (136 n.).

350–369

The relationship of soul and body: (*b*) refutation of two fallacies, (i) that the body itself does not feel (350–58); (ii) that the eyes themselves do not see, but the *animus* through them (359–69). Various philosophical schools held these or similar views; some scholars have thought that L. has the Stoics principally in mind. The section is parenthetic to the main argument.

350 quod superest 'next', 'another point'; this formula does not always mark the last item in a sequence.

refutat 'tries to disprove'; but the 'conative' or 'inceptive' use of the present tense is not reliably attested in Latin before the Augustan period: Bennett I 26; G. Landgraf, *Hist. Gramm. d. lat. Spr.* III I (1903) 112 (both Ciceronian examples irrelevant); Hofmann–Szantyr 316. Lambinus' *renutat* 'denies' is a very plausible correction: L. uses this rare word at 4. 600. The construction with acc. and inf. is in either case by analogy with *negare*; cf. 766 n.

351 animam: sc. *solam*; cf. 144 n.

352 nominitamus for the unmetrical *nominamus*; the frequentative force is not felt. Cf. 505 n.

353 uel manifestas 'quite clear', the usual appeal to the evidence of the senses. The order of words, with the preposition *contra* in the middle, is designed to throw the two emphatic adjj. into relief, and does so at the expense of the metre, creating a false verse-ending after the second foot.

354–5 'For who will ever tell us what bodily sensation is, if not the actual sights and lessons of experience?' Only the senses can tell us about sensation.

354 corpus sentire is treated as a substantival phrase = *corporis sensus* (other Lucretian examples listed by Bailey 102). Greek, possessing a definite article, makes a much freer use of this construction.

adferet, sc. *rationem*, 'will explain'.

355 palam…dedit 'has made plain', literally 'has placed in public'. *do* here has the sense 'place', 'make' rather than 'give'. On the confusion of what were originally two distinct roots see the note of Ernout–Robin on 1. 288; A. Ernout–A. Meillet, *Dict. étymol. de la langue lat.* I (1959), s.v. *dō*. Cf. 603 n.

356 at introduces an objection put into the mouth of the other side.

357   enim 'yes, for...', i.e. 'admitted, but...'; cf. the similar use of γάρ. The emphasis is 'what the body loses is something that did not belong to it (*proprium*)'; that is, sensation is inherent in the *anima*, but not in the body, to which however the *anima* communicates it, so that it does truly participate in sensation. L. is stating briefly an argument which was somewhat more explicitly developed by Epicurus (*Ep. ad Hdt.* 64, 20 Us.), who said that the body when alive does not possess sensation 'in its own right'.

in aeuo 'in life'; cf. 344.

358   multaque 'and many other properties', such as heat (215), motion, etc. Sensation, that is to say, is not the only bodily attribute that is not *proprium*.

perdit cum expellitur aeuo: this early correction gives good sense and is reasonably close to the text of the MSS. Munro's conjecture accounts ingeniously for the presence of *quam* in the MSS (for the order *quam...ante* cf. 973), but gives a less appropriate sense, for the idea that the body loses some attributes, such as strength or beauty, *before* death is less relevant to the point made in 357.

360   animum: L. has just been arguing that the *anima* cannot undergo sensation without the body. He now argues similarly that the *animus* cannot perceive on its own. The view that he is refuting is stated very clearly by Cicero, who attributes it to the Stoics (*Tusc.* 1. 46). That passage shows that L. has selected one sense, eyesight, as typical and assumes, though he does not say so, that his demonstration applies equally to hearing and smell.

foribus: *fores* are the valves of a door, the parts that open; L. appears to be rendering θυρίδες in his Greek source. Cicero's *fenestrae*, which are properly window-openings, blurs the image.

361   difficilest 'is impossible'; 328 n.

contra cum sensus ducat eorum 'seeing that our eyesight itself leads us the other way': understanding *nos* as object of *ducat*. There is no appeal from the evidence of the eyes themselves.

362 'Our eyesight pulls and pushes us to the eyes and nowhere else', that is, what happens when we see shows conclusively that the seeing is done with and in the eyes; but L. expresses the idea by a vigorous development of the image begun with *ducat*. For *trahit*...

detrudit cf. Plaut. *Capt.* 750 *et trahi et trudi simul* (quoted by Smith); the idea that the facts of the matter physically compel adherence to the correct doctrine is characteristic, cf. 2. 869 *ipsa manu ducunt et credere cogunt*. A reader who is properly receptive to L.'s highly concrete kind of metaphor (cf. 37 n.) will not be puzzled.

363   praesertim cum: this is an especially obvious case. For the indic. in a quasi-causal sense after *cum* cf. 112 n., 441.

cernere 'distinguish'; the original sense of the word is 'sift'. For the agricultural origin of much Latin metaphor see J. Marouzeau, *Quelques aspects de la formation du latin littéraire* (1949) 7–25; O. Weise, *Language and character of the Roman people*[3], tr. H. A. Strong and A. Y. Campbell (1909) 18–20.

364   lumina luminibus 'our eyes...the light'. Ancient readers were extremely responsive to this type of verbal point, which indeed goes back to a state of belief in which words and the things represented by them were regarded as intimately connected. Etymology was (and still is) a serious poetic ploy: cf. E. Fraenkel on Aesch. *Ag.* 687. The remarks of commentators on 'puns' and 'false antitheses' are largely beside the point. Cf. e.g. 295, 378–80, 414–15, 449–52 nn.

365   qua 'through which', sc. *uia* 'by which way'.

365–6   We ourselves (*ipsi*: cf. *ipse* at 863) are to an actual door – on the theory here rejected – as the *animus* is to the eyes; but a door, however bright the light that comes through it, is not dazzled, whereas our eyes are: therefore our eyes are not comparable to a door. The argument, which is in effect syllogistic, depends on a very rigid interpretation of the door analogy, which L. goes on to ridicule by a characteristic *reductio ad absurdum*.

366   suscipiunt 'undergo'.

reclusa 'by being opened': 171 n. The scansion *rēcl-* is on the whole avoided by Augustan poets; cf. 502 *rēflexit*.

367–9   This reasoning, which was to excite the contempt of Lactantius ('ineptissimum' is his comment at *De Opif. Dei* 8. 12), is characteristic of L., who delights to round off a passage by imparting a flippant or ironic twist to the argument. Thus at 1. 919–20, at the end of his polemic against the theory of *homoeomeria*, the atoms are sarcastically imagined as laughing and crying.

368   iam 'in that case', as at 676.

369   postibus ipsis 'the doors, posts and all', literally 'even the posts', so necessarily the doors. L. was perhaps influenced by the Greek use of αὐτός in phrases like αὐτῆσιν ῥίζῃσι 'roots and all' (Hom. *Il.* 9. 542) and αὐτοῖς ἀνδράσιν, used of ships taken 'with their crews'. If so, the idiom seems to have gained no further foothold in Latin.

370–395

The relationship of soul and body: (*c*) refutation of the teaching of Democritus about the arrangement of the soul- and body-particles. Like its predecessor, this section is only loosely connected with the main argument.

370   illud in his rebus: 319n. L. is fond of the phrase to introduce, as here, a rebuttal.
      possis: 213n.

371   Democriti . . . sancta uiri sententia: the commentators tend to treat *sancta* as a 'transferred' epithet referring to Democritus (for examples of this usage in the poets see Bell 315–29; and cf. 972–3n.). However, the natural respect which L. felt for Democritus (cf. 1039–41) would attach also to his opinions, even when erroneous; and the phrasing may have been suggested by Lucil. 1316 M. *Valeri sententia dia* (imitated by Horace, *Sat.* 1. 2. 32 *sententia dia Catonis*).

372–3 'That the atoms of body and soul are arranged separately, one by one, in alternation, and so bind our limbs together.'

372   priuis: sc. *principiis*, for the unmetrical *singulis*.

373   alternis: adverbial, not an adj. agreeing with *priuis* (*principiis*).
      uariare: here intransitive.

374–6   cum . . . tum 'as . . . so', i.e. 'both . . . and', like μέν . . . δέ.

374   animae elementa: the only other hiatus in L. is at 6. 755 *loci ope*. The early poets seem to have avoided eliding the *-ae* of the genitive, which was felt as a true diphthong (F. Leo, *Plautinische Forschungen*[2] (1912) 334–60); at 1. 139 *linguae* (*e*)*t* is a case of aphaeresis rather than true elision (Soubiran 181–2). It is interesting that Virgil does not elide *-ae* (gen. or dat.) in the *Eclogues*, but admits it in hiatus: 7. 53 *castaneae hirsutae*; cf. *G.* 2. 144 *oleae armentaque laeta.* These considerations should make an editor hesitant to accept Lachmann's easy correction *elementa minora animai.* See the important discussion of hiatus by Goold, *Phoenix* 23 (1969) 189–95.

elementa 'particles' rather than 'atoms': 180n.

375 quibus e: L. not infrequently postpones prepositions (anastrophe) for metrical convenience; cf. 839, 858.

376 numero...concedunt 'are fewer'; the point which was merely touched on at 278 (see n.) is now developed.

377 dumtaxat ut hoc promittere possis 'to the extent that one may guarantee the following...'. *dumtaxat* 'at least' restricts *ut*; the clause and the statement that it introduces define the hitherto unspecified degree of *raritas.*

378–80 'The intervals between the particles of soul in our bodies are as great as [i.e. cannot be smaller than] the smallest objects which can cause sensation when they touch us.' We do not feel the touch of very small objects: this is because they impinge on us *between* the widely-spaced (*rara*) soul-particles from which sensation arises. In other words, the interval between soul-particles must be larger than the largest objects of which we cannot feel the touch. The usual argument from common experience follows. Munro, commenting on the double sense in which the words *corpus* and *primus* are used, speaks of L.'s 'usual indifference to ambiguity' (cf. the instances collected by him and by Ernout–Robin at 1. 875); in fact L., so far from displaying indifference, was clearly cultivating an effect for which the term 'ambiguity' is not really appropriate. The construction of the sentence is extremely careful, and the placing of the words within the correlative clauses is deliberately contrived to exploit the word-play: *quantula prima...* | *corpora...corpore, tanta* | *...prima.* Cf. 364n.

378 prima: the smallest, the first as we go up the scale of size: contrast 380.

379 corpora 'objects', such as those illustrated in the following verses.

380   exordia prima = *primordia*: L. has clearly gone out of his way to find an equivalent that gives scope for his word-play.

381-2   adhaesum corpore 'its adhesion to the body'; cf. *membris...sidere*. Verbal nouns are occasionally constructed with a direct or indirect object in Latin: Plaut. *Amph.* 519 *quid tibi hanc curatiost rem? = cur hanc rem curas?* The usual case with *adhaereo* or *adhaeresco* is dat.; cf. however 6. 897 *in taedai corpore adhaerent.* The word *adhaesus* is peculiar to L., who affects such fourth decl. abstract nouns (Bailey 135).

382   incussam sidere = (probably) *incussam insidere*; cf. 261 n.

   cretam: perhaps an allusion to the use of chalk as a cosmetic: Plaut. *Truc.* 294 *buccas rubrica, creta omne corpus intinxti tibi,* Ov. *A.A.* 3. 199 *scitis et inducta candorem quaerere creta* (Micyllus: *cera* codd.).

383   araneï: scanned as a trisyllable by 'synizesis'; cf. 877 *eĭcit,* 918 *reĭ.*
   tenuia: 232 n.

384   obretimur 'we are ensnared as we go', for the usual *irretimur*; L. may have coined this form, which occurs nowhere else in Latin, to amplify the notion of encounter contained in *obuia.*

385   supera = *supra.* If his MSS may be trusted, L. uses both spellings indifferently.

385-6   uietam uestem: the 'old garment' of the spider is usually taken to mean his web, and the phrase was evidently so understood by Q. Serenus (*P.L.M.* III) 957 *ex oleo necti uestis debebit arachnes.* Since this seems to repeat the point just made (unless L. is distinguishing between webs *in situ* and falling gossamer), and since elsewhere in L. (3. 614, 4. 61) *uestis* is used of the discarded skin of a snake, it has been suggested that the word has a similar meaning here: not the spider's skin, for L. would no doubt have known perfectly well that spiders do not shed their skins, but its withered and desiccated body. This seems unlikely, for (i) such an extension of the meaning of *uestis* cannot be paralleled; (ii) L. takes his illustrations from the incidents of common life, and whereas to walk into spider's webs or to feel gossamer blowing into one's face is an everyday experience, bombardment by the dead bodies of spiders must be rare.

This illustration, like those of the feathers and thistledown which follow it, is not nearly so relevant to L.'s original point as those of the dust and chalk; 387 shows that he now has lightness rather than smallness in mind.

386   pappos 'down', from plants.

387 'Which fall as a rule not lightly through their great lightness', with a pun on the literal and the extended senses of *grauatim* 'heavily' and 'with difficulty'. L. is now making a rather different point (385-6 n.); but it is not easy to be sure (i) whether he is conscious of the fact; (ii) whether he means that a very light object affects by its fall only the surface atoms of the body, leaving the atoms of the *anima*, which lie below the surface, unaffected; or that a very light object touches the surface only with a part of itself that is too small to span the distance between the nearest soul-atoms.

388   itum 'comings and goings'; the uncompounded form of the verbal noun is rare.

   cuiusuiscumque 'each and every', a combination of *quiuis* and *quicumque*, apparently emphatic, as at Mart. 14. 2. 1 *quouiscumque loco* 'at each and every place you choose'.

389   priua 'each separate footprint' = *singula* (372 n.). The feet of these insects are so close together that they touch no more than one soul-atom at a time: a new point, but one that arises from the preceding argument with perfect propriety.

390   et cetera: L. presumably felt that any more explicit mention of body-vermin, a favourite source of jokes in comedy and epigram, was inconsistent with the dignity of didactic epos.

391-5 'So many atoms spread throughout our bodies must first be stirred into motion before the soul-atoms are shaken into sensation and, jostling in the wide spaces between them, can clash and combine and leap apart again.' The text and the sense are disputed. Marullus' transposition of 392 and 393 allows a straightforward construction of the Latin; in the text as transmitted *multa* 'many things' is unacceptably vague and the syntax is contorted: it is only when the verses are reread that the reader perceives that *semina* and not *primordia* is the subject of *sentiscant*. L. does not set traps of this sort for his readers. In 394 Wakefield's *tantis* gives easy sense: the intervals between the soul-atoms are 'so great' compared with those between the body-atoms (278, 376nn.). Lachmann's *quăm in his* (for the 'prosodic hiatus' see 1082n.) is neat, but *his*, referring back to 380, is unexpected. Turnebus' *quam sis* 'their intervals', i.e. those assigned to them, gives good sense, but *sis* = *suis* occurs elsewhere in L. only in a quotation from Ennius (1025n.).

391   multa ciendum: L. often uses the gerund with an object rather than the more usual gerundive (Hofmann–Szantyr 373, 375). Cf. 626.

393   semina: soul-atoms: cf. 143, 217, 276–7. They are so far apart that many must be moved from their places before they can begin to interact and so cause sensation.

392   primordia: soul-atoms again, but L. may now be thinking of them as grouped in particles: cf. 180n.

sentiscant concussa 'are shaken and (so: 171n.) begin to feel'; *sentisco* is used absolutely, cf. 249 *persentiscunt.*

394–5 A new detail in the description of sensation: the *sensiferi motus* entail that the soul-atoms cease to keep their usual interval and interact *by contact* with each other.

394   tantis intervallis 'in spite of the size of the intervals', which are normally too great to allow contact. For the abl. cf. 293n.

396–416

The relationship of soul and body: (*d*) the dominant role of the *animus* in sustaining life. (Cf. 136–60, where it was shown that in sensation the *animus* regulates the *anima*.)

396   magis...coercens = *coercentior*; the force of the participle is adjectival, as in *dominantior* in the next verse.

uitai claustra: for the metaphor cf. 324n.

397   dominantior ∼ 138 *dominari.*

398–401 L.'s reasoning is open to criticism. It is true that so long as a man retains consciousness (402) he must be alive, but the converse is not necessarily true. Even before the invention of modern techniques of prolonging life a man with concussion or a stroke might lie in a coma for some time without any sign of mental or emotional activity. If *mens animusque* refers to the outward and visible signs of consciousness, L.'s observation of the phenomena is at fault; if to the part of the *animus* that is responsible for maintaining life, his argument is circular. The passage has no exact counterpart in extant Epicurean sources: is L. perhaps embroidering on his own account?

398 mente animoque: 94 n.

399 temporis...partem pars...animai: the chiastic word-order and the word-play impart emphasis; cf. 402 *manet...remansit.*

400 comes insequitur 'follows in its train', sustaining the image of *dominantior.*

403 quamuis est: the construction with indic. is characteristic of verse from L. onwards and of post-Augustan prose; classical prose preferred the subj. (Hofmann–Szantyr 603–4). Cf. 705–6, 415 n.
   caesis...membris 'by having its limbs cut away': 171 n.

404 truncus 'the trunk'; the adj. *truncus* = 'mutilated' is probably not ante-Augustan.
   adempta anima circum membrisque remota 'despite the loss of vital spirit released from the limbs' (Latham). *membris* must be taken ἀπὸ κοινοῦ (189 n.) with both participles. Though the limbs, containing only *anima*, die almost instantly, as has just been explained, the trunk, where the *animus* resides, can survive; the anaphora of *circum* emphasizes the contrast. *membris* is more usually interpreted as 'body', but the abrupt change of meaning from the preceding verse seems here to lack all point (cf. 378–80 n.), and 'limbs' gives perfectly satisfactory sense. The old correction *remotus* obviates the difficulty and gives easy sense, but merely repeats what was said in 403 and so spoils the point brought out by *circum...circum.*

405 aetherias: the distinction between *aether*, the upper air, and *aer*, the lower atmosphere, is not strictly observed by the poets, even by L.   Lachmann's *aerias* is hypercritical.

406 omnimodis 'altogether' = *omnino*; among writers of the classical period peculiar to L.

409 cernundi: the original spelling of the gerund and gerundive in the 3rd and 4th conjugations; cf. 626 *faciundum*. In the normalized orthography with which we are familiar it occurs principally in *eo* and its compounds and in legal formulae (*quaestio de pecuniis repetundis*, etc.), but a good many other instances are preserved by MSS of classical authors, and it is not uncommon in L. (Neue–Wagener III 331–40).

uiuata 'living'; cf. 558, 680. The word occurs in the poem only in this book.

411 et 'and so long as you do not...'; the force of *ne* is still felt (cf. Housman on Manil. 4. 909 and 730 n.). Some of the surrounding tissue of the eyeball (*orbis* = *oculus*) must be left: the pupil (*acies* = *pupula*) cannot function in complete isolation.

412 id quoque...: a condensed way of saying 'Just as the *anima* cannot be completely removed from the body without death ensuing, so the complete separation of eyeball and pupil will entail the destruction of both.'

eorum: n. pl., sc. *orbis et pupulae*: 136 n.

413 tantula pars...media illa 'that middle part, small as it is'; cf. 5. 593 *tantulus ille...sol.*

414–15 The vocabulary (*occidit, tenebrae, splendidus orbis*) is proper to a description of the setting sun; cf. 364 n.

415 incolumis...alioqui 'though otherwise unharmed'.

quamuis: *est* must be understood (403 n.), but it is doubtful if it need be supplied: Kannengiesser's *alioquist* gives a repellent clash of consonant-groups (*-st sp-*).

416 uincti: normal Lucretian usage would require *uincta*: 136 n. Here the masc. may be due to the proximity of *animus*: cf. 66 n. A striking analogy at Livy 21. 50. 11 *rex regiaque classis una profecti*, where however *classis* = *classiarii* (Kühner–Stegmann I 52). For similar variations of concord see Hofmann–Szantyr 435.

B. THE SOUL IS MORTAL

417–424

The central section 417–829 is the core of the book; 94–416 have cleared the ground for it, and 830–1094 are in effect a celebration and an examination in terms of the practical consequences of the great truth that it establishes. To indicate its importance L. dignifies it with a second prooemium addressed (420) to Memmius.

417   nunc age: a formula taken over from Greek didactic; cf. Nic. *Ther.* 359 νῦν δ' ἄγε, al. L. uses it to indicate that he is embarking on a new and important topic, as does Virgil in the second prooemium of the *Aeneid* (7. 37).

natiuos...mortalis: L. denies the existence of the soul both before birth and after death; these leading ideas frame the line (since *nunc age* stands outside the structure), the second being reinforced by the spondaic ending (191 n.).

418   leuis 'light', an anticipation of subsequent arguments, but the idea is easily inferred from the previous discussion.

419 A literary formula: Heinze compared the 'sweet cares', γλυκυτάταις ... φροντίσιν, of Pind. *Ol.* 1. 19; 2. 730–31 *nunc age dicta meo dulci quaesita labore* | *percipe...* The reference is to L.'s poetic shaping of his material rather than to his philosophical researches; the emphasis on technique (*labor = ars*) is pointed (Kenney 366–7).

420   digna 'so as to be worthy of', predicative.

tua...uita 'your (great) calling': cf. the compliments paid to Memmius at 1. 26–7 *Memmiadae nostro, quem tu, dea, tempore in omni* | *omnibus ornatum uoluisti excellere rebus*, 140 *tua...uirtus*. For *uita* in this sense = βίος cf. Virg. *A.* 6. 433 (Minos) *uitasque et crimina discit*; *Laus Pisonis* (*P.L.M.* 1) 5–6 *hinc tua me uirtus rapit et miranda per omnes* | *uita modos*. The interpretation favoured by some scholars 'to be the rule of your life' cannot be extracted from the Latin.

The verse offers the same interplay of endings in long and short *a* as 13 and has the same effect of solemnity.

421   tu fac...iungas: both the emphatic pronoun (after the similar use of σύ by Greek poets) and the periphrastic imperative are characteristic of the high didactic style.

utrumque. . .eorum: *animus* and *anima*: 136 n.

uno sub. . .nomine: the separation of preposition from noun is more drastic than at e.g. 10 *tuisque ex, inclute, chartis*. No metrical necessity prevented L. from writing e.g. *uno iungas sub nomine*; perhaps he wished to drive home his point by the peculiar placing of *iungas*.

422–3 The distinction between *animus* and *anima*, important in the preceding Section A, becomes for the most part immaterial in what follows; but see 446 n.

422 uerbi causa 'for example'.

dicere pergam very nearly = *dicam*; *pergam* is even more colourless than at 178, 420.

424 quatenus: 218 n.

est. . .est 'they are'; but the verb, as often, takes the number of the predicate; cf. Ter. *Andr.* 555 *amantium irae amoris integratiost*; Ov. *Met.* 15. 529 *unumque erat omnia uulnus* (Kühner–Stegmann 1 40–41). Since then *est* is equivalent in sense to *sunt*, *inter se*, though unusual, is perfectly intelligible Latin.

unum inter se coniunctaque res 'a single entity and a united thing'. The variation (*unum. . .res*) and the interlacing (*coniuncta* must be read as constructed ἀπὸ κοινοῦ to refer also to *unum*: 189 n., Bell 272–8), together with the placing of *est. . .est* to frame the utterance, are clearly intended to emphasize the point. Boyancé suggests (160) that L. has in mind the view held by some authorities that the soul had a mortal and an immortal part.

(i) *The soul does not survive the death of the body*

425–444

(**Proof 1**)* The soul is made of far smaller particles than water, mist, or smoke; but when a vessel containing water is broken the water runs away, and mist and smoke can be seen to disperse: therefore when the body, which is the vessel of the soul, is damaged, the soul must be dissolved into its atoms. The form of the argument is syllogistic; it is interrupted by the amplifying parenthesis at 428–33: see 428, 434 nn.

* The proofs are presented according to the numeration of Bailey. Cf., however, Boyancé 161 n. 1.

425   **tenuem constare:** sc. *animam*, not explicitly mentioned until 437.

426   **docui:** at 177–230.

427   **quam liquidus umor aquai:** sc. *est*, as at 456 (*ceu*), 614 (*ut*). Contrast 2. 456–7 *omnia postremo quae puncto tempore cernis | diffugere, ut fumum nebulas flammasque . . .*; but this, which Bailey (89) calls the 'normal' construction, is in fact a secondary development (Kühner–Stegmann II 465; E. C. Woodcock, *A new Latin syntax* (1959) 211–12). L. varies the prosody of *liquidus* according to the incidence of the verse ictus: cf. 4. 1259 *crassaque conueniant liquidis et liquida crassis* (cf. 145 n.). For *umor aquai* cf. 339.

428   **nam:** L. scrupulously advances a proof of what he has just asserted, since, though it follows by implication from the discussion at 179–230, it was not there explicitly demonstrated. The *anima* is more *mobilis* than water, etc., and must therefore be more *tenuis*. Lachmann's *iam* tightens the syntax (434 n.) but, as Munro crisply notes, 'inverts the argument'.

429   **tenui . . . magis:** take together.

430–33   The atoms of the soul are so fine that it is moved, even in sleep, by 'images' of smoke and cloud. These 'images' (*imagines, simulacra* = εἴδωλα) are the films which, according to Epicurean theory, were constantly given off from the surface of every body; they impinge on the eyes – or, in sleep, directly on the *animus* – and so cause vision. L. anticipates his full discussion at 4. 45–521, 722–857. The *simulacrum* of smoke is almost inconceivably fine; but the soul is much finer even than that. This amplification of the point made at 428–9 is loosely constructed and reads like a series of afterthoughts.

430   **quippe ubi** 'seeing that', a common argumentative formula in L.

431   **in somnis** 'in our dreams', to be taken with *cernimus*.

432   **uaporem** 'heat', as always in L.; the phrase *uaporem fumumque* = 'hot smoke', an example of hendiadys: 346 n.
   ferreque: probably here = *efferre* after *exhalare*: 261 n. On *-ĕque* cf. 163 n.

433   These *simulacra* really (*procul dubio*) do come from outside and are not produced by the mind itself. Being conscious that all this part of his argument hinges on doctrine that is as yet unexplained, L. adds a further parenthetic explanation. The text is doubtful. *geruntur*, the reading of the MSS, cannot mean 'are brought': Creech's *feruntur* gives good sense and is printed *faute de mieux*, but it is not easy to account for the corruption. Lambinus' *genuntur* 'are begotten' explains the corruption (cf. 4. 143, 159, where this verb was rightly restored by him) but does not give satisfactory sense. The point that the source of the *simulacra* is external to the *animus* is made only in so far as it is implicit in *feruntur* – if they are 'carried' it can only be from outside. Bentley's *hinc* is too vague.

434   **nunc igitur quoniam** appears to hark back to *quoniam* at 425, but in fact L. now moves on to the second stage of his argument, the minor premiss of the syllogism (425–44 n.). Syntactically there is thus an anacoluthon, i.e. the first *quoniam*-clause lacks its expected apodosis; logically nothing is amiss. Cf. 554 n.

undique qualifies the verbs in the next verse, not *quassatis*.

uasis: cf. 440, 555, 793. The idea that was touched upon at 323–4 (see nn.) of the body as protector of the soul is now developed using a different metaphor: the body as a vessel holding the soul together. The comparison was in fact a commonplace: Cic. *Tusc.* 52 *corpus quidem quasi uas est aut aliquod animi receptaculum.*

435   **diffluere umorem et laticem discedere:** 'linear' variation (cf. Introd. 24–6), with chiasmus and repetition of prefix (17–18 n.).

436   **discedit** agrees with the nearer of its two subjects: 66 n. After *discedere cernis* at 435 the sense is 'likewise disperses, as you may see'.

437   **perire:** perhaps for *disperire* after *diffundi*: 261 n.

438   **ocius et citius:** sc. than water, mist or smoke, because so much more tenuous.

441   **cum:** temporal; but cf. 363 n.
cohibere: cf. 323 *tenetur*.

441–2   **conquassatum...rarefactum** 'if it should be shaken...':
119, 171 nn.

442   ac 'or', as at 164 (cf. 150n.). L. seems to have in mind the fact that the body does not have to be completely shattered (*conquassatum*) for death to occur: if enough blood is lost, the body may lose coherence (*rarefactum*) to the point of allowing the *anima* to escape through its interstices (*foramina*, πόροι); cf. 458 *fatisci*. The analogy with the *uas* is still present to the mind, though not explicitly sustained.

443-4   When the body ceases to enclose the soul, the surrounding air, which is much rarer than the body, must allow it to escape.

443   qui...ullo 'how can any air hold it in?'; the rhetorical question, expecting a negative answer, is equivalent to a statement *nec...ullo. nullus* in early and colloquial Latin is sometimes used as a stronger form of *non*: cf. Plaut. *Bacch.* 90 *tu nullus adfueris, si non lubet* 'you needn't put in an appearance at all if you don't want to'; Lucret. 1. 426–7 *spatium...* | *si nullum foret* 'if void did not exist at all'. For the variant here cf. Cic. *De Leg.* 2. 15 *Zaleucum istum negat ullum fuisse* 'he says Z. never existed at all'. See Hofmann–Szantyr 205; J. B. Hofmann, *Lat. Umgangssprache*[3] (1951) 80; Fordyce on Catull. 17. 20.

444   incohibescit 'which (though) rarer than the body (yet) strives to hold it in'; a strained interpretation which lays more weight on the inceptive sense of the verb than it will bear and is not in any case really pointed in the context. Lachmann's *is cohibessit?* (= *cohibuerit*: Neue–Wagener III 510) would give good sense if it were certain that the pf. subj. is appropriate in a question of this type (Kühner–Stegmann I 178). Bergk's *incohibensquest* gives good sense but a word-order which is not demonstrably Lucretian: 'which is rarer than the body and more incapable of containing (the soul)' = *c. q. n. magis rarus est magisque incohibens*. Other suggestions seem even less probable, and the obelus has for once been employed.

445-458

(**Proof 2**) The growth and development of the soul is parallel to that of the body. This idea was a commonplace.

446-8   The play on words in '*sentimus...senescere...tenero... sententia tenuis*' reinforces the logic. For the Epicurean implications of this technique see Friedländer, *passim*. Cf. 720n.

446   sentimus: the appeal to observation is not, strictly speaking, applicable to *gigni*.

mentem: cf. 448 *animi...sententia*, 450 *consilium*, 453 *ingenium*; L. has the *animus* in mind, but at 455 he applies the argument to the *anima*. Cf. 422–3 n.

447–8   infirmo...corpore: for the abl. cf. 293 n.

447   uagantur 'walk unsteadily'.

448   sequitur 'accompanies', 'matches'; i.e. the mind, like the body, *uagatur*.

tenuis: 232 n. Does *-uĭs* prefigure *uīs* in the following verses? Cf. 446–8 n.

449–52   L. plays on the senses of *uis*: physical power, mental power, the metaphorical power of time. Cf. 378–80 n.

451   quassatum: cf. 434, 441; but the image now is of the body tottering under physical assault, as of a battering-ram: see next n.

452   obtusis 'battered' rather than 'dulled'; the word agrees grammatically with *uiribus* but refers in sense to *artus*. L. likes to express the destructive powers of time in physical terms: 5. 314 *ualidas aeui uiris perferre patique*, 379 *immensi ualidas aeui contemnere uiris*.

453   The language of this succinct depiction of old age is carefully chosen. *claudicat* 'limps' (sustaining the idea of physical damage, which the mind shares with the body) indicates slowness in apprehension; *delirat* 'wanders' (with an eye on the original literal sense 'stray from the furrow' in ploughing: 363 n.), inability to keep to the point (the tongue is *animi interpres*: 6. 1149); *labat* (Lachmann's almost certain supplement) 'totters', indecision and inaction.

454   omnia: both the physical and the mental faculties.

deficiunt...desunt: cf. 435 *diffluere...discedere*.

uno tempore 'together'.

455   quoque: sc. along with the body; cf. 445–6, 457 *pariter*.

conuenit 'it is right and proper', i.e. consistent with the facts just adduced: cf. 462.

456   ceu fumus: the comparison that was hinted at in 436 is now made explicitly. Epicurus is said to have held that at death souls were scattered like smoke, καπνοῦ δίκην σκίδνανται (*Phys.* 337, 227 Us.), but the image was old, both literary (Hom. *Il.* 23. 100: the apparition of Patroclus disappears ἠΰτε καπνός, 'like smoke') and popular (Plat. *Phaed.* 70a). The stately language of *in altas aeris auras* lends dignity to the idea of dissolution and oblivion. For the nom. *fumus* cf. 427n.

458   fessa fatisci 'grow weary and worn' (cf. 5. 308), with 'figura etymologica', since both words come from the same root; but the literal sense of *fatiscor* 'fall apart' is no doubt felt (cf. 442n.). In view of 445–6, which 457–8 obviously echo, the n. pl. must refer to both body and soul (136n.), but since only *anima* is mentioned in the immediate context there is some harshness in the language.

<h3 style="text-align:center">459–462</h3>

(**Proof 3**) Just as the body suffers disease and pain, so the mind suffers grief and fear; (but the body is mortal): therefore the mind is mortal. This proof, which still concerns the *parallel* experiences of body and soul, is syllogistic in form; it paves the way to those which concern their *shared* experience.

459   huc accedit uti 'furthermore', a regular formula to introduce a new argument.

corpus ut ipsum 'like the body too': 128–9n.

460   suscipere 'undergo' (cf. 366); to govern the inf. *uidemus* must be supplied from the preceding *uideamus*.

461   animum: here and at 464 the reader is left to infer that the dissolution of the *animus* entails that of the whole *anima*.

462   conuenit: 455n. The syllogistic logic (459–62n.) is spurious: the 'pains' suffered by the mind are so called by analogy with physical pains (cf. 461 *acris*), but the use of this metaphor does not prove that the mind dies with the body. The arguments from actual derangement that follow are somewhat more cogent. Cf. 484–6n.

<h3 style="text-align:center">463–473</h3>

(**Proof 4**) In disease the mind can be seen to share the derangement of the body.

463   morbis in corporis: in such phrases the genitive is regularly treated as if it were an adj. in agreement with the noun, and the preposition is sandwiched between the two.

auius errat 'wanders'; cf. 453 n., 464 *delira*. Enn. *Sc.* 241 V.² (202 Jocelyn) *incerte errat animus* refers to infirmity of purpose rather than to madness.

464   animus: 461 n.

dementit: the word is not found before L. and may be one of his coinages. That the idea of straying (cf. 453, 463 nn.) was fully felt in *demens* is shown by Enn. *Ann.* 202–3 V.² *quo uobis mentes, rectae quae stare solebant | antehac, dementes sese flexere uiai?* Cf. Festus, p. 150 L. ⟨de⟩*mens, quod de sua* ⟨*mente decesserit*⟩.

465   lethargo 'coma': L. uses the Greek technical term, perhaps thinking *ueternus* insufficiently precise. The reference may be to a form of malaria: W. H. S. Jones, *Malaria and Greek history* (1909) 68.

466   aeternum...soporem 'unbroken sleep', i.e. coma, not death, in spite of 921 *aeternum...soporem* and analogous expressions elsewhere. For *aeternus = perpetuus* cf. 907.

oculis nutuque cadenti 'with drooping eyes and head', perhaps a condensed way of saying *oculis cadentibus et capite nutanti* (cf. 346, 614 nn.); but this may rather be an instance of what Bell 272–8 calls 'synchysis or distribution'. For *cado* in this sense cf. 4. 952 *bracchia palpebraeque cadunt. cadenti* agrees with the nearer noun: 66 n.

468   reuocantes: one of the *signa letalia* is recorded by Pliny (*N.H.* 7. 171) as *a somno mouentium neglectus*; cf. Cels. 3. 20 *si...continens* [cf. *aeternum*] *ei somnus est, utique excitandus est.* However 469 seems to show that L. has in mind rather the week-long mourning ritual of the *conclamatio*: only when this had been faithfully performed was the corpse judged to be securely dead (Serv. *ad* Virg. *A.* 6. 218; Schol. Ter. p. 59. 10–13 Schlee).

469 The description of the mourners is perhaps more scornful than compassionate: 904–8 n.

471   penetrant...contagia morbi 'the disease enters and affects the mind': for *contagia* = 'contacts' cf. 345, but here the sense of 'infection' (6. 1236) must also be present.

472–3 These verses form a necessary part of the argument, even though L. appends them as something of an afterthought. They are indeed the minor premiss of his syllogism: bodily disease affects the mind; but pain and disease in the body lead, as we know, to death (472–3): therefore the mind must perish as the body perishes.

472 fabricator 'architect', a striking metaphor, as Heinze remarks, since disease is thought of as a destroyer.

473 perdocti 'thoroughly instructed': 179–80 n.

476–486

(**Proof 5**) The effects of drunkenness. Whereas disease attacks the body, which then communicates its effects to the mind, drunkenness attacks the *anima* directly (483): thus the argument of the preceding section is reversed. Drunkenness, its effects and their implications, was a topic much discussed by ancient philosophers.

477 Food – and, we must presume, drink – was thought to be distributed through the body by the veins (2. 1125, 1136, 4. 955); as the *anima* is *per totum dissita corpus* (3. 143) it follows that wine first affects the *anima*, which in turn affects the body. L. however leaves this sequence of events to be inferred by his readers.

ardor: a popular notion; Epicurus himself held that wine might be either heating or cooling according to circumstances.

478–80 This catalogue of symptoms is in itself no doubt a matter of common observation, but it is vividly expressed in L.'s manner: cf. 154–6 n. It is also artfully arranged to lead to a climax: the phrases decrease in length and culminate in a sequence of single words, *clamor singultus iurgia*, which convey a picture of mounting loss of self-control, finally summed up in the expressive *gliscunt*.

478 grauitas: because the *anima* can no longer hold them up: 5. 556–7 *nonne uides etiam quam magno pondere nobis | sustineat corpus tenuissima uis animai...?*

479 The rhythm is unobtrusively appropriate to the sense: a slightly stumbling effect in *crura uacillanti* (perhaps to mirror the exaggerated care of a drunken man's walk?), the long slow *tardescit*, the alliteration and monosyllabic ending of *madet mens*. For the structure of the verse cf. 453.

tardescit occurs nowhere else in Latin and is no doubt a coinage of L.'s to fit the special requirements of his description.

madet: the word is commonly used of the drunkard himself, but L. no doubt means that the atoms of the *anima/animus* are permeated by those of the wine: cf. 485 *insinuarit*.

480   nant 'are awash', an expressive metaphor not found before L. It is applied by Virgil and Ovid to sleep and death as well as to the effects of drunkenness.

gliscunt 'grow'; an old word, originally it seems of agricultural application (363 n.), since Columella uses it to mean 'thrive': *paleis...etiam gliscit*, sc. *asellus* (7. 1. 1). As a poetical synonym of *crescere* it is a favourite word of Tacitus'.

481   cetera de genere hoc: a formula, cf. 744 and often elsewhere. The dry and summary character of the verse, which the commentators call 'weak', reflects L.'s unwillingness to describe the more disgusting phenomena of drunkenness in his poetry: cf. 390 n.

482   uemens uiolentia uini: the alliteration implies a reference back to the beginning of the section: 476 *uini uis*.

483   animam: cf. 477 n.
corpore in ipso: 128–9 n.

484–6 This is the argument on which the whole demonstration from 463 to 525 is based, though L. appends it to the section on drunkenness. He reasons from probability: the behaviour of the soul in delirium, drunkenness, etc., does not *prove* conclusively that it dies with the body, but if it can be so grievously affected then it is fair to suppose that the consequences must extend finally to dissolution. Cf. 462 n.

484   quaecumque 'anything which'; the reference is to the *anima*.
inque pediri: 343 n.

485   insinuarit 'has found its way in', i.e. into the atomic structure of the *anima*. L. uses the word both intransitively, as here, and transitively. Cf. 502, 671, 1061 nn.

486   causa 'disease' = αἴτιον in the medical sense, and so equivalent to *morbus*. Cf. 502 *morbi...causa*.

aeuo 'life', as at 344, 357.

487–509

(**Proof 6**) The effects of epilepsy. L.'s evident interest in the disease need not lead us to believe that he was an epileptic: cf. 154–6, 478–80 nn. Epilepsy was much discussed by medical writers, and L. may well have known that Julius Caesar suffered from it (Suet. *Jul.* 45). If he was looking for examples of the disturbance of the *anima* in disease he could hardly omit this, one of the most striking of all.

487   subito ui morbi 'suddenly, by a violent stroke of the disease'; the instantaneous onset of the attack is conveyed by opening the sentence with this phrase and postponing the subject to the next verse and the verbs to the verse after that; cf. 488–9 n.

488   ante oculos aliquis nostros: it is a fact of common experience – and a Roman crowd would have had few inhibitions about staring.

488–9   ut fulminis ictu concidit: the simile and the enjambment of the verb contribute to the description.

489   spumas agit 'foams at the mouth': cf. 493. The same details at Cels. 3. 23 *homo subito concidit, ex ore spumae mouentur, deinde interposito tempore ad se redit et per se ipse consurgit.*

artus: acc. of respect; cf. Virgil's imitation, *G.* 3. 84 *micat auribus et tremit artus.*

490   desipit: cf. 464 *dementit.*

extentat neruos 'his muscles grow rigid', literally 'he tightens his muscles'. Latin not infrequently says 'do' for 'allow (or 'suffer') to be done', 'to have happen to one': cf. 877, 1090 nn.

491 A skilful marriage of rhythm and sense to express the uneven breathing and thrashing movements of the patient.

492–4 'Obviously because the violence of the disease is dispersed throughout the body and as it forces out the breath stirs up foam, as in the ocean the waves. . . .' The text given here, which is that printed by Büchner, represents the smallest possible departure from the text of the MSS that gives acceptable sense. (i) *qua* is meaningless, and *nimirum quia* is a Lucretian formula (194, 226, 566). (ii) *spumas* is an easy correction of *spumans*; the error was phonetic, engendered by the preceding nasal syllables in '*agens* anim*am*'. (iii) A syllable is missing after *spuma(n)s*, and a conjunction is needed: *ut* is more likely to have been lost than *quasi*. The only serious objection to this solution is that nowhere else is *distracta* used = *dispersa*: it always = 'torn apart', as at 501, 507 immediately below; cf. also 590, 799. It is possible that L. used the word here only = 'violently dispersed' in order to emphasize his point by applying to the disease itself the word that is to be used of its effects on the *anima*. MacKay's *districta* 'stretched taut' (cf. 490) entails 'the transfer of the epithet from the *artus* to the *vis morbi* that causes the tension of the *artus*' (*C. Ph.* 56 (1961) 104); this is ingenious, but L. nowhere else uses *distringo*. Since 499–501 seem to imply a fuller explanation than is to be found in the text as we have it, it is possible that, as suggested by Giussani, some verses have dropped out.

493 turbat agens animam spumas = *spumas turbat agens animam*, i.e. *dum animam agit*: *animam agere* usually = 'breathe one's last', but at Catull. 63. 31 *furibunda simul anhelans uaga uadit animam agens* it means 'gasp'. If however it is thought that *spumas agit* at 489 absolutely enforces the construction of the two words together here also, the phrase can be taken = *turbat animam agens spumas*, i.e. *ut spumas agat*, which gives practically the same, or even better, sense, but word-order which is not demonstrably Lucretian. We should not rule out the possibility that L. has deliberately confused his syntax for descriptive purposes.

salso: a purely ornamental epithet on the Homeric model, common in Ennius; the whole sea-simile is emphatic, picturesque and 'literary'.

496 omnino 'in general', implying that the role of pain is secondary.

semina uocis: L. assumes, what he will demonstrate later, that sounds are composed of atoms: 4. 533–4 *haud igitur dubiumst quin uoces uerbaque constent | corporeis e principiis*.

497   eiciuntur 'are forced out'; Lambinus' correction is necessitated by the sense: cf. 495 *exprimitur. eliciuntur* is far too mild; contrast 58 n.

glomerata 'in heaps', pell-mell: the sounds are inarticulate, not properly formed by the tongue as described at 4. 549–52.

498   et sunt munita uiai 'and (where) there is a paved road (for them)', a curious metaphor. It is used at 5. 102–3, much more aptly, of the evidence of the senses as 'the paved road of belief, the nearest way to the mind of man', *uia qua munita fidei | proxima fert humanum in pectus templaque mentis.* L. makes considerable use of periphrases of the type *strata uiai, saepta domorum, prima uirorum,* no doubt primarily for metrical convenience.

499   desipientia: the word, coined from *desipere* on the model of *sapientia,* occurs nowhere else in classical Latin. L. explains this feature of the seizure by recalling that the *animus* is involved with the *anima.*

500   ut docui: at 492, but unless something has fallen out the lesson was not very clearly expressed: 492–4 n.

seorsum: L. uses both this form and *sorsum* as metrically convenient, with a preference for the latter. See Introd. 22 n. 4.

501   eodem: sc. that I have already mentioned.

ueneno: the *uis morbi*; cf. 1. 759–60 *deinde inimica modis multis sunt atque ueneno | ipsa sibi inter se.*

502   reflexit 'has turned back', intransitive; cf. 485 n.

reditque = *rediitque*; cf. 1042 *obît.*

503   in latebras: 'comme un serpent venimeux' (Ernout–Robin).

umor: medical writers ascribed epilepsy to a temporary excess of one or another of the 'humours' (bile, serum, phlegm = χολή, ἰχώρ, φλέγμα; not identical with the 'humours' familiar in medieval and Elizabethan literature). L. does not specify which *umor* is responsible (the question was in fact disputed), nor does he explain how the overflowing of the *umor* sets off the violent processes previously described. Cf. 4. 664, where fever is ascribed to excess of bile.

504   uaccillans: the word is nowhere else scanned with its first syllable metrically 'heavy'; cf. 479. The spelling with -*cc*- is found in

Nonius Marcellus (p. 50 L.), who attributes it to Cicero (*Phil.* 3. 31), and it occurs in MSS; it may be due to false derivation from *uacca*. For other scansional variations cf. 648, 994 nn.

primum: take with *uaccillans*.

consurgit: cf. 489 n.

omnis: acc. pl.

505 **receptat** = *recipit*; the frequentative, as at 352, for metrical convenience.

506–9 These verses sum up the argument by recurring to the point made at 440–44: if the soul can be so affected within the body it is unlikely to be able to exist outside it. As with 484–6 (see n.) the reasoning is from probability.

506 **haec:** *animus* and *anima*: 136 n.

tantis...morbis: the reference is to coma and drunkenness as well as to epilepsy.

corpore in ipso as opposed to *sine corpore* at 508; cf. 483, 128–9 n.

507 **iactentur...laborent:** for the causal subjunctive after *ubi* Ernout–Robin compare 4. 193–5 ...*quod paruula causa | est procul a tergo quae prouehat atque propellat, | quod superest, ubi tam uolucri leuitate ferantur*; the grammars seem to offer no other instances. *ubi* + indic. in a causal sense is also very sparsely attested: Hofmann–Szantyr 652. Cf. 363 n.

miseris...modis: cf. 1. 123 *simulacra modis pallentia miris*. Such pl. expressions with *modus* are common in the comedians and perhaps had a colloquial ring.

laborent: 176 n.

509 **cum ualidis uentis:** the fragile soul could hardly survive in this robust company: the suggestion of ironical personification is maintained in *aetatem degere* = 'live'; contrast 512 *uiuere*.

510–525

(**Proof 7**) Medical treatment entails alteration in the atomic structure of the mind; but change implies death: therefore the mind (and hence the soul) is mortal. The minor premiss of the syllogism is an Epicurean axiom: see 517–20 n.

510   mentem: sc. *aegram*. This proof concerns only the *animus*.

511   flecti 'influenced', 'changed' (516n.), but perhaps referring also to the idea that the sick mind is astray: 453, 464nn.

512   praesagit 'predicts', a slightly unexpected word, perhaps with special reference to *mortalem*; to demonstrate that the soul is mortal is to foretell its eventual death.

    mortalem uiuere 'lives under sentence of death', a calculated oxymoron.

513–16 Change of any kind entails addition, subtraction, or re-arrangement of the atoms.

513   traiecere = *traicere*, the old spelling (W. M. Lindsay, *Early Latin verse* (1922) 140).

    aequumst 'he must', *eum* being understood as antecedent of the following *quicumque*. Cf. 455, 462 *conuenit*.

514   aliquid prorsum...hilum 'something, if only a very little'. *hilum* is generally used after a negative (220n., 518, 783, al.) or a virtual negative (4. 515 *si ex parti claudicat hilum*). Here the word reads almost like an afterthought; cf. 518, where it echoes and reinforces *quicquam*.

515   adoritur et infit 'attempts and begins'; the pleonasm, of which *quaerit* in the next verse is a further variation, does not seem particularly expressive.

516   aliam quamuis naturam 'anything else whatever': the principle (fundamental to Epicurean theory) admits of no exceptions.

    flectere 'change': cf. 511, 522, 755.

517–20 What is immortal cannot change, for change implies death. An Epicurean axiom: 519–20 are repeated several times elsewhere in the poem (see app. crit.). Only the atoms themselves are eternal and unchanging; their combinations are subject to change, i.e. are mortal. Cf. 701, 715–16, 756.

517–18   transferri...tribui...defluere are passive variants for *traiecere, addere, detrahere*. L. nowhere else uses *defluere* = 'flow *away*'; this is probably a deliberate variation of the usual *diffluere* to respond to *detrahere* – an interesting example of L.'s masterful attitude to the language.

517   nec...uult 'forbids': *nolo* and *non uolo* often mean something much stronger than 'be unwilling'.

518   quicquam: 220, 514nn.

519   finibus: an important idea. The great panegyric of Epicurus at the beginning of Book 1 ends with a summary of his teaching: *unde refert nobis uictor quid possit oriri, | quid nequeat, finita potestas denique cuique | quanam sit ratione atque alte terminus haerens* (75–7). The 'boundaries' and the 'boundary-stone' represent the fixed properties of the atomic combinations: any substance that 'quits its limits' ceases as such to exist.

520   continuo 'immediately', but since the sequence of events is logical as well as temporal, almost = 'accordingly', 'thereby'.

521–5 Formally (*ergo* answers *at* in 517) part of the syllogism of this proof, but like 484–6 and 506–9 (see nn.) the summary is relevant to the whole sequence of argument from 463. *animus...aegrescit* rounds off the paragraph in the usual way with a reference back to 463–4.

521–2   mortalia signa mittit: the placing of the main clause between the two subordinate clauses embodies in physical form the idea on which L. insists in the following verses, that all logical escape routes from the Epicurean position are blocked.

523–5 The two arguments are personified as adversaries; the true argument cuts off the retreat of the false, brings it to bay, and hews it down in open combat. L.'s readers might well remember the debate between the Unjust and the Just Reasons in Aristophanes' *Clouds* (see the ed. by K. J. Dover (1968) lviii); and the title Καταβάλλοντες, 'Throws', by which one of Protagoras' works sometimes went, shows that the idea of debate as combat was something of a commonplace. The violent and aggressive turn which L. gives to the image, however, is peculiar to him. Cf. the panegyric of Epicurus at 1. 62–79, esp. 78–9 *quare religio pedibus subiecta uicissim | obteritur*; Sykes Davies 34; Boyancé 306–7.

524   eunti 'as it tries to escape' = *abeunti*: 526n.

525   ancipitique refutatu 'with two-edged refutation', referring to the dilemma posed in the *siue...seu* clauses at 521–2; but also clearly with the literal sense in mind, cf. 6. 168 *ancipiti...ferro* 'a double-edged axe'. *refutatus* appears to be a coinage of L.'s (cf. 381–2n.); the unusual rhythm of the verse gives the sense of a mighty weapon descending once and no more – after which Truth stands erect and triumphant over the prostrate corpse of Falsehood.

<h3 style="text-align:center">526–547</h3>

(**Proof 8**) Often a man is seen to die gradually; this proves that the soul is destroyed piecemeal. The section has no very close connexion either with what precedes or with what follows; and 538 *ut diximus ante* seems to refer most naturally to 580–91 below. On internal grounds therefore Giussani's suggestion that it belongs after 669 has much to commend it. Cf. Introd. 13.

526–30   L. may have had in mind Plato's famous description of the death of Socrates (*Phaedo* 117e–118a).

526   ire 'die', for *obire*: cf. 319, 524nn. In this sense *eo* is found elsewhere in L. (6. 1243 *contagibus ibant | atque labore*, 2. 962) and occasionally in later writers.

527   The slow departure of life is reflected by the heavy spondees and the rhythm, with diaeresis after the second foot and caesura in the fourth foot only.

   membratim 'limb by limb': L. shares with other early writers a fondness for adverbs in -*im*. The idea in the common *paulatim* is taken up and embellished in the more recherché *membratim...tractim* (530)...*particulatim* (542).

529   post inde 'next, from there...'.

530   tractim 'draggingly', a picturesque way of saying 'slowly'.

   gelidi uestigia leti: the personification of death may be purely 'literary'; cf. 1. 852 *leti sub dentibus ipsis*. However, the distinction between death itself, a natural and necessary (even, as being necessary for the survival of the species, a beneficial) phenomenon, and the real adversary, fear of death (37), is not always kept in view. Over which of these things does the triumphant affirmation of 830 proclaim victory?

531 The general sense is obvious: since the soul is torn apart in the process of dying it must be mortal. The transmitted text has two faults: (i) L. does not postpone *atque* (or indeed *et*: see E. Norden, *P. Vergilius Maro Aeneis Buch VI*³ (1934) 402–3); (ii) the reference ought to be to the *anima*, not to the *animus*. None of the solutions hitherto proposed is free from objection. Munro's *itque animae hoc* postulates a fairly simple process of corruption: *itque* (for which cf. 526 *ire*) > *atque* and *animae hoc* > *animo haec* (through interchange of terminations); but *hōc = ergo* regularly begins the sentence. On this ground Bailey retains *haec*; but *natura* stands in need of no such definition, and the elision of *-ae* before *haec* is extremely dubious (374 n.). There is a good deal to be said for deleting *haec*, as Büchner does, explaining its presence as due to an original double reading *animō͞e* in the archetype. The necessary connexion with what precedes could then be achieved by accepting Bernays's *aeque* (which in capital script is very like *atque*), but at the expense of the meaning: Bailey's gloss 'equally with the body' ignores the fact that the body is *not* severed or split. Heinze's *ergo* gives excellent sense (for its position + elision cf. 184, 969), but it is too far from the transmitted text to command general acceptance – which is by no means tantamount to saying that it is not what L. wrote.

531–2 uno tempore: 454 n.

532 sincera exsistit = (apparently) *integra exit*, both words being used in an unusual sense. *sincerus* properly = 'unmixed', 'unalloyed'; in the sense 'intact' it occurs again at 717 (but for the contrary view see Housman, *C.Q.* 3 (1909) 63–5). For *exsistere* = 'emerge' cf. 2. 796 *in lucem exsistunt primordia rerum*, 5. 212 *liquidas exsistere in auras.*

533–5 Obviously this was a standard objection to the Epicurean position; whose is not known.

533 ipsam 'of its own accord', rather than accepting dispersion through the pores of the individual limbs; but the sense 'without losing its integrity' is also possible.

534 partis: sc. *suas.*

537 'Ought to have more sensation', since the degree of acuteness of sensation depends on the concentration of soul-atoms. *in* very nearly = *cum* (cf. 581 n.); for the abl. cf. 293 n.

538 qui: probably, in view of *nusquam*, to be referred to *locus* rather than to *sensus*.

ut diximus ante: if this section is in its right place the reference must be to 531–2, but cf. 526–47 n.

539 dispargitur: L.'s MSS sometimes retain the original *a* in compounds of *spargo*; cf. 661.

540 si iam libeat 'even if one *were* disposed, for the sake of argument'; for this use of *iam* cf. 766, 843.

541 dare 'allow', 'grant', as at 876.

542 particulatim: 527 n.

543 necesse: sc. *est*. If L.'s MSS are a reliable guide to his practice, he occasionally omits *est* in such phrases for the sake of variety; cf. 796.

543–7 The argument, as Bailey remarks, is weak. L. takes as proved what he is seeking to prove, namely that the soul perishes with the body, and asserts that perish it does, whether piecemeal or after concentrating itself. But *obbrutescat* (545) begs the question: the possibility that the soul leaves the body 'in one piece' is not eliminated.

544 per auras: L. tends elsewhere to distinguish between *per auras*, used of motion through the air, and *in auras*, used of arrival in and dispersal through the air (but cf. 4. 569 *perit frustra diffusa per auras*); it is the second of these senses that is required here. Duff remarked that 'the argument deals entirely with the state of the soul before it leaves the body' and proposed *per artus*; this gives excellent sense, opposing the piecemeal death of the soul as each part of the body dies to its 'fading away' in concentrated form. However, as the phrase *per artus* was used at 533 of the concentrating process it is perhaps unlikely that L. applied it almost immediately to the process of dispersal.

545 contracta suis e partibus 'drawn together ⟨so as to make a whole⟩ out of its different parts'; that the *partes* are those of the soul is shown by 534.

obbrutescat 'becomes stupid', no doubt with the root meaning 'heavy' (βαρύς: cf. 6. 105 *bruto...pondere pressae*) in mind, as the rhythm suggests (191 n.). In classical Latin the word is otherwise attested only in the Republican dramatist Afranius (Festus, p. 201 L.). L. assumes without proof that on the rejected hypothesis the soul somehow grows dim and then dies (cf. 543–7 n.).

546–7 These verses summarize and repeat 526–30. The rhythm and phrasing mirror the even and inevitable departure of sensation and life: *magis ac magis...minus et minus* have an almost soothing effect.

546 **totum:** there are no 'pockets' of sensation as postulated by the rejected theory.

548–557

(**Proof 9**) The mind is as much a part of the body as the organs of sense and can no more exist apart from it than they can. The premiss of this proof was argued at 94–7, 136–40, and occurs again below at 615–23, 784–97.

548 **una** 'an individual', further defined by the following relative clause.

550 **alii...qui...cumque** 'all the other senses that...'; for the tmesis of *quicumque* cf. 940, 1075.

sensus 'sense-organs', as at 626 and, probably, 562. Another instance of *patrii sermonis egestas*, for Greek distinguished αἴσθησις 'sensation' and αἰσθητήριον 'sense-organ'.

551 **atque...-ue:** -*ue* is connective, not adversative: 34 n. *uel* is similarly used in enumerations: 5. 965 *glandes atque arbita uel pira lecta*.

naresue in spite of *aures* at 549, not merely to save the metre, but because the removal of the external flap of the ear (which is what 'ear' suggests to most people) does not destroy the hearing.

552 **secreta** 'if removed': 441–2 n. For the n. pl. cf. 136 n.

nequeunt sentire nec esse 'can neither feel nor exist' = *neque sentire neque esse queunt*.

553 **tamen** 'on the contrary'.

tabē: cf. 1. 806 *ut tabe nimborum arbusta uacillent*. In Augustan verse the form *tabĕ* is usual (Neue–Wagener I 374). Cf. 732 *famēque*, 734 n.

554 **sic** answers formally to *ueluti* at 551, which continues *uelut* at

549. Logically, however, 554–8 form the conclusion of a syllogism whose premisses are: (i) the mind is an organ of the body like any other (548–50); (ii) the other organs cannot exist independently of the body (551–3). Therefore, the conclusion follows, neither can the mind. Syntactically the passage is anacoluthic, since the *quoniam*-clause that introduces the first premiss has no grammatical apodosis. For a similar discrepancy between syntactical and logical structure cf. 434 n.; again the argument is not seriously impaired.

554–5 sine corpore et ipso...homine 'without the body and the man himself', sc. of whom the body forms part; for the phraseology cf. 346 n., but the case is here somewhat different: *ipso homine* (as Heinze remarks) is not only explicatory but also parenthetic, since *quod* can only refer to *corpus*.

555 uas: 434 n.

556–7 For the point now made the vessel-image is inadequate, since it does not represent the atomic interconnexions of body and soul; the soul is *nexam per uenas uiscera neruos* (217; cf. 325, 331, al.) and must therefore share in the dissolution of the bodily structure.

556 ei: always a spondee in L. and always at the end of the verse. The comic poets use both $\bar{e}\bar{i}$ and $\widehat{e\bar{i}}$ (W. M. Lindsay, *Early Latin verse* (1922) 168); $\bar{e}\bar{i}$ is rare in all periods, partly because of the general avoidance of the oblique cases of *is* by Augustan and later poets (Neue–Wagener II 378–9; B. Axelson, *Unpoetische Wörter* (1945) 70; J. A. Richmond on [Ov.] *Hal.* 34; Fordyce on Catull. 82. 3).

557 The body is said to cling to the soul rather than the soul to the body because the point at issue is the description of the body (by the vessel-image or some other metaphor) in relation to the soul.

558–579

(Proof 10) The soul cannot function without the protection of the body. This is in effect the converse of the position argued at 323–49.

558 uiuata: 409 n.

559 coniuncta 'because they are joined': 171 n. The periphrasis *corporis atque animi...potestas*, being pl. in sense = *corpus atque animus*, is treated as if it were grammatically pl., and the participle is, following the usual rule (136n.), neuter. This construction is essentially an extension of the usage which is normal with nouns of multitude (*turba*, *pars*, etc.: Hofmann–Szantyr 436–7); it is perhaps rendered less harsh by L.'s 'linear' style of composition (Introd. 24–6), in which a verse apiece is allotted to subject and predicate.

560 edere 'perform', very nearly = *dare*; cf. 2. 311 *proprio dat corpore motus*.

561 animi: because, as explained at 159–60, it is the *animus* that initiates these motions. However, 565 shows that L. has the whole soul in mind in this section: cf. 446n.

   nec autem 'nor on the other hand'.

562 sensibus probably refers, as at 550, to the sense-organs. The eyes, etc., are still there in the dead body but without soul they are useless.

563 radicibus 'from its anchorage': the notion of *radix* embraces the place in which a thing is rooted.

564 ipse 'on its own'.

   sorsum 'apart from', for the usual *sorsum a*, if the text is sound; apparently a unique instance.

565 uidetur: sing. because *anima atque animus* are thought of as a single whole; contrast 559n. (66n. is somewhat different).

566–79 The analogy of the eye, which perhaps appealed to L. because of his general interest in light and vision, was incidental to the main argument, to which he now returns: the intimate interconnexion of body and soul.

566 mixtim: 527n. *mixta* in Q, which gives perfectly good sense (cf. 283), is a 'correction' of *mixti* in OV. This sequence, accidental alteration followed by a deliberate (and almost always incorrect) attempt to mend the damage, is a frequent source of error in texts.

567 tenentur 'are protected'; cf. 323n. The subject is *primordia* in the next verse.

568 magnis interuallis 'so as to leave wide spaces (between themselves)'; for the abl. cf. 293n.

569–70 mouentur...motus 'make motions'; this kind of 'internal' or 'cognate' acc. occurs from Plautus onwards in phrases like *pugnam pugnare, uitam uiuere, somnium somniare* (C. F. W. Müller, *Syntax des Nom. und Akk. im Lat.* (1908) 4–55; Hofmann–Szantyr 38–40). It is even commoner in Greek.

570 in auras: take with *eiecta* in the next verse.

572 tenentur: sc. *ab aere*.

573–5 'For air will be body and what is more (*atque*) a living thing, if it is going to be able to contain the soul within itself and confine it to those motions which it used to make within the sinews and inside (*ipso*: 128–9, 483nn.) the body.' Some alteration of the transmitted text is inevitable if the point is not to be obscured: *aer* must be the subject and *anima* the object of the verbs *cohibere* and *concludere* (cf. 569 *conclusa*, sc. *corpore*) and Wakefield's correction achieves this economically. If the soul could stay together in the air after leaving the body, that could only be because the air was performing the body's function of holding the soul together, in which case it would receive life from the soul – which is ridiculous. The *reductio ad absurdum* is characteristic: 367–9, 624–33nn.

576–7 resoluto corporis omni tegmine: a translation of a phrase of Epicurus (*Ep. ad Hdt.* 65, 21 Us.) τοῦ στεγάζοντος λυθέντος, 'when the protecting agent is dissolved'; cf. 323n. *tegmen* recurs at 604, but nowhere else, in this metaphorical sense.

577 uitalibus auris 'breath', cf. 405. The use of *aura* in this quite different sense so soon after *auras* at 570 is probably inadvertent; but cf. 378–80n.

578 sensus animi is less pointed than at 98 and seems to be little more than a convenient periphrasis for *animum*.

579 coniunctast causa duobus 'what kept them alive is linked for both', sc. body and soul. *causa* is 'cause of life' rather than 'cause of destruction'; cf. 348 *coniunctast causa salutis*, 559 *coniuncta ualent*.

580–591

(**Proof 11**) The manner in which the dead body decays shows that both body and soul are shattered by death.

581 discidium: 342 n.

in taetro...odore: the 'foul smell' reflects the collapse and decay of the body (584–6), which can only be caused by a corresponding collapse of the soul. For *in* cf. 537 n.

582–8 The soul, in disengaging itself from its atomic interconnexions (*ex imo penitusque coorta*) in the recesses of the body and making its escape through the pores, shakes the fabric of the body to its foundations: the language (*putre...conciderit...fundamenta*) figures the decaying body as a tenement crumbling into ruins. This is the converse of the process described at 2. 944–51; cf. also 3. 327–30 (compared by Heinze).

583 uti fumus: 456 n.

584 putre 'in ruins', predicative.

586 emanante: Wakefield's correction of the impossible text of the MSS is preferable to Lachmann's as picking up *emanarit* from 583.

587 uiarum omnis flexus 'all the winding paths', with perhaps a suggestion of a pell-mell flight from a threatened city: 586–8 have a breathless jostling rhythm. Cf. next n.

588 foramina 'pores', but the word can also refer to the exit from a building, etc. (*T.L.L.* VI. 2. 1032. 79ff.). The rhythm and phrasing of the verse, with diaeresis after the second foot, seem unduly abrupt with modern conventions of punctuation, but in reading no long pause should be made after *foramina*, for what follows is closely connected.

589 dispertitam 'only after being separated into its parts': 144, 392 nn. The idea is repeated and expanded in the next two verses.

590 sibi distractam 'torn apart from itself' = *discidio functam*; *sibi* is best regarded as dat. of disadvantage.

corpore in ipso: 128–9 n.

591 prolapsa...enaret 'slipped and floated out': *prolabor* connotes both forward motion and collapse. The sense is not necessarily potential = 'before it *could* emerge'; L. occasionally uses subj. after *priusquam* in a purely temporal sense (Kühner–Stegmann II 370; cf. Hofmann–Szantyr 601).

592–606

(**Proof 12**) In a fainting-fit the soul is clearly so greatly shaken that dissolution cannot be far off. The illustration resembles that of drunkenness at 476–86.

592   **finis...intra:** for the anastrophe cf. 375n. *finis* is not purely metaphorical: the 'boundaries of life' are the surface of the confining body, cf. 256.

   dum 'even while': *tamen* in the next verse imparts a concessive flavour. Cf. 112n.

   uertitur 'moves', for *uersatur*.

594   **ire:** 526n.

   toto 'completely'; the reference is to the soul as much as the body. The soul, already shaken (*labefacta*) and hence partially detached from its anchorage, is on the point of casting loose completely.

   uelle 'is ready to', 'is on the point of', cf. μέλλειν (Hofmann–Szantyr 314).

595   **quasi supremo...tempore** 'as if its last hour had come', sc. of death.

   uultus 'expression', almost 'eyes'.

596   **molliaque exsangui:** both adjj. are predicative.

   cadere omnia corpore membra: this early correction reads better than Lachmann's, giving in fact a 'golden' line (345n.). Bailey's objection, that the reading of OQV in 594 presupposes *omnia membra* here (see app. crit.), is no obstacle to acceptance: the corruptions in 596 and 594 took place, in that order, at two different stages of copying.

597   **cum perhibetur** 'when, as we say'. There were two popular or colloquial phrases for 'faint': for the first cf. Plaut. *Mil.* 1331–2 *animo male | factum est huic repente miserae*; for the second *Mil.* 1347 *animus hanc modo hic reliquerat*. Several variations occur. L. uses *anima* in the next verse for the normal *animus* because he is dealing with the soul as a whole: cf. 600 *mens animaeque potestas*.

598   **trepidatur** 'there is general alarm', impersonal. The brief description of the scene reinforces the usual appeal to experience: cf. 468–9. There is also an implicit contrast between what the participants

and onlookers do and what the reader (as instructed by L.) knows
is actually happening.

599   reprehendere 'hold on to'; the image is that of a boat held by
a single remaining mooring (*uinclum*).

600–1   conquassatur...collabefiunt: 253 n.

601   haec: n. pl. in accordance with L.'s usual practice (136 n.) even
though in this case all the nouns are fem. Cf. 559 n.

603   tandem strikes, as often, a note of impatience: 'how can you
possibly doubt?'
    prodita 'thrust forth', sc. *anima*; cf. 591 *prolapsa*. For *do* = 'place'
see 355 n.

604   imbecilla foras in aperto tegmine dempto: the structure of
the verse, with the three adverbial phrases, increasing in length (a
fundamental rhetorical technique) and in asyndeton, serves to
heighten the pathetic effect, the notion of the soul's helplessness in its
alien environment.
    tegmine: 576–7 n.

605   aeuum: here masc., as shown by *omnem*. The form *aeuus* occurs
also in L. at 2. 561 and at Plaut. *Poen.* 1187. For similar variations of
gender in other words see Neue–Wagener 1 789–808.

606   minimum quoduis...tempus 'however small a time', a
slightly irregular expression.

607–614

(**Proof 12 A**) The soul is felt by the dying to depart gradually, not
to leave the body as a whole at one place. Editors have puzzled
themselves to discern a connexion with what precedes, but none of
the alternative positions suggested for the passage is a clear improvement. In fact a logical connexion can be shown to exist (607 n.), and
there seems to be no reason to deny the passage the status of a
separate proof.

607   nec...enim: L. has argued in 580–91 and again in 592–606
from outward and visible signs; he now argues from the personal

experience of the dying. At 603–6 he asked how it is possible (on the basis of the evidence produced) to believe that the soul can remain intact outside the body; he now states that a dying man *knows* that it does not issue from the body intact. The key to the connexion of thought lies in *incolumem* at 608 (cf. also *de corpore toto* ~ 594 *toto...de corpore*).

uidetur 'it is clear': 164n. The argument from experience is for obvious reasons open to criticism in this case. If challenged, L. might presumably have appealed to the analogous phenomena of fainting-fits or epilepsy, the experience of which men can afterwards communicate.

608   incolumem 'intact'; cf. 532n.
    toto: 594n.

609   ad iugulum et...fauces: the particularity is ironical. The view here rejected was in fact the popular one: 122n.
    supera: adverb. For the spelling cf. 385n.

610   certa 'its own'. The dying man feels in each part of his body the dulling of sensation that betokens the piecemeal dissolution of the *anima*; the idea is amplified in the next verse.

611   sensus alios in parti quemque sua 'each sense in its own place'. The phrase appears to represent a conflation of *sensus alios in alia parte* and *sensum in parte quemque sua*; cf. perhaps 333–4n. This seems preferable to explaining *alios* as a Grecism = 'as well', sc. as the *anima*: for (i) there is no acceptable parallel in L. for such a usage; (ii) the senses do not in fact undergo dissolution 'as well' as the *anima* but as part and parcel of its dissolution.
    parti: archaic abl.; cf. 132 *Heliconi*.

**612–14   At first sight these verses read like a *non sequitur*; but this is L.'s sarcastic way of saying that if the soul were immortal it would not behave in the fashion just described. For his habit of rounding off a sequence of argument with an ironical flourish cf. 367–9n.

612   quod si immortalis: for the 'quasi-caesura' cf. 174, 258nn.

614   sed magis: for the expected *quam potius* after *tam*. The phrasing leads us to look for another verb opposed in sense to *conquereretur,* e.g. *gauderet*: for those who believe in the immortality of the soul have always tended to entertain a corresponding contempt for the body and to consider the soul well quit of it; cf. the Greek saying that the body is a tomb, σῶμα σῆμα. If the text is sound, this is an extreme instance of the type of ellipse known as zeugma, in which one part of an expression must be supplied from the other part, which here is actually opposed in sense. Heinze compared a striking example in Livy (45. 20. 9): *...orantes ne noua falsaque crimina plus obesse Rhodiis aequum censerent quam antiqua merita, quorum ipsi testes essent*, sc. *prodesse*. Cf. also Virg. *G.* 1. 92–3 *...ne tenues pluuiae rapidiue potentia solis | acrior aut Boreae penetrabile frigus adurat*, where some such verb as *diluant* must be understood as the predicate of *pluuiae* (Bell 312); *A.* 2. 780 *longa tibi exsilia et uastum maris aequor arandum*, where Servius notes 'subaudiendum *obeunda*' (but see R. G. Austin *ad loc.*); 5. 340–41 (see R. D. Williams *ad loc.*). On zeugma in general in Latin poetry see Bell 304–14; R. J. Getty, *M. Annaei Lucani De Bello Ciuili I* (1955) lxii–lxiii; Hofmann–Szantyr 831–4; the last authority, however, obscures the important distinction between true zeugma, such as the present case or 'See Pan with flocks, with fruits Pomona crown'd' and the much commoner syllepsis, such as Ov. *A.A.* 1. 551 *et color et Theseus et uox abiere puellae* or the departure of Miss Bolo 'in a flood of tears and a sedan chair'.

ire foras: sc. *incolumem*.

uestem: the image of the body as the garment of the soul is Platonic (*Phaedo* 87 b–e, 91 d).

anguis: nom. sing.: 427 n.

615–623

(**Proof 13**) The mind, like everything else in creation, has its fixed place in the scheme of things. The relevance of this paragraph is not made explicit, but to judge from the way in which the same subject is developed below (784–99) L.'s point must be that the mind cannot exist outside the place appointed for it. The two passages do not duplicate each other: the second forms part of the case against the pre-existence of the soul; here L. is arguing against its survival after death. Cf. 617, 620–21 nn.

615   animi...mens consiliumque: cf. 94–5, 139, 450.

616 in capite: cf. 140n., 791.

616–17 unis sedibus et certis regionibus 'in a single fixed place', already defined at 140 as the chest; for the form of the expression cf. 346n. The plurals are dictated by metrical convenience (*-ibus* giving a dactylic ending), hence the unusual occurrence of *unus* in the pl., found also at 2. 919, 5. 897.

617 omnibus 'for all men'; the word can hardly be construed with *regionibus*, which has its own epithet *certis*, but there is undeniably a slight awkwardness in expression which may be due to lack of revision; cf. 620–21 n.

619 quicquid 'each thing', for *quicque*; cf. 618 *cuique*. The reference is general, to each and every created thing; cf. 787.

620–21 'And (where) it can exist, though with its parts diversely distributed, yet in such a way that the order of its members is never reversed.' The writing is compressed and not entirely lucid. If the text is sound there is an awkward, because only implied, transition from the idea that each thing has its fixed place in the scheme of creation (618–19) to the idea that within each thing each of its parts similarly has its fixed place. Hence Munro suggested a lacuna after 619 in which specific reference was made to the human body. This does not dispose of all the difficulties, for the arrangement of the parts of the human body or of the body of a member of any given species is *not* 'diverse', *multimodis*, but uniform – as L. indeed expressly indicates at 621. The translators and commentators either gloss over the difficulty or offer explanations that are linguistically unacceptable. *multimodis* must refer to the diversity of *species*, and that this is the point is suggested by the restrictive *ita...ut* construction = 'provided that', 'only to the extent that' (Hofmann–Szantyr 641): however differently the parts of, say, an octopus are arranged from those of a bird, the arrangement in any individual octopus or bird is the same. Such compression goes beyond what is usual in L. and may indicate that this passage lacked the author's final revision.

620 multimodis 'diversely', sc. in different species: see preceding n.

   partitis: Bernays's correction is much closer to the nonsensical reading of the MSS than Lachmann's *perfectis* and is apter in sense: cf. 710.

622–3 Instead of drawing the expected conclusion L. ends the paragraph by a general restatement of the principle.

622 res rem: sc. things of the same kind, as the following examples show.

623 fluminibus: understand *in* from *in igni* following. This type of ellipse, classified under ἀπὸ κοινοῦ (189 n.), is common with prepositions in Latin poetry: in L. cf. 4. 147–8 *sed ubi aspera saxa aut in materiam ligni peruenit...*, 1024, 6. 1116–17, and see W. V. Clausen on Pers. 1. 131. It occurs also in Greek, especially in Hellenistic poetry: see e.g. R. Pfeiffer on Callim. fr. 714. 3.

 igni gignier algor: the assonances *gn–g–gn–g* lend emphasis and possibly a flavour of contempt for the view attributed to L.'s opponents. *algor* is one of a number of such abstract substantives affected by L.: *amaror* 'bitterness', *aegror* 'sickness', *leuor* 'smoothness', *luror* 'yellowness', *stringor* 'touch' (693 n.). These formations were clearly considered strange and archaic; they occur sparsely, usually with a consciously archaic flavour, in later writers.

624–633

(**Proof 14**) In order to continue to exist independently of the body, the soul would need to be equipped with sense-organs – which is absurd. Another Lucretian *reductio ad absurdum* (cf. 573–5 n.), syllogistic in form (631 *at*, 633 *igitur*), but depending on a deliberate and (in the context) highly sophistical identification of sensation with the possession of sense-organs. This line of argument is discussed by Cicero in the *Tusculans* (1. 37, 50).

625 sentire: identified with life, cf. 633.

626 quinque, ut opinor 'all five, I take it': the tone is sarcastic.
 faciundum est 'we must hold that'; for this sense of *facio* cf. 878. For the construction with the gerund cf. 391 n.
 sensibus auctam 'furnished with sense-organs', cf. 550 n. *augeo* = 'enlarge', sc. by the possession of, hence 'equip with'. For the phrase cf. Catull. 64. 165 *nullis sensibus auctae* (sc. *aurae*).

627   nosmet: no particular emphasis seems to be intended.

628   infernas animas: for *manes*.

uagari: Q's *uagare* is accepted by some editors as an archaism, and the active form is occasionally attested elsewhere (Neue–Wagener III 99); but L. normally uses the deponent form (15 instances), and there is no reason why he should have varied his usage here.

629   pictores...et scriptorum saecla priora: probably hendiadys = 'the painters and poets of old': cf. 346n. L. is no doubt thinking of the ghosts in Book XI of the *Odyssey*, who drink blood and converse with Odysseus; there was at Delphi a famous painting of the scene by Polygnotus (*c*. 475–445 B.C.).

630   introduxerunt is generally printed by editors as two words on metrical grounds, but *introduco* = 'bring on to the scene' is a semi-technical term, treated by writers contemporary with L. as a fully compounded verb. In any case a caesura would be felt after *intro-*: 174n. In antiquity texts were written without word-division: see Reynolds and Wilson 4, 151–2.

632   animae: dat.

633   per se 'by themselves', i.e. apart from the body, like *sorsum* in 631–2, but now referring to the soul.

possunt: sc. *animae*, understood from 630.

634–669

(**Proof 15**) When the body is divided the soul is divided too: it cannot therefore be immortal. A point already touched on at 526–47 (cf. also 580–614) is here discussed in a somewhat different light, with the appeal now lying to the experience of sudden and violent mutilation. Death and wounds in battle must have been familiar to many of L.'s readers, but his chief illustration is second-hand: see 642–56n.

634–5   toto...totum: the point made by the repetition is fundamental.

635   animale 'alive', sc. *corpus*.

636   subito...celeri: also fundamental to the argument as ruling out the alternative hypothesis of a gradual withdrawal of soul from one part to the other (cf. 533–9). In this case there is obviously no time for that to happen.

medium 'in two', common predicative use of *medius* with verbs like *diuidere*.

638–9 dispertita...discissa...dissicietur: cf. 435–7, 702–4, 17–18n.

638 uis animai: a periphrasis for *anima*, cf. 583; but perhaps also with a reference to *uis* in 637: cf. 364n.

639 dissicietur: this etymologically incorrect spelling is not infrequent in MSS and may be used for metrical reasons, since the spelling with *-ii-* was not used in compounds of *iacio* (cf. Munro at 2. 951) and the correct spelling might have been misunderstood as indicating the scansion *dĭsic-*.

640 discedit 'is divided', virtually = *scinditur*.
ullas 'at all'; *ullus* is generally used with a negative or conditional clause: here *quod* is felt as being equivalent to *si quid*.

641 scilicet 'obviously'.
abnuit 'denies', the sole use of the word by L. For the personification cf. 517 *uult*.

642–56 A vivid description in L.'s best manner; as is shown by *memorant* (642), it is based on literary sources. Scythed chariots were an Oriental importation into Greco-Roman warfare; they evidently made a profound impression on those who encountered them. Livy (37. 41) describes in some detail their use by Antiochus III at the battle of Magnesia in 189 B.C.; the battle was also celebrated by Ennius in his *Annales*, and L. may have drawn on his account (cf. 654n.).

642 falciferos: the usual word is *falcatus*, but L. affects compounds in *-fer*: 11 *floriferis*, 240 al. *sensiferos*, 1012 *horriferos*, etc.

642–6 The enjambments (642–3 *abscidere...de subito*, 644–5 *ab artubus...abscisum*) help to give the verses a breathless quality in keeping with the scene described.

643   de subito: a variation for *subito*, cf. 636. The phrase, like others of the same type, is archaic and colloquial; classical Latin preferred to form such adverbial phrases with *ex*.

permixta caede calentis: the phrase recurs at 5. 1313, where it is used, with more obvious propriety, of lions mad with battle. Here *calentis* (acc. pl.) seems to be primarily literal 'reeking with carnage', but with a secondary figurative sense, referring to the crews of the chariots, 'inflamed by the promiscuous destruction', sc. that they have created. The analogy of 5. 1313 assists the secondary meaning.

644   tremere...uideatur: thus proving that there is still *anima* in the severed part.

645   cum 'although': 107n.
   hominis uis: cf. 8n.

646   mobilitate mali: cf. 636n. For this and for the details that follow cf. Q. Curt. *Hist. Alex.* 4. 15. 17 *quippe amputata uirorum membra humi iacebant, et, quia calidis adhuc uulneribus aberat dolor, trunci quoque et debiles arma non omittebant, donec multo sanguine effuso exanimati procumberent.*

647   et simul...quod: referring back to *cum...non quit* and giving an additional reason for the man's unawareness of his mutilation; for *et simul* used in this way cf. 4. 1276 *et simul ipsa uiris Venus ut concinnior esset.* This entails beginning the following description with a rather abrupt asyndeton, perhaps no more abrupt than that at 1060 (compared by Heinze); but the alternative solution of punctuating after 646 seems even harsher.

   in...studio...dedita: a rare variation of the common construction with dat.; cf. 4. 815 *quibus est in rebus deditus ipse.*

648   rēlicuo: the invariable scansion in L.; cf. 656. The word originally had four short syllables; this arbitrary 'weighting' of the first syllable evidently did not commend itself to the Augustans, who avoid the word altogether. The trisyllabic form *reliquus* is not found before Persius.

   petessit 'tries to get to', sc. *homo* understood from 645.

649   nec tenet 'and does not grasp', exactly as in English.

650   abstraxe = *abstraxisse*: cf. 1. 233 *consumpse*, 5. 1159 *protraxe*. Later poets on the whole avoid such contractions of consonant-stem verbs; contrast 683n.

rotas falcesque rapaces 'the wheels with their snatching scythes': 346n.

651   cum scandit et instat 'while he perseveres in climbing', sc. on to the chariot, to get at the driver. The phrase is a kind of hendiadys (Bell 261–2): it is more emphatic than *instat scandere* and throws the man's demented perseverance into relief.

652 A somewhat unusual rhythm, with 'weak' caesura in the third foot, followed by a bacchiac word ($\cup--$), no doubt illustrating the awkward efforts of the wounded man to rise. Cf. 773n.

653   cum 'although': 107n.
propter 'nearby', adverbial.

654–6 There is a marked resemblance to a famous fragment of Ennius' *Annales* (472–3 V.[2]; the location of the verses in the poem is unknown): *oscitat in campis caput a ceruice reuulsum | semianimesque micant oculi lucemque requirunt*. It was adapted by Virgil, *A*. 10. 394–6 *nam tibi, Thymbre, caput Euandrius abstulit ensis; | te decisa suum, Laride, dextera quaerit | semianimesque micant digiti ferrumque retractant*. Servius, our authority for the Ennius fragment, tells us that Varro Atacinus borrowed the first verse as it stood, and it seems reasonable to infer that the description was a celebrated one and that L. too had it in mind here. Possibly Virgil's transformation of the blinking eyes of the original into twitching fingers was suggested by L.'s verse 653.

654   et caput: sc. yet another man's.
uiuenteque: 163n.

655   uultum uitalem 'the expression of life'.

656   rēliquias: 648n.

657–9 'Or if you should choose to hack into a number of pieces a snake, with its flickering tongue, its threatening tail, and its long body...' Many attempts have been made to emend and explain this passage; the text presented here represents the least alteration of what is offered by the MSS that yields acceptable sense. *serpentis...*

utrumque cannot possibly mean 'both parts of a snake'; and the idea of a division in two stages, first into halves and then into smaller pieces, is irrelevant (and not to be justified by reference to 637). Nor, in spite of *utrumque* at 668, can the words mean, as suggested by Nicoll (*C.R.* N.S. 20 (1970) 140–41) following Diels, 'body and soul of a snake'. Marullus' *serpentem* is an easy alteration that provides an object for *discidere* and allows the three descriptive ablatives to qualify the snake directly. His *utrimque* 'on this side and that' is palaeographically easy but incurs similar objections to those already raised against *utrumque*. Giussani's *truncum* (keeping *serpentis*: cf. 404 n.) is palaeographically more difficult and entails an awkward reference for the abl. phrases. The obelus has therefore been used, *faute de mieux*, at the end of the verse.

The description of the snake emphasizes head, body and tail, as at Virg. *G.* 3. 422–4 *iamque fuga timidum caput abdidit alte,* | *cum medii nexus extremaeque agmina caudae* | *soluuntur, tardosque trahit sinus ultimus orbis*; it is calculated to contrast its normally menacing and collected appearance with the frenzy of self-centred activity that follows its mutilation. *minanti*, however, spoils the picture, being at variance both with the facts of natural history (which L. might have been expected to know) and with traditional descriptions: cf. Virg. loc. cit. 421 *tollentemque minas et sibila colla tumentem, A.* 2. 206–11, *Cul.* 170–73. Lachmann's *micanti*, however, weakens the effect by substituting a word which merely echoes *uibrante* and which is elsewhere applied to the snake's *tongue*: Virg. *G.* 3. 439, *A.* 2. 475.

658   procero: perhaps, as Heinze suggested, stretched for attack.

659   sit libitum '(if) you should take it into your head'. The combination of subjunctive protasis and indicative apodosis (*cernes*) is normal from Plautus onwards (Bennett 1 274–6); there is no irregularity and no suggestion of vividness (cf. Kenney, *C.Q.* N.S. (1958) 63 n.2; 9 (1959) 246–7; to the references there add F. Leo, *Ausgew. kl. Schr.* 1 (1960) 103, 237).

discidere 'cut apart', a very rare word, found in classical Latin only here, at 669, and possibly at Ter. *Adelph.* 559.

660   omnia...sorsum 'each part separately'.

ancisa 'hacked', literally 'cut around', from *am(bi)* + *caedo*;

cf. *amputo*, *anquiro*. The word occurs in literary Latin only here: see Varro, *L.L.* 7. 43, Isid. *Orig.* 18. 12. 3.

661   tortari 'writhe', another very rare word.

 conspargere: 539 n.

 tabo 'gore', a word almost peculiar to epic poetry.

662–3 'And the front part you will see attack itself backwards with its mouth in order to bite (itself), smitten with the burning pain of the wound.' The elements of 662 are arranged to reinforce the description, hind part first, front part last: *retro...petere* straddle *partem*, so that though *partem* agrees grammatically with *priorem* it is also felt as appositional to *ipsam se*, almost = 'its own hinder part'.

662   ipsam seque: the two words cohere so closely that it is natural for -*que* to follow the second. Cf. 939, 962.

 petere: perhaps felt as = *repetere* after *retro* (261 n.). L. likes to play on *retro* and *re-*: 1. 785, 1059, 2. 130, 283, 4. 310, al.

663   morsu premat 'bite', sc. *ipsam se*, not 'assuage'. The suggested corrections (see app. crit.) show that some editors have felt a certain awkwardness in the phrasing; but L. may have intended the word-order to reflect the broken writhing of the snake. There is no sign of carelessness in the composition of this elaborately written passage.

665   particulis: the *partes* of 659, for L. a somewhat unusual use of the word; contrast 708.

665–6 Another *reductio ad absurdum*.

666   unam: *animans* is always fem. in L. (Neue–Wagener 1 916).

667   una: the *anima*.

667–8   simul cum corpore: a very strong enjambment to reinforce the idea of the connexion of soul and body.

668   utrumque: both soul and body.

669   disciditur: 659 n.

(ii) *The soul did not exist before the body*

670–678

(**Proof 16**) The soul does not remember any previous existence.

670 praeterea: at 417–18 L. announced his intention of demonstrating that souls are *natiuos et mortalis* (417n.); 425–669 have shown that the soul is *mortalis*, i.e. that it cannot survive the death of the body. In turning to his second thesis, that it is *natiua*, i.e. cannot have existed before the body to which it belongs, L. does not announce it as a new topic, since the idea of immortality also necessarily entailed that of pre-existence, as was assumed by those philosophers, such as Plato, who held that the soul was immortal.

671 nascentibus insinuatur: the same phrase in the same connexion at 1. 113; cf. *extrinsecus insinuatas* at 689, 698 below. *insinuatur* 'is put in', sc. as an existing entity. L. uses the verb both transitively (either, as here, passive or reflexive + *se*) and intransitively; cf. 485n.

672 super 'as well', sc. as the events of this present life.

anteactam aetatem 'past life', when the soul was occupying another body (cf. 673, 675) rather than when it was 'between bodies'. In early Latin and Cicero the acc. is commoner than the gen. with verbs of remembering (Bennett II 88, 213; Kühner–Stegmann I 471–2).

672–3 In fact, as is well known, Plato did hold that there was some such 'recollection', ἀνάμνησις, though it probably did not extend to the memory of specific events. For an account of the Platonic doctrine see the edition of the *Meno* by R. S. Bluck (1961) 30–61.

674–6 An appeal to the principle that change = destruction: 517–20n.

675 retinentia 'grasp', i.e. 'memory', for the metrically impossible *memoria*. The word is unique in Latin; the sense is made clear by *tenemus* at 673. Cf. 318n.

676 non...id ab leto iam longius errat 'that state of affairs is in that case (*iam*: cf. 368) no great distance from death'. *longius* '(not) very far', as at 789 (= 5. 133), a use analogous to the common *saepius, citius* (Hofmann–Szantyr 168–9); there is no reason to prefer the otherwise unattested *longiter* offered by the grammarians or their common source (see app. crit.), for though L. has a slight penchant for adverbs in *-iter* (cf. e.g. 839, 846), he uses the normal form *longe* consistently elsewhere, and *longius* is good and idiomatic Latin.

errat: a slightly unexpected metaphor, but cf. perhaps 67 for the idea of death as a place to which one moves.

677   quae fuit ante 'this soul that "previously existed"', sc. as you maintain: in point of fact it was quite a different soul and perished with its possessor. L. here bestows only a passing mention on the theory of metempsychosis; see 741–7n.

679–697

(Proof 17) The soul is far too intimately connected with the body for it to have been introduced as an entity.

679   iam perfecto 'when it is already complete': *iam* qualifies *perfecto* rather than *si* (cf. 540n.). This was the Pythagorean doctrine expressed by Ennius in lines with which L. may well have been familiar: *Ann.* 10–12 V.² *oua parire solet genu' pennis condecoratum | non animam: et post inde uenit diuinitu' pullis | ipsa anima.*

680   animi: in spite of 422–3 (see n.) it is a little odd that L. should use *animus* here, especially as he unobtrusively changes to the fem. at 684 *solam* and thereafter speaks of *anima*. At 674 the idea of the intellect was uppermost, and L. may still have had the *animus* in the forefront of his mind.

uiuata: 409n.

681   gignimur 'are born', not 'conceived'; cf. 671 *nascentibus.*

uitae...limen: only here of life, though the phrase *leti limen* occurs elsewhere in the poem several times.

682   haud...conueniebat 'it would not be suitable', sc. *animam inferri* or perhaps better *uiuere*: cf. 684. For the impersonal *conuenit* cf. 455n. The impf. indic. is idiomatic, an extension of the regular usage with verbs connoting potentiality, as in *poterat, potuit* = 'could have', or obligation, as in *debebat, debuit* = 'should have', etc. In Augustan and Silver Latin a further extension takes place: cf. the common *tempus erat* = 'it is (high) time'. In the present passage the occurrence of *conuenit* (685) so soon after *conueniebat* shows that there is no real difference in sense. See G. Landgraf, *Hist. Gramm. d. lat. Spr.* III 1 (1903) 149–51; Hofmann–Szantyr 327–8.

683 uideatur: present tense-sequence, as the sense dictates: 'it would not be consistent for it to live in such a manner that it can be seen to grow...'.

in ipso sanguine: the idea of a close connexion between the blood and the soul is nowhere else developed by L., though there may be a hint of it at 442 (see n.).

cresse: for *creuisse*, but equivalent in sense to *crescere*. For this 'timeless' use of the pf. inf. (rather like the Greek aorist) cf. Bennett I 427–8. In Augustan elegy it becomes something of a mannerism. Contrast 69 n.

684 cauea 'den', 'cage', 'prison': the word implies disparagement of the rejected theory, and the following *per se sibi...solam* 'all on its very very own' also conveys ridicule. For *per se sibi* cf. 145.

685 conuenit 'it would follow': 682 n.

ut...tamen 'but only on condition that': the implication is that the stipulation is inconsistent with *in cauea uiuere*.

affluat 'abounds in'.

686–7 These verses reiterate, like 677–8, the two essential points of the whole section, that souls are both *natiui* and *mortales*; cf. 711–12.

688–97 The gist of the passage is: 'the soul does not pre-exist, for it is too closely connected with the body for that to be possible; nor, for the same reason, can it survive the body'. There is some awkwardness of construction, for 690–94, illustrating by examples the close connexion of body and soul, form a parenthesis in the sequence of thought and obscure the fact that *nec* in 695 looks back to *neque* in 688. Cf. 472–3 n. Lachmann's transposition, however, which several editors accept, if anything impairs the sequence of thought still more and has the added disadvantage that it entails the expulsion or emendation of 685, a verse which is perfectly satisfactory and indeed helpful to the argument.

688 nam: the two points to be made (see preceding n.) are those already reiterated at 686–7, as the repetition of *putandumst* shows.

adnecti 'fastened *on*', as opposed to the true state of affairs indicated by 691 *conexa*, 695 *contextae*; L. nowhere else uses *adnecto*.

689   insinuatas 'if they entered': 441–2 n.

690   'But that the whole thing happens in the opposite way is shown by the clear facts of the case.' The expression is formulaic (cf. 4. 1088 *quod fieri contra totum natura repugnat*) and forms, in the context, a somewhat harsh transition, for the illustrations that follow do not bear directly on the impossibility that *animas extrinsecus insinuari* (to which the *quod*-clause refers) but on the close connexion of body and soul which is the premiss of the argument.

691   Cf. 217. Note the unmetrical transposition in OQ (app. crit.).

692   ossaque 'and even the bones', the teeth being so classified. Cf. 250.

  sensu: for the abl. the commentators compare Plaut. *Mil.* 262–3 *non potuit quin sermone suo aliquem familiarium | participauerit.* Contrast 462 *participem leti.*

693   morbus 'toothache', for the usual *dolor dentium*.

  stringor 'touch', found here only: 623 n.

694   'Or (150 n.) the biting on a rough stone if one should be lurking in the bread.' The reading of the MSS is indefensible; but the idea of suddenness is appropriate, and MacKay's *subito sub*, with a deliberate play on words (*U. Cal. Publ. Class. Phil.* 13 (1950) 441), is attractive. A. C. Clark's *subsit si* is preferred, however, as nearer to the transmitted text.

  oppressus 'bitten on': cf. 663 *premat.*

  frugibus 'bread', as at 4. 1093 *laticum frugumque cupido.*

695   nec...uidentur 'and equally clearly they cannot...'; cf. 688–97 n.

695–6   exire...incolumes...et saluas exsoluere sese: the combination of chiasmus and variation, coupled with alliteration and word-play ('*sal*uas ex*sol*uere') emphasizes the evident absurdity of the notion. Cf. next n.

697   neruis...ossibus articulis(que): the list is composed according to a well-known rhetorical principle exemplified often elsewhere in L. and throughout Latin literature, the tricolon crescendo ('Gesetz der wachsenden Glieder'), of words of $2+3+4$ (5) syllables, to emphasize the extent and the consequent hazards of the disengagement that the soul would have to undergo while yet preserving its identity.

698–712

(**Proof 18**) If the soul cannot exist separately, *in cauea*, it must permeate the whole body at birth; but it could not do this without losing its original identity. This is the other horn of the dilemma broached at 679. No known Epicurean doctrine appears directly to underlie the passage. The argument relies heavily on the (dubiously appropriate) analogy of food: see 704n.

698   quod si forte: picks up *si* from 679. *forte*, as often, is scornful.
insinuatam 'after having entered'.

700   tanto quique magis 'all the more'; the phrase recurs at 5. 343 but nowhere else. *quique* is evidently abl. (738n.), but its precise syntactical function has not been satisfactorily explained.

fusa 'by being combined': 171n.

701   Cf. 517–20n., 756.

702–10   Some emendation is necessary: the transmitted text of 702 and 705 will not scan. The solution adopted is Lachmann's; it gives good sense and a straightforward structure to the paragraph. The only objection that can be made to it is that there is no mention elsewhere of food being distributed *per caulas*, only *in membra atque artus* (703) and *in uenas* (2. 1125, 1136, 4. 955, 6. 946). L.'s argument, however, seems to entail that he is referring to two processes: (i) the distribution of food through the veins to the different parts of the body; (ii) its final dispersion when it gets to its destination, *per caulas corporis*, at what in modern terminology would be called the molecular level. It is this second process – to which L. nowhere else refers (but see 702n.) – which is analogous to the permeation of the body by the soul. This interpretation is corroborated by the responsions *per caulas...in membra atque artus* (702–3) ~ *per caulas...in artus* (707).

702–4   dispertitus...diditur...disperit: cf. 435–7, 638–9, 17–18n.

702 **dispertitus** 'by being spread about'; cf. 700 *fusa*.

　caulas: here and at 707 not, as elsewhere, 'pores' on the surface of the body or of its parts, but the tiny spaces within the body. Athenaeus (3. 102) quotes a passage from a comedy in which a cook professing profound Epicurean learning and displaying much technical vocabulary speaks of 'juice' or 'flavour' being distributed evenly 'into the passages', εἰς τοὺς πόρους; the poet may or may not have been using the word accurately.

704 **disperit** 'loses its identity'.

　aliam naturam 'another substance'. There is no real analogy between the *change* of food into blood, flesh, bones, etc. and the *rearrangement* of the atoms of the original *anima* to form a different one.

705–8 **anima atque animus...animi natura:** throughout this part of the discussion it has been the *anima* that L. has chiefly had in mind (but cf. 680n.), and at 712 *natura animae* rounds off the paragraph in the usual way by a reference back to *natura animai* at 670. Here he briefly and somewhat obscurely introduces the *animus* into the argument: obscurely, since in 705 *anima* and *animus* seem to be envisaged as entering the body together, while in 708–10 the reference is to the creation of a new *animus* (defined as such by *dominatur*: cf. 138–9) only. Since L. is in any case confuting a theory that he disbelieves it is not easy to be sure what exactly he purports to be describing. Cf. 796n.

705 **integra:** n. pl.: 136n.

　recens 'new-born'.

706 **eunt:** 403n.

　dissolŭuntur: 330n.

707 **quasi:** perhaps to apologize for the difficulty of the idea rather than to indicate that it is not L.'s own view; cf. 729. He did not so excuse himself at 702, but cf. 131, 280nn.

708 **particulae** 'soul-particles'. The word occurs only five times in the poem; here and at 2. 833, 4. 261 it refers to the grouping of atoms into larger combinations. Cf. 180n.

709–10 **nunc...tunc:** the reader is left to infer for himself that the *animus* is formed by the re-concentration of soul-particles that have

first been dispersed through the body. The notion that L. is de-
molishing may be one attributed to his adversaries for polemical
convenience rather than a doctrine actually held.

710   tunc: emended to *tum* by an early editor, followed by Lachmann and Munro. Before a guttural Latin poets tended to avoid
tunc for reasons of euphony; here however L. may have wished to
emphasize the correlation with *nunc*. 1. 130 *tunc cum primis* (cited by
Bailey) does not support *tunc* here: see A. E. Housman's edition of
Juvenal (1938) xxi n. 1, where it is shown that the sense there
demands *tum*. On the tendency for *tunc* to oust the less emphatic *tum*
cf. Hofmann–Szantyr 519–20.

711–12   This final variation on the theme of 417–18 (cf. 677–8,
686–7) is deliberately anthropomorphic: the soul has a 'birthday'
and a 'funeral' (the original sense of *funus*). The effect is to identify
the existence of the soul with that of its host. *priuata...expers* seems to
suggest that the soul enjoys a common privilege – sound Epicurean
doctrine.

713–740

(**Proof 19**) The appearance of maggots in the decaying body proves
that the soul-atoms are dispersed. The beginning of the paragraph
seems to recur to the issue of survival rather than pre-existence, but L.
throughout treats the topics as connected (670 n.), and the real point
here is the origin of life in the maggots. The argument proceeds by
posing a series of dilemmas.

713–14   To this question it is soon seen that L.'s answer is 'yes'.
What he said at 398–401 (and cf. 425–44) ought seemingly to have
led him to answer 'no'; however, it appears from *partis* at 718 that,
though he does not say so explicitly, he assumed that some soul-atoms
remained within the body and some were dispersed outside it.

713   necne: very rare in direct questions for *annon*: Hofmann–
Szantyr 465 quote three examples only, all from Cicero.

715–16   Cf. 517–20 n.

715   haud erit ut...possit 'in no way will it be possible', emphatic
periphrasis for *haud poterit*. Cf. 725–6.
    merito immortalis: for the 'quasi-caesura' cf. 174, 258 nn.

717   ita sinceris membris 'with its limbs so intact', *sincerus* being used, as at 532, = *integer*. That the phrase can only refer to the soul is clear from the responsions of the passage: *sinceris membris* answers *partibus amissis* as *ablata profugit* answers *libata* [of which *ablata* is very nearly an anagram] *recessit* (716); cf. also 718 *nullas partis*. The objection by literal-minded critics that L. nowhere else speaks of the soul's having limbs takes no account of his highly developed sense of irony: cf. 727–31.

719   The verse has caesuras only in the first and fourth feet.

   rancenti: for the unmetrical *rancido*. The word recurs only in L.'s imitator Q. Serenus (*P.L.M.* III) 969; cf. 721 n.

   uermis: acc. pl.

720   exspirant...animantum: L. asks 'how does it come about that the dead body breeds creatures *endowed with soul*?', sc. unless they get their *animae* from the *anima* of the corpse. Instead of making his point explicitly he conveys it by a play on words: *anima* is 'breath' as well as 'life' or 'soul', and the 'airy' nature of the soul has been previously established (232–6 n.). The dying body 'breathes out', not the soul, but – maggots: we may render 'imparts animation to'. Cf. Read, *C.J.* 36 (1940) 38–40; but Wakefield had already seen the point: '*Exspirant*, quasi *animas* scilicet, *animatos uermes*'. For the force of '*exspirant...animantum...tanta*' cf. 446–8 n.

721   A vivid and gruesome depiction of the writhing mass of white maggots. *exos* is a rare word, recurring like *rancenti* (719 n.) in Q. Serenus (670); and *perfluctuat* is unique.

   tumidos: probably 'swollen' or 'bloated', its normal sense, rather than 'heaving' (Munro).

723   priuas: i.e. one soul per maggot; cf. 372 n.

724   nec reputas 'without stopping to consider'.

724–5   An interesting appeal for economy in explanation that perhaps suggests Occam's Razor, 'entia non sunt multiplicanda praeter necessitatem'.

725–6   '...there is still, it seems, this question to be investigated and brought to a decision'; the rather pompous periphrasis (cf. 715 n.) paves the way for the heavy irony that follows.

727–8 This picture of souls hunting for maggot-particles and building individual domiciles out of them seems too ludicrous to be anything but L.'s own invention. As Heinze remarks, his method is to attack a general position by refuting an absurd special case of his own devising.

727 **semina quaeque:** the appropriate particles of each type.

728 **uermiculorum:** for the unmetrical *uermium*.
   ubi sint 'a place to live in'.

729 **quasi:** 707 n.

730 **neque cur...quareue** = *neque cur...neque cur*; cf. 411 n.
   ipsae 'of their own accord', i.e. when there is no need; perhaps rather more emphatic than at 728.
   laborent 'put themselves out'.

731 **suppeditat** 'it would (not) be easy', literally 'it is (not) at hand', impersonal.

732 **algu:** a rare and archaic word, which occurs almost exclusively in the abl. sing.

733 **his uitiis adfine laborat** 'is liable to suffer from these afflictions': *uitiis* is to be construed both with *adfine*, literally 'in contact with' (as at Cic. *De Inu.* 2. 33 *aliis adfinem uitiis*; cf. 734 *contage*) and with *laborat*. This figure is called amphibole: Bell 293–303. Cf. 773–5 n.

734 **contagē:** for the unmetrical *contagio*. The word *contages* does not occur in classical Latin outside L. and was no doubt invented by him (cf. 345 n.). He declined it to suit himself: contrast 4. 336 *contagĕ*. Cf. 553 n.
   fungitur 'suffers', cf. 168 n. In old Latin *fungor* normally takes the acc. Cf. 801, 940, 956 nn.

735 **quamuis...utile** 'as useful as you like', sc. to admit.

736 **cui subeant** 'for them to enter'; one would perhaps expect the acc. rather than the dat., but Bernays's correction of the *cum* of the MSS is easy and economical.

738–40 So far L. has been dealing with the first horn of the dilemma (727–8); he now treats the second (729) by restating in summary fashion the arguments already deployed at 688–97.

738 **utqui** = *ut*, an emphatic form found also in Plautus and probably colloquial; cf. *atqui*. *qui* was the old abl. of the pronoun, here used as an enclitic like Greek πως; for the commoner sense 'how' cf. 443.

740 'And the interconnexions (*contagia*) that belong to (i.e. are essential to) common sensation (*sensus* = συμπάθεια, cf. 153 n.) will not occur.' Lachmann's correction of the transmitted reading *consensu* seems inescapable, since the physical interconnexions do not take place as a result of *consensus*, but vice versa: cf. 331 *implexis . . . principiis* = '*it is because* the atoms are so closely interlaced . . .' (see n.).

  conexae . . . consensus contagia: 17–18 n.

741–747

(**Proof 20**) Mental, as well as physical, characteristics remain constant in a species: this shows that soul and body grow together. Cf. 445–58 for the application of this argument to prove that the two also perish together. L. now turns to demolish the doctrine of metempsychosis, transmigration of souls, associated particularly with the Pythagoreans. He has referred to it in passing at 677 (see n.), and his criticisms of Ennius in the Prooemium to Book 1 had entailed a rejection of the Pythagorean position (cf. Kenney 373–8). His method of argument by anticipation (see 754–9, 760–64, 765–8 nn.) shows that this was familiar ground.

741–2 **triste . . . seminium** 'the grim breed'; *seminium* seems to have been a technical term of breeders, to judge from Varro, *R.R.* 2. 1. 14 *tertia pars est, quo sit seminio quaerendum*.

742 **sequitur** 'goes with', cf. 448.

743 'It is from the sire that their instinct for flight is transmitted, and from the sire comes the fear that sets their limbs in motion.' This emphasis on the transmission of characteristics through the male recalls the idea that the female was no more than a receptacle for the male seed and was not truly related to her offspring; Aesch. *Eum.* 657–66, Diod. 1. 80. 4 (who ascribes it to the Egyptians); cf. J. Needham, *A history of embryology*², rev. A. Hughes (1959) 43–6. Could L. have held such a view? It is not possible to escape the difficulty as several interpreters do, by rendering *patribus* as 'parents' and *patrius* as 'inherited': there is no reliable instance of *patres* = 'father and mother' in literary Latin before the age of Ausonius and Claudian (cf. R. G. Austin on Virg. *A.* 2. 579). The grounds on which Lambinus' learned friend (approved by Lachmann and Munro) suspected the verse were different; but satisfactory syntax is restored, as Lambinus himself allowed, by the easy change in 742 of *ceruos* (assimilated to the construction of *sequitur* by a copyist paying attention only to the verse on which he was engaged) to *ceruis*.

744 'And all other such characteristics'; cf. 481.

744–5 membris...ingenioque: L. emphasizes the close connexion of body and soul *ex ineunte aeuo*, from the moment of generation (cf. 344), and their consequent common growth.

745 generascunt 'come into being', a curious Lucretian coinage for *gignuntur*; possibly the inceptive form is intended to convey the idea of common development.

746 certa 'fixed', referring as much to *semen* as to *uis animi*.

semine seminioque 'in virtue of its seed and breed'; for the jingle cf. 753. For the abl. cf. 293 n.

747 quoque makes an additional point, that this happens in each individual of each species: cf. 769. The alliterations in '*c*rescit *c*um *c*orpore *quo*que' are studied and effective; the fact that, with *quoque*, three successive verses end in *-oque* may, on the other hand, be accidental: one can hardly be sure that L. would have avoided such a sequence. *toto*, preferred by some editors, gives what is something of a cliché (109, 138, 276, 281, 329, 351, 564, 608); in such a case the critic asks '*utrum in alterum abiturum fuit?*', i.e. in which direction is accidental change more likely to have occurred? (Reynolds and Wilson 150).

748–753

(**Proof 21**) Characteristics do not pass from one species to another. Cf. 784–6 n.

748   mutare 'pass from one to another', like Greek ἀμείβειν; cf. 755–6. L. is probably playing on words to bring out the fundamental incompatibility between immortality and change.

750   Hyrcano: the Hyrcani lived on the Caspian Sea and were popularly supposed to possess dogs that interbred with tigers and other wild animals: Grattius, *Cyn.* 161–6. The tradition of such unions was at least as old as Aristotle (*H.A.* 8. 607a). However, in this context the idea seems slightly inopportune, and L. probably cites this breed merely to exemplify extreme ferocity.

751   incursum 'attack', as uncharacteristic for a stag as flight for a dog: cf. 752n.

751–2   tremeret...fugiens 'would flee in alarm'.

752   ueniente 'coming on', of a hostile advance, as at 821–2, 833.

754–759

(**Proof 22**) (Anticipation of a counter-argument.) To say that the soul changes when it enters a different body is to admit that it is mortal.

754   'They are wrong who say that': *illud* is picked up by *quod aiunt*.

755   immortalem 'while still remaining immortal': the word is placed to complement *flecti* (= *mutari*, as at 516) at the end of the verse and so to emphasize the paradox.
   mutato corpore 'with a change of body'; cf. 748n.

756   ∼ 701; cf. 517–20n.

757–9   Once it is conceded that the parts of the soul can be transposed it follows that they can be dissolved through the limbs and perish with the body. The point briefly stated at 756 is developed more explicitly in a parenthesis.

757   traiciuntur...ordine migrant: cf. 513.

758   debent posse 'they must be able'.

759   denique 'in the end', temporal rather than logical, though the latter is in L. the more usual sense.

ut: consecutive rather than final, but there is, as often, an ambiguity which English 'so that' fortunately retains.

760–764

(**Proof 23**) (Anticipation of a counter-argument.) If the theory is amended to provide that souls remain constant to a particular species, this takes no account of the fact that the mind of a child or young animal is obviously undeveloped.

760–61   hominum...humana: sc. and animals likewise, cf. 764.

762   prudens 'discreet'.
puer 'child'.

764   doctus 'well trained'.
fortis equi uis: 8n.

765–768

(**Proof 24**) (Anticipation of a counter-argument.) Nor will it do to say that the mind grows young again when it enters a new body, for change entails mortality (cf. 754–9n.).

765   tenerascere 'becomes young'; the word was probably coined by L. (cf. 745n.) to convey the point that he refutes, that the mind grows young because it is *in* (note the positioning of the word in the phrase *in tenero...corpore*) a young body.

766   confugient 'will take refuge (in the position that)', used like a verb of saying with *oratio obliqua*; cf. for a partial parallel 350n. Cf. also 1. 582 *discrepat*+acc. and inf. = 'is inconsistent with the fact that...'.
si iam: 540n.

767   mutata per artus: cf. 758 *dissolui...per artus*.

768   tanto opere qualifies *mutata*, which is causal 'through being changed so much it loses...' (171n.).
amittit uitam: cf. 759 *intereant*.

769-771

If body and soul grow to maturity together they must have originated together: an argument of rather general application that does not seem to be closely connected with the preceding train of thought but serves to round it off. Cf. 772–5 n.

769   quoque: sc. the individual body whose fate it shares. Cf. 747 n. and compare the rather different pattern of alliteration.

770   On the metre cf. 83 n.

772-775

If the soul were immortal it would have no reason to quit its habitation when the body dies. This argument does not cohere very closely with what has preceded, but it makes a fine scornful flourish in L.'s best manner to conclude the paragraph. Formally it is united by the correlation *quoue* (769) . . . *quidue*.

772   quid . . . sibi uult . . . exire 'what does it mean by leaving?'; apparently a variation of the common *sibi uelle* idiom, with the inf. *exire* treated as a noun and subject of the sentence.

senectis 'aged'; the adj. does not occur after L., though the fem. sing. *senecta* as a noun = *senectus* is common in poetry of all periods.

773-5   metuit . . . manere . . . ne . . . obruat 'does it shrink from remaining for fear that . . . ?': *metuit* does double duty, with *manere* and with the *ne*-clause. Cf. 733 n.

773   Another rhythmically unusual verse: the only strong caesura is in the second foot, since the elided syllable of *manere* is felt (Soubiran 536–8); cf. 83, 652 nn.

774   domus: a traditional comparison, allied to the σῶμα–σῆμα idea. It was used by Bion (see Introd. 17–19 and cf. 931–77 n.): 'just as we are evicted from a house when the landlord removes the door or the roof or blocks up the well, so when landlady Nature takes away the use of eyes or ears or limbs I am evicted from the body' – ἐκ τοῦ σωματίου ἐξοικίζομαι (Hense 15–16; cf. Cic. *De Sen.* 84; Sen. *Ep.* 120. 14, cited ibid. cxvi). Cf. also Eur. *Suppl.* 534–5 οὔτι γὰρ κεκτή-μεθα | ἡμέτερον αὐτὸ [sc. τὸ σῶμα] πλὴν ἐνοικῆσαι βίον, 'our tenure of the body is that of a life-tenant only'.

775 obruat 'collapse in ruin', an unusual intransitive usage. The pause after the first dactyl and the position of the verb are descriptive; in later epic this effect becomes almost a cliché (S. E. Winbolt, *Latin hexameter verse* (1903) 13–16).

immortali: anything, that is, which is really immortal.

776–783

(**Proof 25**) It is absurd to imagine souls struggling or queueing for the next available body. L. winds up the series of arguments against pre-existence in characteristic style (cf. 772–5 n.) with one in his most sardonic vein. That the position which he attacks was not in this case purely an Aunt Sally of his own devising (cf. 727–8 n.) seems to be shown by the neo-Platonist passages cited by Heinze.

776 conubia...Veneris = *concubitus*, apparently, in view of the following *partusque ferarum*, referring to human beings. The scansion of *conubia* has occasioned much debate: Munro argues powerfully for *conūbia* (rather than *conūbja*), and his reasoning was approved by R. S. Conway (*ad* Virg. *A.* 1. 73).

777 esse...praesto 'are on the spot'.

778–80 The sarcasm is heightened by the combination of anti-thesis, assonance, alliteration and special vocabulary (779 n.).

778 immortalis: acc. pl. For the word-play cf. 869 n. and the next n.

779 innumero numero: the same jingle at 2. 1054; L. may have had in mind a verse from the epitaph supposedly written for himself by Plautus (p. 32 Morel) *et numeri innumeri simul omnes conlacrimarunt*. Perhaps a cliché? (see next n.).

certareque: 163 n.

praeproperanter 'in a tearing hurry', a Lucretian variant of the usual *praepropere*. L. had a weakness for adverbs of this type: cf. 1063 *praecipitanter*.

780 prima potissimaque: this collocation seems to have been a favourite of Livy's. It may have had a suggestion of cliché (779 n.), like our 'first and foremost'.

781 si non forte 'unless we are to suppose', ironical.

782 uolans aduenerit: sc. from some sort of limbo or extra-terrestrial waiting-room.

783 hilum '(not) at all', adverbial acc., as at 813, 830. Cf. 220n.

(iii) *Some general considerations*

784–799

(**Proof 26**) Everything in nature has its place, and that of the soul is within the body, without which it cannot exist; cf. 615–23n. Most of this passage recurs in Book v (see app. crit.), slightly adapted to fit it for its new context (Boyancé 217–18). This is the first of a short series of general arguments against the immortality of the soul with which L. concludes his case; some of them have been touched on earlier.

784–6 Two different kinds of unnatural and impossible phenomena are in question. (i) Trees in the sky, clouds in the sea, fish on land (cf. the more elaborate series at 1. 161–6) are Lucretian variants of a familiar literary device, the *adynaton* (impossible). Cf. in particular Theoc. 1. 132–6, 5. 124–5 and the notes of A. S. F. Gow *ad locc.* The absurdities at 750–53 also belong to the same type, as the resemblances with Theocritus show. See E. Dutoit, *Le thème de l'adynaton dans la poésie antique* (1936) 31–4, 62–5; Rowe, 'The *ADYNATON* as a stylistic device', *A.J.P.* 86 (1965) 387–96. (ii) Blood in wood and sap in rocks are specifically Epicurean, recalling the technical discussion and rejection of the theories of Anaxagoras at 1. 875–920; cf. esp. 881–4 *conueniebat enim fruges quoque saepe minaci | robore cum saxi franguntur mittere signum | sanguinis aut aliquid, nostro quae corpore aluntur, | cum lapidi in lapidem terimus, manare cruorem.* L.'s point here is different, but these illustrations were almost certainly suggested by the earlier passage. See further 785n.

784 in alto: Lachmann emended to *salso* because 5. 128 reads *salso,* but this would ruin the alliterative scheme of the verse. It is clear that 5. 128 has been reworded to suit its new context; it begins with *sicut* instead of *denique* (cf. 784–99n.).

785 pisces uiuere in aruis: the scientific literature of antiquity offers occasional reports of fish being unearthed by the spade or the plough; one such case is recounted by Livy (42. 2. 5) in a list of prodigies of the year 173 B.C. which included a celestial apparition, a miraculous crop of dark wool, showers of stones and a plague of locusts (see also J. E. B. Mayor on Juv. 13. 65). It is possible that L. was tilting at what he would undoubtedly have considered an old wives' tale: so Dutoit, op. cit. (784–6 n.) 65. Heinze plausibly suggested that 786 may be intended to refer to bleeding and sweating statues, a type of portent familiar in both ancient and modern times. On the *adynaton* as belonging to 'the area of popular speech and beliefs' cf. Rowe (art. cit. 784–6 n.) 392–5; he shows that poets employed it in full awareness of such associations. L. is already modulating into the diatribe style (Introd. 17–19).

787   quicquid = *quidque*: 619 n.

  crescat et insit: cf. 797 *durare genique* and contrast 795 *esse crescere*. In such word-groups Latin does not always concern itself with 'logical' order: Tibullus' *uir mulierque* (2. 2. 2) no more implies male domination than Ovid's *femina uirque* (*Am.* 1. 10. 36, al.) implies the converse; *itque reditque* (*Tr.* 5. 7. 14) and *it redit* (*Fast.* 1. 126) and *redit itque* (*A.A.* 1. 93, *Met.* 2. 409) all mean exactly the same thing. The handbooks call this *hysteron proteron*: see Bell 270–71; Hofmann–Szantyr 698–9; and cf. Postgate, *Proc. Brit. Acad.* 3 (1908) 167. It is uncommon in L.

788   animi: the reference is specifically to the *animus*, as 790–92 show.

789   longius: 676 n.

790–97   If the *animus* could exist outside the body it could, *a fortiori*, exist anywhere inside the body; but it has a fixed place within the body: therefore it cannot exist outside it. There are difficulties in 790–93. (i) The combination of *quod* and *enim* was condemned by Lachmann as a solecism; the commentators cite Varro, *R.R.* 2. 4. 8 ...*ut uolutentur in luto, quae enim illorum requies*, which is admittedly parallel, but Varro was a more colloquial and a less correct writer than L. (ii) The asyndeton between *manere* (793) and the preceding inff. is harsh. However the verses recur without variation at 5. 134–7 as part of a passage evidently adapted by the poet to its new context (784–99 n.), and it seems hazardous to tamper with them.

790   quod...enim: if this was what L. wrote (see preceding n.) he nodded, producing a phrase which was an amalgamation of *quod si posset* and *hoc enim si posset*. In the colloquial *quod enim* and *quia enim* the force of the *enim* is affirmative = 'indeed' (Hofmann–Szantyr 508, 575); whereas here *enim* cannot be so explained, since the argument calls for an inferential rather than a connective particle. In other words, the phrase cannot be excused as colloquial; if not corrupt, it is in the context bad writing.

prius = *potius*, sc. than existing outside the body: cf. 793 n.

animi uis = *animus*; cf. 788 *animi natura*, 8 n.

793 'So long as it remained in the same man and the same container'; *tandem* = 'at all events'. Logically this is the main point: rather than exist outside (790 n.) the soul would in fact stay in its container, the body. Syntactically however the clause is subordinated to what precedes as a qualification of *quauis in parte*, with *manere* dependent on *soleret* and in asyndetic parallelism with *esse* and *innasci*. This is awkward writing, as the attempt to describe it perhaps shows.

in eodem homine atque in eodem uase 'the man to whom it belongs, who is its container': *eodem* very nearly = *suo*. For the identification of body and container cf. 555; *atque* practically = 'viz.', cf. 346 n. On the *uas*-metaphor see 434 n.

794–6 As has previously been explained: see 140 n. The alliteration is striking.

794   quod quoniam 'but since', like *quod si*. *quod quoniam* does not recur in L., but it is Ciceronian; on this type of *quod*-phrase see Hofmann–Szantyr 571–2.

quoque: as in the rest of the universe; cf. 787 *certum ac dispositumst.*

796   anima atque animus: as has been remarked (788 n.), the argument of this section can only refer to the *animus*, since the *anima* is diffused through the body. In bringing the *anima* into his conclusion L. can hardly have been guilty of dishonesty, for the flaw in logic is too blatant (one would think) for him to have risked it. For similar negligence cf. 705–8 n. Cf. 798–9 n.

797   totum...extra corpus 'right outside the body'; the emphasis of *totum* is important. If even inside the body the mind can only exist in a fixed place, how much less likely is it that it can exist at all when completely separated from the body. The spondaic metre reinforces the point.

durare genique 'be born or continue to exist'; the *-que* is disjunctive (150 n.). For the word-order cf. 787 n. *geni = gigni*; *geno* is the original form of which *gigno* is a reduplication. It has been restored to L. elsewhere by conjecture: 433 n.

798–9 The preceding argument has been concerned with the genesis (788 *oriri*, 792 *innasci*, 797 *geni*) of the *animus*; this conclusion relates to the destruction of the *anima* (cf. 796 n.).

798 interiit, periisse: the repetition is for emphasis; there is no difference in sense. An Augustan poet might have written *ubi periit, periisse*; possibly L. disdained this as too obvious. Cf. Introd. 22–3.

799 distractam: cf. 589–91.
in corpore toto: appropriate only to the *anima*; cf. 798–9 n.

800–805

(**Proof 27**) The union of mortal (body) with immortal (soul) is grossly improbable. L. has been arguing from observed fact; he now changes to a more aprioristic line of reasoning which paves the way for his concluding arguments (806–29). A return to first principles in fact makes a suitable close for this main section of the book.

800–2 A very effective structure: a series of substantized infinitives conveying the rejected view and then polished off, so to say, by the crisp *desiperest*. Cf. the really monumental example of this technique at 5. 156–65.

800 iungere: a short way of saying 'postulate that they can be joined'.

801 consentire...fungi: coupled, as at 168–9, to represent συμπάσχειν; cf. 153 n.
fungi mutua 'mutually interact' (Latham). *mutua* is adverbial acc.: cf. 2. 76 *inter se mortales mutua uiuunt*.

802–5 The sentence begins as if L. meant to ask 'what two things could be more different and incongruous than the mortal and the immortal?'; it ends as if he had asked 'What could be more unlikely than that the mortal and the immortal could co-exist?' Nevertheless the sentence is artfully constructed. The emphatic *diuersius...disiunctum discrepitansque* (cf. 638–9, 702–4, 17–18 n.) does not merely restate the same point three times: there is a transition from the idea of *difference*, via that of *incongruity*, to that of *inconsistency* (exploiting two distinct but allied senses of *discrepito*, apparently a coinage of L.'s own). This is assisted by the deliberately ambiguous (not, as Bailey would have it, grammatically impossible) *inter se*, which refers both backwards and forwards: backwards to the idea that the mortal and the immortal are *res inter se diuersae et disiunctae*, forwards to the idea that the hypothesis of 804–5 is *inter se disiunctum discrepitansque*, i.e. internally inconsistent, not self-consistent.

805 concilio: a technical term (on the metaphor see Sykes Davies 37), though L. does not elsewhere apply it to the union of body and soul; but since that union is at the atomic level the term is perfectly apt. In this verse too the thought is compressed and the point is made by implication: if body and soul are linked in a true *concilium* (sc. such as from observation and argument we know their union to be) it is unthinkable that the body should be affected by the stresses and strains of life (*saeuae procellae*: a strong and unexpected metaphor; but cf. 509 n.) while the soul is unaffected. But (the reader is expected to remember), if the soul *is* affected, the familiar axiom entails that it is mortal. This is a different point to that made at 800–1.

806–818

(**Proof 28**) What is immortal must satisfy certain conditions; these requirements are met only by the atoms, the void and the universe as a whole. These verses recur in Book v (see app. crit.) as part of the proof that our world is not eternal. There the corollary that the world does not satisfy the conditions is explicitly drawn; here, unless we postulate a lacuna after 818, the reader is left to deduce it for himself. Since the third example of an immortal thing, the universe, though perfectly appropriate in Book v, is much less relevant here, it seems likely that the passage was originally written for its other setting and (unless there has been damage to the text) imperfectly assimilated by

L. to its new context. Lachmann's deletion is generally rejected by modern editors as excessively drastic: see 819–29n.

806   necessest: this is the usual form, but at 5. 351 (and in a few other places) the MSS give *necessust*; and *necessumst* also occurs here and there (see Munro on 2. 710). It would be rash to try to normalize L.'s usage; this is one of the rare cases where the critic has no option but to follow the MSS in default of more reliable guidance.

807   solido: without void, a technical term: cf. 1. 510 *sunt igitur solida ac sine inani corpora prima.*

808   sibi: dat. of disadvantage.

809–10   artas...partis 'their tightly-packed parts', which of course, being atoms, *solido cum corpore*, they do not have. The jingle is no doubt deliberate, to round off the emphatic series of alliterations.

810   ante: at 1. 503–50; cf. esp. 528–30 *haec neque dissolui plagis extrinsecus icta | possunt nec porro penitus penetrata retexi | nec ratione queunt alia temptata labare.*

813   neque ab ictu fungitur hilum 'and is not in the smallest degree affected by blows'. *ab* = 'as a result of', not quite parallel to *ab* at 820, with which the commentators compare it. *fungitur* is passive (cf. 168n.). For *hilum* cf. 783n.

814   fit: Lachmann's correction (also at 5. 359) of *sit* is demanded by the preceding indicc. at 807 and 812; the distinctions drawn between this *quia*-clause and the first two by the defenders of *sit* are too tenuous to merit serious consideration. *fit* means no more than *est*; cf. 6. 829 *magna mali fit copia circum.*

815   quasi: almost 'if they could'.
   dissolūique: 330n.

816–18   Cf. 2. 303–7 *nec rerum summam commutare ulla potest uis: | nam neque quo possit genus ullum materiai | effugere ex omni quicquam est extra, | neque in omne | unde coorta queat noua uis irrumpere et omnem | naturam rerum mutare et uertere motus.*

816   summarum summa: the universe, elsewhere called *summa, rerum summa, omnis summa,* etc. The 'superlative' genitive (as it may be called) identifies: not 'the *summa* formed by adding all *summae*', but 'the *summa* par excellence', 'the one and only *summa*'. In classical Latin this usage is rare and has a colloquial flavour (Hofmann–Szantyr 55–6). *summa summarum* is used by other authors in various senses: 'crowning achievement' (Plin. *N.H.* 7. 99); 'what it all boils down to' (Sen. *Ep.* 40. 14); at Plaut. *Truc.* 24–5 *Venus,* | *quam penes amantum summa summarum redit,* 'the supreme command'.

neque does double duty (i) = *non enim* (cf. 150n.), (ii) looking forward to the second *neque*. The clause which it introduces depends on *sicut*; to refer it to *quia* in 814 entails tautology.

817   quis 'any', used after the negative for the more usual *ullus* or *quisquam*. An Augustan poet would avoid beginning a verse, even when there is, as here, close enjambment, with an indefinite pronoun. Both *quis* and *qui* are used adjectivally (Hofmann–Szantyr 540–41), but the variation between the forms here and at 5. 362 (see app. crit.) is more likely to be due to the accidents of transmission than to the poet. The variation between the verbs, however, is pretty clearly authorial.

819–829

(**Proof 29**) The soul enjoys no special protection: it is afflicted not only by the ills of the flesh but by other maladies peculiar to itself. At first sight these considerations seem to follow pat on 805, a fact which would support Lachmann's deletion of the intervening verses. However, the connexion may not be so close as at first appears: cf. 819n. Giussani's suggestion that 819–23 refer to a fourth class of eternal beings, the gods, is attractive as relating the passage to what has gone before, but it receives no solid support from extant Epicurean texts. The concluding verses of the section (see especially 825–7) assist the transition to the Conclusion of the book, for it is precisely these self-tormenting tendencies in men that provide L. with much of the material for his great peroration. There may be deliberate irony in the suggestion that these fears, in which fear of the hereafter predominates, prove, if rightly understood, that there is no hereafter.

819   magis: for the reasons that follow rather than because it satisfies (as it cannot) the conditions rehearsed in the preceding

passage; but there is an implicit antithesis, which serves as a connexion, between the two sets of conditions.

habendast: sc. *anima,* last mentioned at 799. If some verses are
missing after 818 that is probably because L. never wrote them rather
than because they have been accidentally omitted: it seems likely that
this portion of the poem lacked its final revision.

820 uitalibus ab rebus munita 'protected by vital forces'; cf.
2. 575 *uitalis rerum* = almost *res uitales.* For the unnecessary *ab* with
the instrumental abl. cf. 323, 429, 522, 567; the usage is fairly common
in Latin poetry of all periods (Hofmann–Szantyr 122). However, in
other authors (L. is no help) *munire ab* always means 'protect *from*'.
If that is the meaning of the phrase here, *uitalibus* must either be
emended or explained as a euphemism, scornfully employed, for its
opposite. The second alternative is improbable, both because mockery
does not seem particularly apposite or effective here and because
uitalis in its euphemistic sense is confined to things having specific
associations with funerals: *uitalis lectus* = 'bier'; *uitalia,* sc. *uesti-
menta* = 'grave-clothes'. Lambinus' *letalibus* is palaeographically not
implausible, since words are sometimes corrupted into their opposites
(e.g. *captae* to *liberae, magna* to *parua*: Housman on Manil. 5. 463), but
the word is not found elsewhere in L. and probably does not antedate
Virgil.

  tenetur: 323 n.

821–2 aut quia...aut quia: subordinate, not parallel, to the
quod-clause of 820 and offering alternative explanations of the
hypothesis.

821 ueniunt 'attack', as at 752, 833.

  omnino 'at all', with *non.*

  aliena salutis 'hostile to its survival' (Latham): there is an easy
transition from the idea of difference to that of harm. *alienus* with
genitive instead of the usual abl. (cf. 961) is classical but relatively
uncommon: a few instances in Cicero, none in the other poets.

823 quid 'how much', virtually = *quantum.* After 823 a verse or
verses have been lost in which was contained the apodosis of the
sentence, showing or stating that these reasons do not apply to the
soul.

824-5 praeter...quam quod 'apart from the fact that...', leading the reader to expect that L. will proceed *accedit quod* 'there is the additional fact...'; instead he switches to a personal construction, *aduenit id quod* 'there arrives (cf. 821–2 *ueniunt*) that which torments...', i.e. the susceptibility of the mind to anxiety and fear. The writing throughout this last section, with its string of conjunctions and anaphoras (*quod si...quod...quia...quia...praeter enim quam quod...aduenit id quod...adde...adde quod*) seems stiff and ungainly; cf. 819 n., but contrast 827 n.

826 inque metu male habet 'terrifies and vexes it'; the *in* is almost instrumental. *male habere* is a colloquial phrase, frequent in comedy; cf. 597 n.

827 'And even when its misdeeds are past the memory of them returns to torment it.' An artfully constructed verse, employing three perfect participles: *praeteritis* answers *futuris* in 825; *male admissis* is varied by *peccata*. L. uses *remordeo* of the pangs of conscience at 4. 1135 *cum conscius ipse animus se forte remordet*; after him it occurs almost exclusively in poetry, always of mental anguish. Cf. 1011–22.

828 proprium 'peculiar to it', as opposed to the diseases which it shares with the body (824).

829 The 'insistence upon mortality concludes with a dramatic plunge into the black waters of forgetfulness' (Hadzits 97). The image was no doubt intended to suggest a connexion between *lethargus* (here a symptom of mental illness rather than of disease shared with the body, as at 465) and the waters of Lethe, which when drunk induced oblivion; for *nigras* cf. Virgil's description of the waters of Styx (*A.* 9. 104–5).

III. CONCLUSION

830–869

Death then does not concern us: to be dead is the same as never to have been born. From all that has been said it follows that death is not a thing to be feared. In the rest of the book L. develops this theme in terms which are fundamentally Epicurean but which also owe much to the literary-philosophical *consolatio*: see Introd. 31–2. This is practical philosophy, appealing as much to the prejudices and emotions as to the reason of L.'s audience.

830 This famous verse follows closely the words of Epicurus himself, 'death is nothing to us', ὁ θάνατος οὐδὲν πρὸς ἡμᾶς (Κ.Δ. 2, 71 Us., cf. *Ep. ad Men.* 124, 60 Us.). L.'s expansion combines two renderings, a literal and a less literal: cf. Cic. *De Fin.* 2. 100 *scripsit* (sc. Epicurus) ...*mortem nihil ad nos pertinere*. Like other parts of the Epicurean message the sentiment passed, in a debased form, into the stock of popular wisdom, frequently appearing on tombstones: see Lattimore 84–6. One example (*C.L.E.* 1585. 2) seems designed to recall L.'s line: *non fueram, non sum, nescio, non ad me pertinet*. The idea, in different variations, recurs as a *leitmotiv* throughout what follows: 845, 850, 852, 926, 972.

mors: the state of being dead, not the act of dying.

hilum: 783 n.

831   habetur 'is held to be', but in the context the meaning is stronger, 'has been proved to be': cf. 532, 819.

832–42 We shall be concerned by what happens after we die no more than we were by what happened before we were born. L. uses an Epicurean argument ([Plat.] *Axioch.* 365 d) in a Roman setting. His choice of the Punic Wars as illustration is significant. The vocabulary and phrasing of 833–7 suggest that he is imitating, or even parodying, the high epic style (see nn.), and the suggestion of irony is characteristic of the diatribe: these events were, when they occurred, world-shaking and so presented themselves to a great national poet – but what are they to us now? The Romans looked back to the Punic Wars as one of the great crises of their history: Livy represents what was thought to be at stake in language which seems reminiscent of L.: *in discrimine est nunc humanum omne genus, utrum uos an Carthaginienses principes orbis terrarum uideat* (29. 17. 6). No doubt Ennius was their common model: see the echoes at [Virg.] *Cul.* 34, Lucan 1. 304–6. Hannibal continued to haunt the declamatory tradition for centuries (cf. Juv. 10. 147–67); here the tradition is seen near its source, but already a subject for sardonic reflection.

832   anteacto: before we were born; cf. 672.

nil...aegri 'no discomfort', a kind of defining genitive sometimes

13   KLU

called the genitive of the rubric, that is the class to which an individual thing belongs: 'nothing (in the sphere) of discomfort'.

833   ad confligendum uenientibus 'coming on to the attack': cf. 752 n. The transition to the high epic style is signalled by the march-like rhythm, which then increases its tempo and urgency.

834–5   The language recalls Enn. *Ann.* 310 V.² *Africa terribili tremit horrida terra tumultu.* In his adaptation of what was probably a well-known passage L. overdoes things slightly for his own satirical purpose (cf. 832–42 n.).

835   sub altis aetheris oris 'under the lofty regions of aether', a stately periphrasis for 'on earth'. Gifanius' correction *oris* is demanded by the sense and by Lucretian usage: the normal collocations are *aetheris orae* or *aeris aurae* (but cf. 405 n.).

836   fuere: sc. *omnia*, in view of the parallelism *contremuere...fuere,* rather than *omnes humani* extracted from the following indirect question (cf. 843 n.).

utrorum ad regna cadendum 'which of the two it should be to whose dominions all mankind must lapse'. The usual construction with *cadere* = 'fall under the power of' is with *sub* or *in*; but the use of *regna* rather than *regnum* suggests that the idea uppermost in L.'s mind was that of territorial empire rather than 'rule' in the abstract, hence his use of *ad.*

837   humanis = *hominibus*, as at 80.

terraque marique: a cliché, but here pointed, looking forward to 842.

839   discidium: the dissolution of the *concilium* referred to at 805. From all that has been argued in the first part of the book it follows that the separation of body and soul entails the end of sensation, that is the end of existence: so far as we are concerned the two things are identical (841). The dictum of Epicurus quoted above (830 n.) continues 'what has been separated cannot feel and what cannot feel has nothing to do with us': that is, the dispersed atoms of body and soul no longer have anything to do with the *concilium* that was the true 'us'.

quibus e: 375 n.

uniter apti 'fitted into a single being': cf. 846–7.

841   sensumque mouere 'or (150 n.) affect our senses', the only valid test. Epicurus equated death with deprivation of sensation, στέρησις αἰσθήσεως (*Ep. ad Men.* 124, 60 Us.).

842   Not even the final catastrophe in which the world itself will be destroyed will concern us. L. ostensibly refers to the Epicurean doctrine which he is to discuss at 5. 235–415. However, his readers (as he obviously intended) were bound to think of the proverbial saying, the ancient equivalent of 'après moi le déluge', ἐμοῦ θανόντος γαῖα μιχθήτω πυρί, paraphrased by Cicero by a reference to those *qui negant se recusare quo minus ipsis mortuis terrarum omnium deflagratio consequatur* (*De Fin.* 3. 64); cf. Otto 345. What men often speak of lightly is, whether they like it or not, going to happen. The implication is assisted by the syntax: after *non si* one would expect pres. subj., as at e.g. Virg. *A.* 12. 203–5 *nec me uis ulla uolentem | auertet, non, si tellurem effundat in undas | diluuio miscens caelumque in Tartara soluat*; here the future *miscebitur* shows that this is a statement of fact, not a remote eventuality.

terra mari...mare caelo: the Punic Wars were confined to earth and sea (835 n.); in the final destruction the heavens too will be involved. The crescendo is carefully contrived and emphasized by alliteration.

843–61   These lines form a digression or parenthesis within the paragraph. They follow naturally on what precedes (840 *qui non erimus* ∼ 843–4) and are relevant to the theme *mors nil est ad nos*; but little attempt is made to facilitate the transition back to the main argument at 862.

843–4   The construction is: *si iam sentit animi natura animaeque potestas, postquam de nostro corpore distractast...*: the effect seems to be to throw *sentit* into increased relief. Such dislocations of the normal word-order (hyperbaton) occur only occasionally in L. and his contemporary Catullus; in later poets, particularly Ovid and Martial, they become something of a mannerism. Besides the literature cited by Hofmann–Szantyr 689–94 see M. Platnauer, *Latin elegiac verse* (1951) 104–8; Fordyce on Catull. 66. 18. For *si iam* cf. 540 n.; here L. uses the indic.: 'even if the soul *does* continue to have sensation...'.

844   distractast: referring here to the separation of the soul from the body, not its dissolution (501, 507, 590, 799); cf. 330 *extrahere*.
  animi natura animaeque potestas = *anima*; cf. 846.

845–6   comptu coniugioque…consistimus: the repetition of the prefix (17–18 n.) emphasizes that the true 'us' is a *concilium* (839 n.), to which any sensation that might be independently possessed by the soul after it leaves the body is irrelevant. *comptus* subst. = 'union' is unique in Latin, and *coniugium* occurs in L. only here.

847–51   Even if in the course of time our atoms were to recombine in the same form, that would still not be 'us'. This contingency is not admitted, like its predecessor, for the sake of argument: Epicurus seems to have held that it was not impossible, and at 856 L. finds it easily credible. In its original, cyclic, guise the idea was Stoic.

847–9   collegerit…redegerit…fuerint 'if it should have…', pf. subj.

847   si = *etsi*, as shown by *tamen* in 850 (cf. 946, 948), but even without such indication *si* must frequently be interpreted as concessive: Hofmann–Szantyr 671. Cf. 107 n.
  collegerit aetas: time, as often in poetry, is figured as an active agent; compare the famous speech of Ajax (Soph. *Aj.* 646–7), 'All things the long unnumbered years bring out from obscurity and hide again', ἅπανθ' ὁ μακρὸς κἀναρίθμητος χρόνος | φύει τ' ἄδηλα καὶ φανέντα κρύπτεται.

848   ut 'as' rather than 'where', as Munro apparently took it. The local sense of *ut* is rare and there seems to be no certain example in L.; cf. Fordyce on Catull. 11. 3. Cf. 857.

850   nos: the present 'us', the existing *concilium*; cf. 852 n.
  id quoque factum 'even if that did happen': 441–2 n.

851   repetentia nostri 'the ability to recollect ourselves', sc. as we were: *nostri* is objective genitive. *repetentia* occurs nowhere else in classical Latin (cf. 675 n.), but its use by L.'s imitator Arnobius guarantees it. (*memoria*) *repetere* = 'remember' is of course standard Latin.

852   et nunc 'and in our present existence', opposed to *ante*, as at

858. Susemihl's *ut* gives a good logical connexion with what precedes: 'we should not be concerned (in the hypothetical case) just as we are not (in the actual case)'; but the correction is not imperatively demanded by the context. Cf. also 853 n.

ad nos de nobis: the present 'us' is the only one that we are interested in; the former 'us' might just as well not have existed.

853   neque: Lachmann's metrically improved version of Marullus' *nec* is the most natural supplement, giving good rhetorical responsion: *et nunc...neque iam.* Merrill's *nil* gives a less appropriate emphasis.

d(e) illis: cf. Virg. *A.* 6. 38 *grege de intacto*; these, according to Soubiran (404), are the only instances of elided *de* in epic poetry from Cicero to Silius; cf. 159 n. *illis*, sc. our former selves.

854–8   The suggestion that these recombinations are not merely a theoretical possibility but have actually occurred cannot be attributed to Epicurus himself (cf. 847–51 n.); however, if L. is improving on his sources his formulation is suitably cautious.

854–6   cum respicias...possis 'when one looks back...one can': 213 n.

855–6   tum motus materiai multimodis quam sint 'and also how variously the atoms move'. For the structure of the indirect question cf. 208–9 n.; but the adv. *multimodis* is used as if he had written *materies moueatur.* Cf. Sall. *Hist.* fr. 2. 42 M. *L. Octauius et C. Cotta consulatum ingressi, quorum Octauius languide et incuriose fuit, Cotta promptius.*

856   hoc: to be read and scanned before a vowel as *hŏcc*; see W. S. Allen, *Vox Latina* (1965) 75–7. Cf. 914 n.

adcredere: only here in L. The force of the prefix is uncertain: 'believe in addition' or perhaps 'come to believe'.

857   posta = *posita*: cf. 346, 871.

858   quibus e: 375 n.

859   reprehendere = *repetere*; cf. 851 n.

860   inter...iectast: 262 n.

uitai pausa 'a break in existence', cf. 930. After L. *pausa* disappears from Latin except for an occasional antiquarian revival.

860–61 'And the moving atoms have strayed far and wide at large away from the senses': a condensed and emphatic way of saying that the atoms have quitted the controlled motions which produce sensation (cf. 272) to pursue new and random motions. Contrast 923–4.

861   deerrarunt: scanned as a trisyllable.

862–9 The argument now resumes abruptly where it left off at 842 (cf. 843–61 n.): nothing can happen to anybody (*accidere* 841 ~ 864) who is not there to have it happen to him; from the point of view of the individual to die is never to have been born. The intervening passage is relevant inasmuch as it has helped to substantiate the conclusion referred to in 864 *id quoniam mors eximit.*

862   misere...aegreque: a heightened version of the common *male* (*bene*) *esse alicui*; here *cui* must be understood from the apodosis of the *si*-clause.

863 A similar formulation in the ps.-Platonic *Axiochus* (365 d): 'you will not be (there) for it (misfortune) to happen to you', σὺ γὰρ οὐκ ἔσῃ, περὶ ὃν ἔσται (κακόν).

ipse...in eo tum tempore 'the actual self at that actual moment of time': the pleonasm and the sandwiching of *tum* emphasize the point.

864   id: the possibility that he can be there; the following clause expands and varies the point.

esseque: 163 n.
probet = *prohibet.*

865 'The man on whom misfortunes may be conferred.' *conciliare* = 'acquire' usually has desirable objects such as *gratia, fauor, amor, beneuolentia.* L. perverts the normal sense for the sake of a play on words: if there is no *concilium* of atoms there can be no *concilium* of misfortunes.

867–8 It makes no difference whether a man (has been born at some time or) has never been born at all. This kind of ellipse, in which something which is not expressed is inferred from what follows, is technically classified as *e sequentibus praecedentia*: cf. R. J. Getty,

*M. Annaei Lucani De Bello Ciuili Liber I*² (1955) lv. Heinze quotes two examples from Livy (36. 17. 10–11, 44. 25. 11).

868   iam: sc. once death has occurred, looking forward to *cum.*

869   The conceit that death is immortal had been used by Amphis, a comic poet of the fourth century (*ap.* Athen. 8. 336c): 'Death is deathless when once a man is dead', ὁ Θάνατος δ' ἀθάνατός ἐστιν, ἂν ἅπαξ τις ἀποθάνῃ; but what is a mere jingle in the Greek is dignified and sonorous in L., and what is more makes a point. L. is insisting on a basic philosophical and scientific truth, that the death of the parts is the price of the survival of the whole. 'Change is the law of nature for all things that man can know by observation, and change is death. But if the basic matter of the universe is eternal, so are the changes through which it passes, and therefore death is eternal' (Agnes K. Michels, *T.A.P.A.* 86 (1955) 165–6). Cf. 1087–94n.

870–893

Fear of what may happen to the body after death is therefore (870 *proinde*) irrational. The topic was an Epicurean commonplace. This paragraph marks the point at which the diatribe-satirist (see Introd. 17–19) takes control of the argument: a comparison with the treatment of the same idea by the author of the ps.-Platonic *Axiochus* (365c) shows how L. uses rhetoric to enlist the emotional sympathies of his readers. In his evident pleasure in the keen sarcasms with which he rounds off the passage he apparently fails to notice that he has passed to discussing a commonplace which, though related, is different from that with which he began: see 888–93n.

870   uideas: 213n.

870–71   se …indignarier ipsum…fore ut 'treating it as a grievance that…he' (Latham): the construction is best explained as belonging to the 'I know thee who thou art' type (208–9n.), a contrived variation on the usual acc. + inf. (cf. 884) designed to bring out the absurdity of the man's behaviour. The *se ipsum* that he feels so strongly about is not in fact the real 'self' and it will not be 'he' that undergoes these indignities: cf. 882–3. As L. goes on to say, what he is really afraid of, though he will not admit it, is that these things will hurt.

871–5 The alliteration, in which the paragraph is unusually rich, helps to convey L.'s scorn for these silly notions.

871 **putescat:** to be preferred to *putrescat* as closer to the *putes* of OQ and as corresponding to σηπόμενος in the parallel passage of the *Axiochus*.

  posto 'buried': the simple verb for the normal *composito* (or *condito*); cf. 319n.

872 **interfiat** = *interficiatur*, a very rare usage, unparalleled in L.
  malisue ferarum: perhaps a reference to Persian customs (cf. Cic. *Tusc.* 1. 108), still maintained in the Parsee 'Towers of Silence', in which corpses are exposed to birds of prey. It is, however, equally possible that L. had in mind the consequences of death in battle, with which the age enjoyed a terrible familiarity.

873 **non sincerum sonere** 'does not ring true', like a flawed pot: a common image. *sincerum* is adverbial (internal) acc., cf. Enn. *Sc.* 106 V.² (108 Jocelyn) *nam neque irati neque blandi quicquam sincere sonant.* For *sonere* cf. 156n.

874 **caecum...stimulum** 'a hidden prick', sc. of fear; hidden, that is to say, from himself, cf. 878 *inscius.* For *stimulum* cf. 1019, 4. 1082–3 *et stimuli subsunt qui instigant laedere id ipsum | quodcumque est, rabies unde illaec germina surgunt.*

876 **dat** 'grants', 'allows the truth of', for the usual *concedo* (cf. 319n.).

  quod promittit et unde 'neither what he professes to grant [that is, that 'he' will not survive after death] nor what that profession arises from [*id unde* (= *ex quo*) *promittit*: sc. that the soul perishes along with the body]'. In his heart of hearts the man accepts neither conclusion nor premises.

877 **nec...se tollit et eicit** 'he will not uproot and cast "himself" out'. For the idiom cf. 490n.; but here the usage is pointed: an effort of the intellect and will is required, which he shrinks from making. The point is the now familiar one that the 'self' cannot survive the dissolution of the *concilium.*

  eicit is scanned as a disyllable by synizesis: 383n.

878 facit 'supposes'; the original sense of *facere* is 'place'. Cf. 626 n.

esse...super = *superesse*, tmesis.

sui...ipse: see 881 n.

880 uolucres...feraeque: the classic fate of the unburied corpse (882 *proiecto*) in literary allusions from Homer onwards.

881 ipse sui: here and at 878 *ipse* is the man as he is now (879 *uiuus*), *sui* as he sees himself in anticipation; but the point of L.'s argument is of course that the corpse is not 'himself' at all and the man who now exists, *ipse*, will not be there to feel pity. By using both words he sharpens the absurdity: Bailey is wrong to term *ipse* 're-dundant'. Cf. 925 n.

miseret: the personal use of the verb is archaic.

neque...se diuidit: he will not distinguish his true self as it is now (*se*) from the imagined corpse but persists in trying to participate in his 'own' sufferings.

illim = *illinc*, i.e. from the corpse. Cf. 160 *exim*.

882 proiecto 'cast out', almost a technical term for unburied bodies; cf. 6. 1155 *proiecta cadauera*.

882–3 illum se fingit 'identifies himself with it' (M. F. Smith).

sensuque suo contaminat adstans 'and standing there [sc. in his imagination] he infects it with his own sensations', i.e. attributes to the insensate corpse what the living man now feels. *contamino* occurs nowhere else in L.; here it is close to what appears to be the original meaning = *contingo*, but already the familiar sense 'change' or, more specifically, 'spoil', sc. by bringing into contact, is felt.

adstans: cf. 886–7 n.

884 hinc '*this* is why', looking back to 870. *indignatur* ∼ *indignarier*.

885 uera 'as it really is'.

nullum...alium se: there is only one self, which ceases to exist at the moment of death.

886–7 uiuus...peremptum, sibi se, stansque iacentem: the oppositions emphasize the paradoxical character of the notions attacked and round off the argument. *sibi* is most pointed if construed with *peremptum*: the words *sibi se* are carefully positioned to convey the absurdity of a living man mourning for a 'self' that has been bereaved of a 'self'. Bailey's reference to 'the usual Lucretian redundance' is insensitive: cf. 881 n.

887 stansque iacentem: the juxtaposition entails an unusual rhythm, with diaeresis and consequent false verse-ending after the second foot. Cf. 1033 n.

uriue reintroduces the idea of cremation, lost sight of since 872; see next n.

888–93 Up to this point L. has been dealing with the fate of the body after death in general terms, though 880–83 refer to the special case of the unburied. He now proceeds to pour scorn on the belief that it is a misfortune not to have a proper funeral – whatever form that might take in a particular society. This was (and is) the general belief of mankind, and was a favourite Aunt Sally of the philosophers in antiquity. The technique of contemptuous enumeration here followed is characteristic: cf. Bion (Hense 31), Cic. *Tusc.* 1. 103–8. The topic was not Epicurean property: Cicero (loc. cit. 104) quotes a well-known repartee of the Cynic Diogenes on the subject, and as authority for his catalogue of customs he gives the Stoic Chrysippus. Cf. the noble epigram of Lucan (a Stoic) on the unburied dead of Pharsalus: *caelo tegitur qui non habet urnam* (7. 819). Petronius (115. 17–18) incorporates the theme into a burlesque declamation, from which it may be inferred that by the latter part of the first century A.D. it had become intolerably trite. L. develops it more because it offers an opportunity for a series of crushing sarcasms than because it was strictly relevant to his main argument (though on his premisses the views that he criticizes are certainly irrational); and though *uriue* in 887 (picked up by *nam* in the next verse) can be seen as paving the transition, it remains true (as Heinze remarked) that the distinction between the two commonplaces (the fate of the body; decent burial) is blurred by L., perhaps deliberately.

888 The alliteration and word-play (*mălumst mālis*) strike a note of scornful irony that is sustained in what follows.

889 qui 'how'.

**890–93   torrescere...suffocari...rigere...cubat...urgeriue
...obtritum:** the words are all such as impute sensation to the corpse
and so imply the absurdity of the view that is attacked. Conventional
methods of disposal – cremation, embalming and entombment, in-
humation – are just as unpleasant as being devoured by wild beasts.
torrescere is found nowhere else in classical Latin.

891   in melle situm: honey was commonly used for embalming.
In more recent times, before the invention of preservatives such as
formaldehyde, bodies might be transported in a cask of rum or
brandy.

**892   The reference must be to entombment, after embalming (*atque*
in 891 connective not adversative), in a rock-cut tomb, in which the
body was laid out on a slab or shelf of stone. The chilly discomfort
of this situation, in which the body has no covering (*summo...
aequore*) is ironically contrasted with that of the buried body, which has
too much.

**893   The buried body is pressed down and crushed, an implicit
reflection on the conventional pious prayer *sit tibi terra leuis*, a formula
which was worked to death both in literature and in actual use
(Lattimore 65–72).
  urgeriue superne: again an unusual rhythm, this time with the
diaeresis and false verse-ending (on the persistence of the elided
syllable see 83n.) after the third foot (cf. 887n.). The ponderous
metre reinforces the sense.

894–911

Regrets for the loss of present happiness can have no meaning for the
dead. The opening verses of this passage are so often quoted out of
context that there is a danger of overlooking the spirit of irony, rising
at times to parody and overt mockery, that pervades the argument.
Here too L. attacks conventional ideas using the techniques of the
diatribe. There are some effective strokes of satire, but nowhere are
the weaknesses of L.'s case more apparent: cf. Introd. 32–3.

**894–9   Conventional sentiments ascribed by L. to mourners so that
he can demolish them. To put an argument to which you already
know the answer into the mouth of a real or imagined adversary is

one of the oldest of rhetorical devices; it was valued in diatribe and
satire for its dramatic and enlivening potentialities (cf. 931 n.). L. is
clearly rejecting the sentiments that he 'quotes', but the expression
is for the most part not overtly sarcastic, as it is at 904-8 (see n.). For
the conventional nature of the mourners' utterances see Lattimore
172-7; especially close to L. is an epitaph from third-century
Alexandria: 'No longer, Philoxenus, does your mother receive you
and cast her arms lingeringly about your lovely neck, nor do you go
to the famous city with the young men and rejoice in the shaded level
of the gymnasium' (176). Virgil paid L. the compliment of imitating
these verses (*G.* 2. 523-4), and so, in turn, did Gray:

> For them no more the blazing hearth shall burn,
> Or busy housewife ply her evening care:
> No children run to lisp their sire's return,
> Or climb his knees the envied kiss to share.
>
> (*Elegy written in a country Church Yard* 21-4)

894   iam iam non 'never again'. This is an unusual sense, dubiously
supported by Catull. 63. 73 *iam iam dolet quod egi, iam iamque paenitet*
'now at last' (see Fordyce *ad loc.*); but the alternative explanation
that the phrase connotes 'the imminence of the event' seems hardly
tenable in view of the dramatic situation. The man is dead (898
ademit), not dying.

894-5   This punctuation is demanded by both sense and phrasing,
rather than the comma after *laeta* which most editors prefer. The
reader of an unpunctuated text would naturally take *uxor* as the
subject of *accipiet* along with *domus*, and the resulting picture is truer
to life: a Roman matron would not race her children to the door to
greet her husband – and indeed *praeripere* perhaps most naturally
indicates that the children run to kiss their father before their mother
does so. Munro (who however punctuated after *laeta*) noted that
'Virgil and Gray I fancy joined the *uxor* with the *domus*'; and the
point was worth making.

896   praeripere: inf. of purpose, usually after verbs of motion, is
fairly common in old and colloquial Latin, relatively rare in classical
poetry (Bennett 1 418-19; Hofmann–Szantyr 344-5).
  tacita 'heartfelt' (Duff).

897 factis florentibus is best taken as dat. depending, like *tuisque*, on *praesidium* 'you will no longer be able to protect your prosperous affairs or your dependants'. The usual interpretation, that *f. f. esse* is a periphrasis for *florere* = 'prosper' is objectionable on two counts: (i) it entails an awkward construction for *esse*, which is made to do double duty; (ii) this use of the descriptive abl. cannot be satisfactorily paralleled.

898 praesidium is almost a technical term in the vocabulary of personal relationships: see Nisbet and Hubbard on Hor. *C.* 1. 1. 2. At 2. 643 L. uses the predicative dat.: *praesidioque parent decorique parentibus esse*; here the nom. avoids a pointless jingle with *misero*. It seems astonishing that L. should implicitly reject the natural concern of a man for the fate of his family when he is dead: it is a sentiment that, in the speech put by Homer into the mouth of Hector (*Il.* 6. 450–65), forms part of one of the most moving scenes in all literature. Even the austere Epicurean morality allowed that such concern was legitimate; it was to the credit of Epicurus that he 'could not wholly reconcile his philosophy with his humanity' (Sikes 134), and we learn from Diogenes Laertius (10. 16–21) that his will included full instructions for the care of his dependants and the freeing of his slaves. L.'s answer, that these things do not trouble a man *when he is dead*, is totally beside the point.

898–9 misero misere...omnia ademit una dies: here the language becomes deliberately banal. Cf. Cic. *Att.* 3. 23. 5 *quem ego miserum misere perdidi* and D. R. Shackleton Bailey's note; *C.L.E.* 405 *abstulit una dies animam corpusque simitur | arsit et in cineres iacet hic uersum adque fauilla. | supremum munus misero posuere sodales*; 1307. 7–8 *apstulit haec unus tot tantaque munera nobis | perfidus infelix horrificusque dies.*

899 una dies: in the sense of a particular day, as opposed to a period, *dies* is masc. in old Latin and classical prose. L. might, it may be supposed, have written *unu' dies*, but to this licence, which he employs sparingly, he prefers the less obviously licentious change of gender. Cf. 5. 95, 1000; and for *dies* fem. = *tempus* cf. 908 *nulla dies*, 4. 1031 *ipsa dies*. On the whole question see the monumental article of E. Fraenkel, 'Das Geschlecht von *dies*', *Kl. Beiträge zur klass. Philol.* 1 (1964) 27–72, esp. 64.

900   illud in his rebus: cf. 370.

nec 'yet...not', adversative: 340 n.

901   super: 672 n.

unā 'together', sc. 'with you'; but the reference may be to
earum...rerum: the yearning passes along with its object. In any case
Giussani's *ullum* is unnecessary: the point of 922 is different.

902   dictisque sequantur 'and make their words correspond' to
their thoughts.

904–8   The speaker is made to express the feelings of the bereaved in
unmistakably satirical terms: L. is mocking the commonplaces of
the formal *lamentatio* and the epitaph. Grief was recognized by
Epicurus as natural (D.L. 10. 119); L. attacks, not mourning itself,
but its more extravagant manifestations. He seizes on the conventional promise never to forget the dead person (see 907–8 n.) with
all the scorn that he habitually brings to bear on a false philosophical
position. Such rigour, however, belongs to the rhetorical satirist
rather than the philosopher: mourning, as Epicurus undoubtedly
realized (and modern social anthropologists would agree with him),
meets a universal human need for some sort of ritualized comfort,
however slender its logical basis, in bereavement. The reflection that
the dead person's troubles are over does not always do much to
mitigate the sense of loss felt by his friends and family.

904   tu quidem as opposed to *at nos* (906). For the elision cf. 339 n.

aeui: with *quod superest* (905), 'for all time to come'.

906   cinefactum 'turned to ashes', 'incinerated', a curious word
found nowhere else and possibly coined by L. (in derision?) on the
analogy of *tepefactus*, *labefactus*; cf. Nonius (cit. app. crit.).

prope '(standing) nearby', adverbial.

busto: the burnt-out pyre, as explained by Servius *ad* Virg. *A.*
11. 185 '*pyra*' *est lignorum congeries*, '*rogus*' *cum iam ardere coeperit
dicitur*, '*bustum*' *uero iam exustum uocatur*.

907   This famous verse has sometimes been treated with undue
respect. Three metrical features combine to make it probably unique
in serious Latin poetry: (i) the fact that it is composed of three words
only: (ii) its single caesura; (iii) its spondaic quadrisyllabic ending

(191 n.). The effect on the Roman ear must have been grotesque. 'Surely these pathetic rhetorical figures and astonishing rhythms are meant as sarcastic caricatures of the mawkish clichés used by such *stulti* and *baratri*. *Insatiabiliter* for instance is not necessarily an elevated word. Its only other use in Lucretius [6. 978] is of swine rolling in filth' (West 29). L. may be deriding the often limping hexameters found on Roman tombstones: e.g. *C.L.E.* 526, esp. 10–11 *hunc fleuit populus pius, hunc miseri ingemuere parentes | perculsi longo luctu tristitiaque perenni*. So might a modern satirist parody the pathetic verses in the 'In Memoriam' columns of local newspapers.

insatiabiliter: L. had a weakness for formations of this type, which were popular with the older Latin writers but which are relatively rare (with a few common exceptions such as *amabiliter*) in classical Latin. They survived 'underground' (interesting examples among the Pompeian graffiti) to reappear in some of the Fathers. Cf. 779 n. on *praeproperanter*.

defleuimus: the word is almost a technical term for the formal lament. The reading of the older editions *deflebimus* was expelled from the text by Lachmann and is not mentioned in modern editions. It allows *insatiabiliter* its full value, 'our mourning will never be done', and so sharpens the satire; and there is no need to envisage the words of this speaker as necessarily uttered *after* the funeral – they could just as easily be imagined as belonging to the *conclamatio*, the *previous* ritual of mourning (Serv. *ad* Virg. *A.* 6. 218, Don. *Comm. Ter.* 1 346 Wessner; cf. Virg. *A.* 11. 59 *haec ubi defleuit*, referring to words uttered over the body of Pallas). However, *defleuimus* is the reading of the MSS, for what that is worth (the *b/u* confusion being extremely common), and the variation of tenses *defleuimus...demet* may be designed to respond to the preceding *ut es...sic eris*.

907–8 aeternumque...maerorem: one of the commonest sentiments of all epitaphs, ancient and modern: Lattimore 243–6. A recurrent epithet was ἀείμνηστος, 'always remembered'.

908 nulla dies: 899 n.

909 hoc: sc. the speaker.

910 somnum...atque quietem refer back to 904 *leto sopitus*. Death as sleep was and is a popular idea (Lattimore 82–3); for this

as a standard ingredient of the *consolatio* cf. Nisbet and Hubbard on
Hor. *C.* 1. 24. 5. L. as a good Epicurean disdains the trite symbol and
turns it back on the innocent speaker: 'you talk of the dead being
"at rest"; if you believe that, where is the sense in perpetual
mourning?'

si res redit 'if it comes (in the end) to...'.

911   cur depends on *quid sit amari*, 'what bitterness is there so great,
that it can cause a man to...'.

aeterno ~ 907 *aeternumque.*

tabescere 'waste away': the word is used, as it is of the ravages
of love at 4. 1120, with a sneer.

912-930

There is no occasion to regret the loss of trivial bodily pleasures.
L. passes to the superficial complaints of the hedonist, whose philosophy is merely 'let us eat and drink, for tomorrow we die'. This
attitude is no doubt as old as mankind; what is ironical (though
irrelevant to L.'s argument here) is that to the man in the street it
became, quite wrongly, identified with the Epicurean philosophy,
hence English 'epicure'. On the prevalence of a trivialized Epicureanism in the Roman world cf. M. Rostovtzeff, *Soc. and Econ. Hist. of
the Roman Empire*, rev. P. M. Fraser, 1 (1957) 56 and Pl. VII. L.'s choice
of the dinner-table as the setting for this shallow moralizing is
accurate: compare the scene in Petronius in which Trimalchio shows
his guests a miniature silver skeleton and declaims: *eheu nos miseros,
quam totus homuncio nil est!* | *sic erimus cuncti, postquam nos auferet
Orcus.* | *ergo uiuamus, dum licet esse bene* (34. 10); also the ps.-Virgilian
Copa 37-8 *pone merum et talos; pereat qui crastina curat:* | *Mors aurem
uellens 'uiuite' ait, 'uenio'.* L. may, however, intend an even more
specific reference, to sympotic poetry, in which the 'carpe diem'
motif is typical: see Nisbet and Hubbard 134-6. The situation is
piquant: the real Epicurean reproves the false (Martha 143-4).

912-14   hoc...faciunt...ut dicant: the *ut*-clause is attached in a
rather loosely epexegetic fashion, but the writing is informal rather
than 'clumsy' (Bailey) or 'gauche' (Ernout–Robin).

912 discubuere 'are at table'; *discumbo, accumbo* are the normal terms for reclining at a meal.

913 pocula: they are at the maudlin stage.

ora 'temples', perhaps to be classified as an example of synecdoche, *totum pro parte*; more familiar is the reverse, *pars pro toto*, as in *puppis* for *nauis*. Cf. Getty, op. cit. (867–8 n.) liii–lvi.

coronis 'garlands', indispensable wear for festive occasions throughout antiquity.

914 ex animo 'sincerely': *in uino ueritas*.

hic: probably the pronoun (*hĭc*) not the adverb (*hīc*). For the scansion cf. 856 n.

homullis 'poor mortals'; cf. *homuncio* in the quotation from Petronius (912–30 n.), Plaut. *Capt.* 51 *homunculi quanti* ['how little'] *sunt, quom recogito!*

915 fuerit is fut. pf.: 'soon it will be over and done'.

916 'As if when they are dead this is to be the worst of their troubles'; *mali* depends on *hoc*, defining genitive.

917 miseros 'poor wretches', heavily ironical.

torrat: this has become the modern vulgate. A subjunctive is needed, since the reasons given in the *quod*-clauses are not presented as facts but are attributed (of course scornfully) to the speakers of 914–15. For a form *torrēre* bearing the same relationship to *torrēre* as e.g. *feruĕre* to *feruēre*, *tuor* to *tueor*, there appears to be no other evidence. Lachmann's *torres* (= *torris*; the form is attested only in glossaries), translated by Munro 'drought', means literally 'torch'; the image is perhaps not too daring for L., but it is hazardous to attribute it to him by conjecture. Housman's *aridu' torror* (*J.P.* 25 (1897) 237–8), besides departing far from the transmitted text, imports into the poem a word not otherwise known in classical Latin. The objection expressed by Lachmann, and apparently sustained by Housman, that *arida* is 'absurde collocatum' is not very cogent; one may perhaps compare Virg. *A.* 2. 565–6 *corpora saltu | ad terram misere aut ignibus aegra dedere*, and in any case it seems cavalier to emend away the second verb in view of 5. 902 *tam soleat torrere atque urere*. M. L. West's *tortet* (*C.R.* N.S. 11 (1961) 203–4) is palaeographically easy but is not supported by *tortari* at 3. 661 (the only other instance of the word in L.), where the sense is literal.

It is tempting to recur to an older solution than any of these, apparently accepted by Gifanius and more recently by Ernout: to print *torreat*, scanned as a disyllable by synizesis; cf. 383 *aranei*, 918 *rei*. If *torreat* were the original reading the state of affairs in the MSS is elegantly explained: it was miscopied (or 'corrected') as *torret*, corrected, by the addition of *a*, to *torrĕt*, the reading in the common source of OQ (see Introd. 34), which was then misunderstood as indicating, not a correction, but a variant reading *torrat*, which was accepted by one copyist and rejected by the other. Against *torreat* is the fact that no sufficient parallel seems to exist for synizesis of a verbal termination before *ebulliat* at Pers. 2. 10; for the Plautine *eamus* (W. M. Lindsay, *Early Latin verse* (1922) 63) is probably to be explained on the analogy of *eadem* et sim.

918   aliae: gen. sing.; the only other instance of this form in contemporary Latin is at Cic. *De Diu.* 2. 30 *aliae pecudis* (Neue–Wagener II 534).

cuius 'any', since *tamquam* is equivalent to *tamquam si*.

rei: 383n.

919–30 Even when we are only asleep we do not regret the loss of our pleasures: *a fortiori* we shall not regret them when we are dead. L. recurs to the idea of death as sleep to reinforce his point that it is absurd to anticipate a sense of loss that one will not in fact feel. The repetition of the keyword *desiderium* (918, 922) shows that the verses belong where the MSS give them and do not require to be transposed or bracketed, as has been suggested. L.'s implication is that our behaviour is both illogical and inconsistent. This is a special application of an argument that was not specifically Epicurean but belonged among the commonplaces of the philosophical *consolatio*: Cic. *Tusc.* 1. 92 *habes somnum imaginem mortis eamque cotidie induis: et dubitas quin sensus in morte nullus sit, cum in eius simulacro uideas esse nullum sensum?*

919   se uitamque 'the life enjoyed by his waking self': cf. 922 *nostri*.

requirit 'misses', 'feels regret for': *requiro* often means to seek and not to find.

920 sopita: n. pl., cf. 136n. The word is chosen to recall 904; L. exploits a point already admitted by his imagined mourner.

921 sic 'on these terms', referring to the preceding verse. Once we are sound asleep it is all the same to us whether we wake up or not.

922 nostri 'our waking selves', cf. 919n.

923–5 L. anticipates the full account of sleep at 4. 907–61; cf. esp. 4. 916–18 *principio somnus fit ubi est distracta per artus | uis animae partim-que foras eiecta recessit | et partim contrusa magis concessit in altum.*

923 haudquaquam modifies *longe* in 924.
   illa: the atoms concerned, those of the *anima*.

924 For the expression cf. 860–61n.

925 'When a man starts up from sleep and pulls himself together.' *correptus...colligit* convey the idea of a sudden awakening. The point appears to be that the speed with which one can wake up shows that the atoms of the *anima* have not gone far afield: *haudquaquam longe errant* = 'are not at all far away'. This cannot be easily reconciled with 4. 917 (quoted 923–5n.). Winkelmann's *colligat* makes the causal force of the *cum*-clause clear, but is not necessary: 363n.
   ipse: perhaps 'easily' = *sponte*: but cf. 881n.

927 minus...quam...nil: heavily ironical.

928 turba et: Goebel's very simple correction not only gives easier grammar but more Lucretian writing: for the commentators can produce no parallel for the combination of the double genitive and the awkward word-order in *turbae disiectus materiai* = d. t. m. 'displace-ment of the disordered atoms'.
   disiectus: found only here and probably a Lucretian coinage.

929 leto 'in death', *consequitur* being used absolutely as at 478; the commentators compare Virg. *A.* 9. 433 *uoluitur Euryalus leto.* The easy correction to *letum* (cf. W. M. Lindsay, *An introduction to Latin textual emendation* (1896) 13) should be rejected: with the possible exception of 2. 958 L. uses *letum* only of the state of being dead, not for the moment or act of dying.
   expergitus exstat ~ 925.

930 secuta 'has overtaken', a somewhat unexpected verb for *uitai pausa* (cf. 860), but chosen no doubt to pick up *consequitur* (cf. 261 n.) and so round off the paragraph.

931–977

Nature herself is now imagined as admonishing the man who cannot bear the thought of dying. Personification, *prosopopoeia*, is as old as the art of effective speaking. Plato in a well-known passage of the *Crito* (50a) had made the Laws speak; and Epicurus had personified Nature even if he did not put words into her mouth. This device was peculiarly suitable for the diatribe-sermon: besides providing dramatic relief it allowed the speaker to upbraid and remonstrate with his audience in terms that might have been resented if spoken *in propria persona* (cf. 939, 955 nn.). Bion had made Poverty answer his imagined critics in person (Hense 7–8); and in the satires of L.'s great contemporary M. Terentius Varro we meet such personifications as Infamia, Veritas and Existimatio (cf. E. Norden, *Kl. Schr. z. kl. Altertum* (1966) 81–2). The hectoring tone and alliterative vehemence of Nature's harangue are characteristic of the diatribe style. But L. has far transcended his sources. His Nature is no mere anthropomorphic poetical figment: she exists in her own right, as representing the immutable and inexorable laws of the universe that form the subject of the poem. 'The reverence which other men felt in presence of the ceremonies of religion he feels in presence of the majesty of Nature' (Sellar 301). In introducing this stupendous abstraction as interlocutrix in a dialogue with his readers L. has taken a leaf out of Bion's book, but the result eclipses the lowly origin of the device by the grandeur of its implication: it is not the arguments deployed by the poet, nor even the authority of Epicurus, but the very Sum of Things that stands there to convict the fool of his folly.

What Nature is made to say does not mirror specific Epicurean doctrines very closely, but there is a general resemblance to *Ep. ad Men.* 125–7, 60–62 Us.

931–2 si uocem…mittat: almost a formula = εἰ φωνὴν λάβοι: cf. Plato, *Prot.* 361a; Hense 6; Norden, op. cit. (preceding n.) 80–81.

932 hoc alicui…increpet 'levels the following reproach at them'; the construction is more familiar with e.g. *obicere* or *exprobrare*:

contrast Plaut. *Most.* 750 *numquid increpitauit filium?* For the prosody of *hoc* acc. see 856n.

933 'What is it that troubles you so much, that you...?': an elaborate periphrasis for 'why?'. Cf. 1008–9 *hoc...est...quod*; Cic. *Verr.* 4. 43 *quid erat quod confirmabat...?* The phrase may have had a colloquial ring: cf. Plaut. *Men.* 626 *quid tibi aegre est?*; W. M. Lindsay, *Syntax of Plautus* (1907) 79–80; J. B. Hofmann, *Lat. Umgangssprache*[3] (1951) 166. See also 715n.

mortalis is pointed, reminding the man of his condition.

nimis qualifies *indulges* in 934.

935–9 Nature poses a dilemma, of which this is the first horn: if you have enjoyed life, can you not leave it with equanimity? Pervading the entire discussion there is perhaps, as Giussani and Bailey suggest, a specifically Epicurean idea (K.Δ. 19, 73 Us.): that pleasure does not increase infinitely with infinite length of time. This however is not stated or implied until 946–9, in the context of the second horn of the dilemma.

935 si grata: Naugerius' correction satisfies the demands of sense and form: *si* is needed to complement *sin* at 940, and *grata* to respond to 937 *ingrata*, 942 *ingratum*. On the sense of *grata* see 937n.

936–7 The idea that one should be grateful for past pleasures is Epicurean: an old man should be a philosopher so that 'though growing old, he should renew his youth in benefits through thankfulness for the past' (*Ep. ad Men.* 122, 59 Us.); cf. Sen. *De Ben.* 3. 4. 1 *adsidue queritur* (Epicurus) *quod aduersus praeterita simus ingrati, quod quaecumque percipimus bona non reducamus nec inter uoluptates numeremus, cum certior nulla sit uoluptas quam quae iam eripi non potest.* This was also the view of James Mill, who 'used to say, that he had never known a happy old man, except those who were able to live again in the pleasures of the young' (J. S. Mill, *Autobiography* ch. 2). The image of the cracked jar has a homely ring (cf. 873n.), but here there is obviously an allusion to the Danaids as a type of ingratitude: cf. 1003–10n.

937 ingrata 'thanklessly', i.e. without receiving any thanks from you: cf. Plaut. *Asin.* 136–7 *ingrata atque inrita esse omnia intellego | quae* *dedi et quod bene feci, Amph.* 184. The word must be so understood throughout the passage, and so also *grata* at 935 = 'having had its meed of thanks'.

938 Epicurus was alleged to have said, apropos of suicide, *aut bibat aut abeat* (Cic. *Tusc.* 5. 118 = ἢ πῖθι ἢ ἄπιθι): if a man cannot bear his misfortunes he should quit the scene of them. That is a little different from what we find here, where the image is used to recommend cheerful acceptance of inevitable death; this too is how it had been used by Bion (Hense 16) and was used after L. by Horace (*Sat.* 1. 1. 118–19, *Ep.* 2. 2. 214) and Seneca (*Ep.* 61. 4, 98. 15). It belongs in the sphere of popular wisdom rather than Epicurean orthodoxy.

939   aequo animoque: for the position of *-que* cf. 962, 662 n.

   securam...quietem: the phrase has occurred at 211, but we are here meant to think of the equation of death with sleep at 904, 910.

   stulte: so St Paul, 1 Cor. 15. 35–6: 'But some man will say, How are the dead raised up? and with what body do they come? Thou fool, that which thou sowest is not quickened, except it die.' For similarities between the diatribe and Christian homiletic cf. E. Norden, *Die antike Kunstprosa*[5] (1958) 556–8. Cf. 1026 *improbe*.

940–49 The second horn of Nature's dilemma: if you have *not* enjoyed your life, why do you want to go on living? Better to make an end. Nature cannot be forever devising fresh diversions for you.

940   quae fructus cumque es = *quaecumque fructus es*: cf. 550, 1075. For the acc. cf. 4. 1078 *nec constat quid primum oculis manibusque fruantur*, 734 n.; but even in old Latin the abl. is the normal construction with *fruor*.

   periere profusa continues the image of the leaking vessel from 936–7.

941   in offensast 'is hateful': cf. Cic. *Att.* 9. 2a. 2 *quin magna in offensa sim apud Pompeium*. The fact that L. nowhere else uses *offensa* is not in itself a cogent argument against this easy correction. Lambinus' *offensust* is plausible in itself, but elsewhere in L. *offensus* is always literal = 'clash'. The MS reading *offensost* can be defended as an extension of such idioms as *in dubio esse* (Hofmann–Szantyr 153), but L. offers no analogy to this Latinity.

942   male 'uselessly': *male* often reinforces *perdere* and *perire*.

943   The Epicureans did not positively approve suicide, but they allowed it as a last resort (cf. 938n.). L. nowhere discusses the ethics of the question, and it is not really relevant to his argument here; but it is dramatically effective that Nature should take this sharp line in order to emphasize the unreasonableness of continual hoping against hope. She is making a debating point, not expounding doctrine.

945   quod placeat: dependent on, not parallel with, the preceding *quod*-clause.

   eadem sunt omnia semper: that life in the end becomes too monotonous to be borne is an old commonplace: Sen. *Ep.* 24. 26 *quosdam subit eadem faciendi uidendique satietas et uitae non odium sed fastidium, in quod prolabimur ipsa inpellente philosophia, dum dicimus 'quousque eadem?'*; and with what follows in Seneca may be compared the famous meditation of the Preacher (Ecclesiastes 1). As a consolation for the dying the idea is ascribed by Seneca to a Stoic source (*Ep.* 77. 6). There is also a hint in what follows of the Epicurean doctrine that pleasure does not increase with duration: cf. 935–9, 958nn., 1080–81.

946, 948   si = *etsi*, as shown by *tamen*: cf. 847n.

946   non...iam 'not yet', the sense demanded by the context: cf. Plaut. *Asin.* 233 *non omnino iam perii*, Cic. *Pro Quinct.* 40 *non adesa iam sed abundanti etiam pecunia*, al. This sense is considerably rarer than 'no longer'; it seems to occur nowhere else in poetry outside comedy, though Juvenal (4. 101) and Silius (16. 533) use *iam non* = 'not...by this time'. See *T.L.L.* VII. 1. 93. 35–58.

948   omnia...saecla: all generations of living creatures, but the sense is 'any creature, even the longest-lived' rather than 'the entire living creation'. *omnia* is repeated from the preceding verse for emphasis. Contrast 1090, 1. 202 *multaque uiuendo uitalia uincere saecla*. It was well known, and matter for rhetorical exploitation, that some animals live longer than man.

   perges 'though you shall...'; Lambinus' *pergas* is not demanded by the syntax and perhaps weakens the sense.

949   A highly ironical climax, for it is the law of Nature, who is speaking, that forbids such a thing to happen.

950   quid respondemus 'what do we say?' The indic., unexpected
after *mittat* and *increpet* (932), perhaps carries the implication that
there is no answer: Heinze compared Cic. *Att.* 16. 7. 4 *nam si a
Phaedro nostro esses, expedita excusatio esset: nunc quid respondemus?*
However the indic. in deliberative questions was usual in colloquial
Latin: Hofmann–Szantyr 308; Bennett 1 22–4, noting that the usage
is confined to dialogue. For the phrase itself cf. Bion (Hense 8) τί ἄν
ἔχοις ἀντειπεῖν;, Hor. *Sat.* 1. 2. 72 (in a passage of coarsely-phrased
dialogue) *quid responderet?*

950–51   The phraseology has a legal tone: cf. 963, 971 nn. *intendere
litem*, like other such phrases, occurs in both technical and non-
technical contexts; and the same is true of *uera causa*.

952–62   An old man who complains that he must die is rebuked
even more sharply. At 946–7 it was implied that the man addressed is
young or in the prime of life; 952 (*uero*) makes an explicit contrast. Old
men proverbially cling to life: Soph. fr. 63 N.[2] (66 Pearson) τοῦ ζῆν
γὰρ οὐδεὶς ὡς ὁ γηράσκων ἐρᾷ; Arist. *Rhet.* 2. 13. 8 καὶ φιλόζωοι καὶ
μάλιστα ἐπὶ τῇ τελευταίᾳ ἡμέρᾳ διὰ τὸ τοῦ ἀπόντος εἶναι τὴν
ἐπιθυμίαν – 'because they want what they cannot have' (see 957n.).

952   grandior...senior: there is no difference in meaning.

   hic: the adverb (*hīc*), not infrequent in dialogue or narrative =
'hereupon', 'now'.

953   lamentetur: emphasized by its position astride the main
caesura. To use the word of mourning one's own death implies, not
only a misuse of language, but gross self-pity: Pacuv. 268 R.[3] *conqueri
fortunam aduersam, non lamentari decet.*

955   abhinc = *hinc* 'away'; this local sense seems not to be attested
again before Apuleius, but it is clearly what the context requires: cf.
Plaut. *Poen.* 1035 *maledicta hinc aufer.* The usage may be colloquial: see
next n.

   baratre: various interpretations and corrections have been
suggested. (i) *baratre* = βάραθρε 'one who deserves to be thrown into
a pit', hence 'criminal'. The existence of the Greek word is not
reliably attested before the fifth century A.D. (ii) *barat(h)ro* 'spend-
thrift'; the existence of the word is vouched for only by a scholium on

Hor. *Sat.* 1. 2. 2 (ps.-Acro). (iii) *balatro* 'buffoon', a word attested by Varro, *R.R.* 2. 5. 1, Hor. loc. cit. (iv) *blatero* 'windbag', attested by Gell. 1. 15. 20. Of these possibilities (ii) gives the best sense in the context (cf. 956, 958), but in view of the general uncertainty it seems best to print the text as transmitted and suspend judgement. One thing is clear, that Nature is made to employ a colloquial term of abuse, at home in diatribe-satire but alien to the didactic epos.

956 perfunctus: for the construction + acc. cf. 734, 940nn. and contrast 968.

957 Cf. 1082. The idea behind the verse, that one should take no thought for the morrow, goes back through Epicurus to Democritus; it is the idea that, debased and trivialized, stood for Epicureanism in the eyes of the common man (912–30n.). The expression of the thought by L. recalls that it enjoyed the status of a proverb, which was applied in widely differing literary contexts (Otto 81, s.v. *certus*), especially with a moralizing or satirical emphasis. A common example was the well-worn topic of μεμψιμοιρία, discontent with one's lot (Hense 38; Sen. *Ep.* 74. 12; cf. the Aesopic fable of the dog and the lump of meat, Phaedrus 1. 4). Many instances are collected from diverse sources by E. Norden, *Kl. Schr. z. klass. Altertum* (1966) 42–3; cf. also the passage of Arist. *Rhet.* quoted at 952–62n. In short, this is a commonplace, introduced as such by L. to make a point. The old man's foolish behaviour is first described in popular terms, then (958n.) its Epicurean implications are revealed. As not infrequently, one may in translating put inverted commas round the phrase or add a sardonic gloss: 'but since – as you yourself might put it –...'.

abest...temnis: the verbs are in asyndeton; the apodosis of the *quia*-clause begins at 958.

958 imperfecta...ingrataque: *imperfecta*, because he has not yet begun to live: Sen. *Ep.* 23. 9 (the sentiment attributed to Epicurus) *molestum est semper uitam inchoare...male uiuunt qui semper uiuere incipiunt. ingrata*, because he has neglected or misused his opportunities: 936–7n. The thought behind the argument is probably the Epicurean precept that true pleasure, which consists in the absence of pain, must have a limit (see 5. 1412–35, 945n.). It is because the old man has never grasped this truth that he has yearned for unattainable

pleasures and so has missed the real pleasures that he might have
had.

elapsast: positioned so as to blur the caesura (cf. 174n.), perhaps
with descriptive intent since the effect is to accelerate the verse.

959–60 The imagery is deliberately ambiguous. *satur ac plenus* refer
immediately to *imperfecta* at 958, but also to the idea of life as a banquet
at 938. Thus the *lectus* on which the old man lies is at once dining-
couch and bier; and the one becomes the other before he is aware of
what is happening to him.

959   nec opinanti: the old sense of *nec* = *non* survives in this set
phrase: Hofmann–Szantyr 448–9.

caput: the implication is that the man is already reclining: see
preceding n.

adstitit 'has taken his stand': Death comes for the old man
suddenly and unawares.

960 'Before you can fill yourself with good things and so depart':
the emphasis falls on *satur ac plenus*.

rerum: the (good) things of life, cf. 1004.

962   aequo animoque: 939n.

agedum magnis concede: no completely satisfying correction
has been proposed. The context, esp. 964–5, requires that the old man
accept the necessity of giving place to the coming generations, and
this is most simply expressed by Marullus' *iam aliis*: cf. 965 and
Epictetus 4. 1. 106 δὸς ἄλλοις τόπον 'make room for others'.
Bernays's ⟨g⟩*natis* gives a similar sense, but = 'sons' it is of too limited
application, and for the meaning 'the younger generation' there are
no adequate parallels. Traina's *iam annis* (M. F. Smith, *C.R.* N.S. 16
(1966) 264) is less appropriate in sense to the whole, as opposed to
the immediate, context; Merrill's *age nunc annis* eliminates *agedum*
(an easy correction of MS *agendum*), a lively and colloquial expression – 'come on with you' – which fits the tone of Nature's harangue.
M. L. Clarke's *mage dignis cede* (*C.R.* N.S. 20 (1970) 9–10) is palaeographically neat but the resultant jingle *age...mage* is objectionable,
because pointless. For a list of the numerous other attempts see
Vallot, in *Miscellanea critica*, ed. J. Irmscher II (1965) 365–6. Horace's

adaptation of the passage at *Ep.* 2. 2. 213–16 is too free to serve as a reliable basis for reconstructing L.'s text.

963 iure...agat: cf. 950–51, 971 nn.

inciletque means exactly the same as *increpet*, which it reinforces, slowing down the line and adding dignity to Nature's exit. The word is archaic: Nonius (pp. 180–81 L.) quotes a handful of instances from Lucilius and Republican tragedy.

964–77 Death is necessary so that life may go on. The physical doctrines on which this section is based have been mentioned at 1. 263–4, 2. 71–9; cf. also 5. 828–33. In incorporating the idea into his *consolatio* L. may have broken new ground; he was followed by Seneca (*Ep.* 36. 11) and Plutarch (*Cons. ad Apoll.* 10. 106e). To a man who takes a truly philosophical view of things this fundamental biological principle no doubt ought to be consoling, but it does little to reconcile the ordinary person to his own extinction.

964 rerum nouitate...uetustas = *nouis rebus...uetustae res.*
extrusa: the language is unceremonious.

965 aliis aliud: the variation in number can only be due to metrical convenience; contrast 970.

reparare necesse est 'it is necessary to renew'; the subject is unexpressed, but cf. 967 *materies opus est,* sc. *Naturae.*

966 By saying that nobody is sent down to Tartarus L. kills two birds (if not three) with one stone: he states the dogma that matter cannot be annihilated (cf. 967n.) in terms that bring it home to the individual, who is still being addressed (968–9); he also gets in a hit at popular notions of death (which are implied to be absurdly wasteful) and hints at the subject of his next paragraph.

barathrum nec Tartara...atra 'the black pit of Tartarus', a hendiadys. On the 'terrible sound' of the verse see Friedländer 26 (345), comparing Enn. *Ann.* 140 V.² *at tuba terribili sonitu taratantara dixit.*

967 The atoms which compose a human being are needed for new life and cannot be allowed to run to waste in an abyss. There is a touch of satire here, but Bailey has no business to call the argument 'strange' (1150). That the death and decay of individuals are necessary for the survival of the species has long been a biological commonplace.

materies opus est 'matter is a need', i.e. 'there is need of matter': *materies* is subj., *opus* predicate. Cf. 4. 1268 *nec molles opu' sunt motus*; Plaut. *Capt.* 164 *maritumi omnes milites opu' sunt tibi* (and see W. M. Lindsay *ad loc.*). In classical Latin the normal construction is with abl.; but cf. Kühner–Stegmann 1 388; Hofmann–Szantyr 123–4.

969 L. seems to have conflated two ideas: (i) *ergo omnia saecla cecidere cadentque*, rounding off the argument; (ii) *nec minus quam tu* (sc. *cades*) *priora saecla ante haec cecidere*, corresponding to 968. The expression is awkward: the subject *priora saecla* must be inferred from the context, and *haec* is ambiguous, being taken by some commentators not as suggested here but as the subject of the verbs. For *ante haec* Bailey compared 2. 299 *post haec*, where however an earlier editor emended to *posthac*, as Heinze emended to *antehac* here. The verse-ending *cecidere cadentque* recurs at Hor. *A.P.* 70.

970 **alid** = *aliud*, an archaic form used several times by L. in this phrase. Catullus uses *alid* (29. 15; but the reading is uncertain) and *alis* = *alius* (66. 28); otherwise these forms make no certain appearance in literary texts (Neue–Wagener II 531–2).

971 Another commonplace sentiment. Bion had said (Stob. *Flor.* 4. 41. 56) that the rich enjoy their possessions as a loan from Fortune, not as a gift; and several variations on the idea are cited by the commentators from philosophical and literary sources, as also from gravestones. What is particularly interesting is that L. should have chosen to cast the idea into specifically Roman legal terminology. *mancipium* and *usus* were both terms of art (see A. Berger, *Encyclopedic dictionary of Roman law* (1953), s.vv.); and *mancipium* is a word that forms no part of the vocabulary of poetry. It is a striking fact that Roman poets make much more use than their Greek predecessors of legal imagery and metaphor, particularly in love-poetry (Kenney, 'Ovid and the law', in *Studies in Latin poetry*, *Y.C.S.* 21 (1969) 250–51). L.'s point must have been meant to impress his readers the more forcibly for being formulated in contemporary juridical terms: cf. Sykes Davies 35. Cf. further 950–51, 963; Cic. *Tusc.* 1. 93 (*Natura*) *dedit usuram uitae tamquam pecuniae nulla praestituta die*; *C.L.E.* 183 *usurae uitae sortem morti reddidit* (the syntax is opaque but the image is clear). Cf. 1074 n.

mancipio…usu: predicative datt. Some interpreters take them as abll., but though *mancipio* = 'by *mancipium*' can be defended, *usu* must = '*for* use'; cf. the analogy of *dono dare* (see Hofmann–Szantyr 99). For the form *usu* cf. 5. 101 *oculorum subdere uisu*; naturally it recommended itself to poets on account of its metrical convenience (see Neue–Wagener 1 542; but their list is far from complete).

972–7 By returning (for *respice* may be read in a double sense) to the argument of 830–42 L. signals the end of this section and the appearance of a new topic. The series of rhetorical questions in 976–7 also marks a climax and a pause in the exposition.

972–3 anteacta uetustas temporis aeterni 'the whole immense expanse of past time'; the adjj. are interchangeable to suit the sense (enallage), as is shown by 1. 558 *infinita aetas anteacti temporis omnis*. Cf. 371 n.

973 quam nascimur ante = *antequam nascimur*. The tense shows that *nascimur* refers to all successive generations, not merely this one.

974–5 hoc refers to the idea of past time in 973–4, but as usual the pronoun is attracted into the number and gender of its noun: Kühner–Stegmann 1 34–5.

speculum…exponit 'shows a reflection', not, as the translators have it, 'holds up a mirror', for which *exponere* is inappropriate. For this sense of *speculum* cf. Plaut. *Men.* 1062–3 *quid uides? – speculum tuom.* | – *quid negoti est? – tuast imago.* This interpretation allows *hoc* a clear reference = *anteacta uetustas temporis aeterni*: that is what Nature shows us as the mirror-image of *futurum tempus*, and it is, of course – a blank, a reflection of nothing (cf. 972 *nil ad nos*); this is the paradox and the reason for L.'s choice of image. Naturally there is nothing *horribile* or *triste* (976) to be seen, because there is nothing *at all* to be seen.

976 The verse has two concealed caesuras in virtue of the elisions of *ibi* and *horribile*: 83, 174 nn.

977   omni: Latin can say *omni somno securius* or *securius quam ullus somnus*, but the two constructions are not mixed.

securius: sc. what you see. There is a slight anacoluthon: *securius* must be referred to *speculum* or *futurum tempus*, not to *numquid* or *quicquam*.

978–1023

Hell and its punishments do not exist: it is the passions of our life on earth that are symbolized in these stories. We should have expected L. to treat this subject somewhere in the body of the book, since it bulked large in his prooemium (31–93); in fact he treats it so as to make it parenthetic to the main argument. A denial of the torments of hell is appropriate to a *consolatio*, and we find Seneca employing it in his *Consolatio ad Marciam*: *cogita nullis defunctum malis adfici, illa, quae nobis inferos faciunt terribiles, fabulas esse*, etc. (19. 4). It was indeed so much of a commonplace that Seneca elsewhere calls it 'the old Epicurean tune', *Epicurea cantilena* (*Ep.* 24. 18), dismissing it as unworthy of discussion. It is indeed difficult to believe that the educated public of L.'s day took these legends seriously, whatever the common man may have thought; but L. is not primarily concerned to rebut these fears (cf. Introd. 4–5), and he passes straight to his allegorical interpretations. Allegorization of myth was not exclusively Epicurean (Norden, op. cit. (957 n.) 66–9); for its occurrence in the diatribe see below, 980–83 n., and for the idea behind this particular passage cf. Philo, *De Congr. Erud. Gr.* 57 (cit. Boyancé 180 n. 4), stating that 'the true Hades is the life of the wicked man'. L.'s explanations are relevant in general terms to his declared intention of enlightening mankind and freeing them from superstition (3. 14–27), but seem somewhat out of place in the context of a *consolatio*; comparison of content and tone of this paragraph with what precedes will make this point clear. That is not to say that the passage does not belong here: 976–7 (*horribile...triste*) are clearly designed both to round off their own section and to provide a transition to the topic of Hades. No comparable transition, however, is provided at 1023.

980–83 (1) Tantalus. L. refers to a form of the legend in which T. was punished for stealing the nectar and ambrosia of the gods by having a large stone suspended over him, for fear of which he dared not eat or drink (Pind. *Ol.* 1. 55–64). Cicero explains this story as symbolizing irrational fears in general: *omnibus enim, quorum mens abhorret a ratione, semper aliqui talis terror impendet* (*Tusc.* 4. 35; cf. *De Fin.* 1. 60); and it is the version referred to by Virg. *A.* 6. 602–3. L.'s more specific application to the fear of the gods may be original to him (Plut. *De Superstit.* 11 is not really parallel); certainly it exploits etymology in a characteristic way. West (98) has remarked that the rock hanging over Tantalus recalls the appearance of *religio* at the beginning of Book 1 as a monster *standing over* (*super instans* ∼ *superstitio*) grovelling mankind: 1. 65 *horribili super aspectu mortalibus instans*; and this is clearly the point here too: *religio = superstitio = diuum metus*.

The better-known version represented in the *Odyssey* (11. 582–92) and frequently referred to in later poetry has T. standing in a pool of water which receded whenever he tried to drink and surrounded by fruit trees which withdrew whenever he tried to eat. This version was allegorized by Teles (Hense 34–5) as typifying the avarice which cannot profit from its possessions: cf. Oltramare 54 n. 3; Hor. *Sat.* 1. 1. 68–9 *Tantalus a labris sitiens fugientia captat | flumina*, etc.

980 nec looks forward to 984.

981 cassa formidine looks forward to *metus inanis* in the next verse: man's fear of the gods is as unnecessary as T.'s fear of the stone – and he after all never existed.

983 casum = both '(mis)chance' and 'fall', the latter referring to the stone.

ferat fors: the phrase plays on the real or fancied connexion of the two words: cf. Enn. *Ann.* 197 V.² *quidue ferat fors*; Lucret. 3. 44 *fert... forte*.

984–94 (2) Tityos. He was a Giant, son of Earth, who for the attempted rape of Leto was sentenced to have his liver perpetually devoured by vultures as he lay stretched upon the ground (Hom. *Od.* 11. 576–81). L.'s choice of love as the irrational desire, κενὴ ἐπιθυμία, *par excellence* is not necessarily dictated by the nature of T.'s crime, for this is not relevant to his other allegories (see 995–1002 n.). At Hor. *C.* 3. 4. 77 T. is called *incontinens*, not so much 'lustful' as 'immoderate'.

984   uolucres: traditionally vultures, but L. refrains from specifying and uses a word which by its ambiguous grammatical status as noun or adj. paves the way to his allegorical interpretation (see 992–4 n.). For such interaction between 'protasis' and 'apodosis' of the allegory cf. 1002, 1008 nn.

985   magno 'great though it is'; L. expands on the idea in 987–91.

986   perpetuam aetatem belongs in sense to the *quod*-clause.

987 'However huge the extent of his prostrate body': for *proiectu* cf. 882.

quamlibet qualifies *immani* closely: the construction is equivalent to *sit* (cf. 97 n.) *quamlibet immani corporis proiectu*. Neither here nor in the single parallel known to the commentators (Quint. *Inst.* 1. 1. 18) can *quamlibet* be properly said to 'take' the subjunctive; the concessive force of the clause resides primarily in the jussive use of the verb = 'let him be', as at 2. 541–2 *quamlibet esto | unica res = esto res quamlibet unica*. The normal use of *quamlibet* in classical Latin is as an adverb qualifying concessively an adj. or participle, as at e.g. 5. 1116 *quamlibet et fortes et pulchro corpore creti* (Hofmann–Szantyr 604); whereas *quamuis*, originally also an adverb, was freely used as a conjunction (+subj.) on the analogy of *quamquam* (ibid. 603–4).

988–9   qui...qui: consecutive, 'be he such as to...', 'though he'; the anaphora lends emphasis to the irony.

988   nouem...iugera: the usual rendering 'acre' is not an exact translation of *iugerum*, any more than *iugerum* is of πέλεθρον (Hom. *Od.* 11. 577), but the point is in any case a rhetorical one.

dispessis: *dispando*, not *dispergo*, gives the required sense; few confusions are commoner in MSS than that of *sparsus* and *passus*.

989–91 L.'s sarcasm does not obscure a solid rational argument: the story violates the laws of nature.

992–4 The allegorical correspondence is close. L. begins by picking up *iacentem* from 984; *in amore iacentem* implies that the lover, like T., is *fettered* by his passion, but the image behind the phrase is a complex one. There is first the idea of the traditional inactivity of the lover (cf. *Il. Lat.* 265 *dum iaceas in amore tuo, nos bella geremus*, etc., cit.

Fletcher 887); but also, and more important, the conventional picture of the lover tossing and turning on his lonely bed while he bemoans the absence of the beloved or the hopelessness of his passion (Theoc. 2. 86; Meleager, *A.P.* 5. 166, 215, etc.; Ov. *Am.* 1. 2, etc.) or, alternatively, encamped on the beloved's doorstep (Meleager, *A.P.* 12. 72; Asclepiades, *A.P.* 5. 189, etc.; and, of course, L. himself, 4. 1177–9; cf. F. O. Copley, *Exclusus amator* (1956), passim). The *uolucres* of 993, which have troubled interpreters a good deal, may be explained as a scornful reference, exploiting the ambiguity of the word (both 'birds' and, more generally, 'winged things'), to the Erotes, Lat. *Cupidines*, 'Loves'. 'The plurality of the Cupids is abundantly attested' (A. S. Pease on Cic. *N.D.* 3. 60, citing many passages from Aeschylus onwards); in their prettified Hellenistic form, equipped with all the conventional attributes (see T. B. L. Webster, *Hellenistic poetry and art* (1964), passim), they flit in and out of the love epigrams of Meleager's *Garland*, where their function is that of tormenting the lover in various ways for which *lacerare* (993) is scarcely too strong a word: cf. Meleager, *A.P.* 5. 212, 139, 12. 126; Asclepiades, *A.P.* 12. 46, 166; Posidippus, *A.P.* 12. 45, al. For a closer parallel with *lacerant* cf. Theoc. 13. 71 χαλεπὸς γὰρ ἔσω θεὸς ἧπαρ ἄμυσσεν 'a cruel god was rending his heart (lit. liver) within him'; and for a combination of motifs which suggests that another poet before L. had applied the Tityos-image to the plight of the lover see the anonymous epigram at *A.P.* 12. 160 (assigned to the *Garland* by A. S. F. Gow and D. L. Page, *The Greek Anthology*: *Hellenistic Epigrams* II (1965) 559–61): 1–2 θαρσα-λέως τρηχεῖαν ὑπὸ σπλάγχνοισιν ἀνίην | οἴσω καὶ χαλεπῆς δεσμὸν ἀλυκτοπέδης (3776–7 G.–P.), 'stoutly shall I bear the harsh pain in my vitals and the bond of the cruel fetters'. Cf. also 994 n. for another possible allusion to the idea; and for this type of allusion in L. see Kenney, passim. The verses must be read with an ironical inflexion and the aid of inverted commas: 'the real Tityos is the man who "lies" (sc. as they say) lovelorn and is torn by (those) "winged creatures" (sc. of the poet's fantasy) . . .'. (For a fuller interpretation see *P.C.P.S.* n.s. 16 (1970) 44–7.)

992   hic: probably the pronoun (*hĭc*): 'our T. is this man here, whom...', cf. 4. 1058 *haec Venus est nobis*; but the adverb (*hīc*) = *in uita* (cf. 995) would be almost equally pointed. Cf. 1023.

993 'Torn by winged creatures and eaten away by distressful anguish'; *anxius angor* provides a transition to the more generalized allegory in which T.'s vultures are equated with *curae* in general (but see next n.). The verse seems to have impressed Cicero: *Tusc.* 3. 27 *aegritudo . . . lacerat exest animum planeque conficit.*

994   cuppedine = *cupidine*: cf. 504 n. It is possible that L. is still playing with words and that the phrase *alia quauis . . . cuppedine* = 'another kind of (winged) *Cupido*'; in Book IV there is a famous play on the use of *Cupido* as the proper name of the god of love, 4. 1058 *hinc autemst nomen amoris*; and such etymologizing is, as we have seen, characteristic of L. and of much ancient poetry. It would not have been asking too much of his readers to expect them to take the point: *scindunt* shows that the underlying image has not been lost sight of. In any case *curae* must be understood of irrational desires in general.

995–1002   (3) Sisyphus. S. was condemned to roll a large stone up a hill but never to reach the top (Hom. *Od.* 11. 593–600). It was clearly his punishment and not his crime (about which the ancient authorities disagree) which led L. to present him as a special type of *auaritia*, political ambition: cf. 59–64. Avoidance of politics and public life was an Epicurean tenet, dealt with by L. at 5. 1120–35, and touched on in the prooemium to Book II, where we encounter an image of struggle and ascent which clearly foreshadows the Sisyphus-allegory: 12–13 *noctes atque dies niti praestante labore | ad summas emergere opes rerumque potiri.* As with Tantalus (see 980–83 n.) L.'s treatment of the legend may be original to hin; it seems not to be precisely exemplified elsewhere (cf. Phaedrus, *App.* 5. 3–6; Macrob. *Comm.* 1. 10. 15).

996–7   petere . . . imbibit: cf. 6. 72 *ut ex ira poenas petere imbibat* [sc. *deum uis*] *acris.* The sense of *imbibit* is 'forms a deep desire to seek' rather than 'seeks open-mouthed' (Bailey). *petere* and *recedit* are both technical terms of political life (West 100–2); cf. 1002 n.

996   saeuas: a stock conventional epithet but also a recognition of historical fact: on the 'legal murder' of the proscriptions see R. Syme, *The Roman revolution* (1956) 187–201.

998   For the false idea that power confers security cf. 59–86 n. *nec datur umquam* means that the *imperium* that men promise themselves is illusory and unobtainable: at 2. 53 L. has said that the power over *metus hominum curaeque sequaces* belongs to reason alone: *quid dubitas quin omni' sit haec rationi' potestas?*

999   **in eo:** sc. *in petendo.*

1000–2   Highly pictorial writing: the heavy spondees in 1000 for the slow and toilsome ascent; the first-foot spondaic word in 1001 for the momentary pause at the summit; the predominantly dactylic 1001–2 for the headlong descent. Comparison with the famous Homeric prototype shows that L. has (i) treated the whole episode descriptively, employing phonetic and alliterative effects foreign to Greek, whereas Homer's verse makes no attempt to reproduce S.'s *upward* progress; (ii) exercised more restraint than Homer in describing the descent of the stone: Homer's line has (*a*) the maximum five dactyls, (*b*) three 'feminine' caesuras, to give an effect at once swift and bouncing: αὖτις ἔπειτα πέδονδε κυλίνδετο λᾶας ἀναιδής, 'once more down to the flat trundled the stone in its shamelessness'.

1000   **aduerso...monte** 'up the hill'.

   nixantem 'with great effort'; the frequentative form of *nitor* may well have been invented by L.

1002   **plani...petit aequora campi:** a play on words: 'in electoral terms the candidate goes down to the Campus Martius to stand for election again, *descendat in Campum petitor* [= Hor. *C.* 3. 1. 11]' (West 102).

1003–10   (4) The Danaids. For the murder of their husbands they were condemned to draw water for ever in leaking vessels (or sieves); they do not figure in Homer's Underworld, but the story was famous (Hor. *C.* 3. 11, Ov. *Her.* 14). In using the Danaids as a type of ingratitude L. is harking back to Nature's reproach to the old man at 955–63; he is also giving a twist to the argument. His first three examples suggest that the legendary punishments of Hell really refer to suffering (self-inflicted) in this life: *diuum metus* (982), *curae* (994), *durus labor* (999). An inability to be satisfied, ἀπληστία, is a different matter, and the Danaids must be taken as a type of behaviour rather than of suffering: cf. 1005, 1008nn. It is suggested by Heinze that this is L.'s reason for not naming them, but it is a curious fact that they are not named by Plato in the *Gorgias* (493 a–d), where the allegory of the leaky jar first occurs, though they are clearly alluded to. In Polygnotus' famous fresco (Pausan. 10. 31. 9) the two unnamed young women drawing water in broken pots were identified as the un-initiated. Cf. Cousin, 'Lucrèce, les verseuses et la Vita stultorum...', *Mélanges...offerts à A. Ernout* (1940), 97–106.

1003 animi ingratam naturam = *ingratum animum*: cf. 130–31 n.

1004 explere...satiareque are synonymous (cf. 1007 *explemur*) and are both governed by *numquam*, which is placed at the end of the verse to answer *semper* in 1003.
    satiareque: 163 n.

1005–6 quod faciunt nobis 'as the seasons of the year do for us' (Munro, Bailey) not 'as is the case with' (M. F. Smith) or 'the fate we suffer' (Latham). The inff. *pascere, explere, satiare* refer naturally to the seasons, who are the providers of good things. It is worth re-marking that the 'grammatical' punctuation of 1005 as printed would have puzzled an ancient reader, who would have punctuated 'rhetorically': *quod faciunt nobis* ‖ *annorum tempora circum* ‖ *cum redeunt...*; *annorum tempora* belongs in sense quite as much to the *cum*-clause as to the *quod*-clause.

1006 ferunt = *referunt*: 261 n.

1008–9 hoc...id est...quod memorant: cf. 754, 933 nn., but the writing here borders on the inelegant.

1008 aeuo florente puellas: one of the two women in Polygnotus' picture (1003–10 n.) was represented as beautiful, ἔτι ὡραία τὸ εἶδος, but the detail is not in itself particularly appropriate to the Danaids. L. brings it in to cement the allegory by identifying them with the Seasons, ῟Ωραι, who were represented as beautiful women: cf. ὡραῖος = 'beautiful'.

1009 pertusum...in uas: cf. 936. L. presumably has in mind that passage of Plato's *Gorgias* (493 b) in which the part of the soul in which the desires are is compared to a jar with a hole in it, τετρημένος πίθος: it is insatiability, ἀπληστία, not wasted labour, that is exemplified.

**1010	potestur:** pass. with *expleri*, cf. 1. 1045 *suppleri...queatur*; the construction is normal in classical Latin with e.g. *coepi* + pass. inf. (Hofmann–Szantyr 288). The form *potestur* (also at Enn. *Ann.* 611 V.²) is possibly by analogy with *ēstur* from *ědo* 'eat'.

Servius' note on Virg. *A.* 6. 596 refers to L.'s allegorical explanation of the fates of Tityos, Tantalus and Sisyphus (in that order); he then adds *per rotam autem ostendit negotiatores, qui semper tempestatibus turbinibusque uoluuntur*. From this it has been inferred that in the copy of L. used by Servius (or his source) mention was made of Ixion and that there is a lacuna in our existing text. Ixion of course figured in the standard catalogue of notable sufferers: he is in Virgil's Hell (*A.* 6. 601) and is enumerated by Seneca (*Ep.* 24. 18) along with Sisyphus and Tityos (but not Tantalus), followed by *Cerberum...et tenebras*, etc. However, if L. had allegorized Ixion, he would not have been likely to interpret him as the type of the *negotiator*, who would represent merely a particular case of the *curae* dealt with at 984–94. As a type of ambition (Dio Chrysost. 4. 123) Ixion would have duplicated Sisyphus; as a type of those who act without *consilium, ratio* or *uirtus* (Macrob. *Comm.* 1. 10. 14) he would have lacked definition. Moreover he is not represented in the *Odyssey*, as all L.'s three *sinners* (not the Danaids) are. The fact that Ixion comes last (and is not named) in Servius' list may indicate that he is an intruder who really belongs in a note on *A.* 6. 601 (where serious difficulties of interpretation exist) and has been transferred by Servius or his source to follow the Lucretian list. In any case, no hypothesis of a lacuna containing Ixion avails to explain the difficulties of 1011–13 (see n.). If L. did include him, his proper place was *before* the Danaids, e.g. after 1002.

1011–23	The terrors of Hell are equated with the pangs of conscience. This is a general application of the principle enunciated at 978–9, to which we are brought back, in the familiar cyclic movement, by the words *Acherusia...uita* at 1023. The idea was as old as Democritus (69 B 297 DK).

1011–13	The sentence contains one major and two minor causes of offence: (i) it lacks a main verb; (ii) the asyndeton between 1011 and 1012 is surprising when the list is so short; (iii) L.'s usual rule would require *quae*, not *qui*, in 1013 (136n.). Difficulty (ii) was eliminated by the early correction of *egestas* to *egenus*, but other similar asyndeta are found elsewhere in L. and the word *egenus* is not. Marullus' *haec* for *qui* in 1013 gives easy sense and syntax (for resumptive *haec* after a list cf. 1. 458), but the corruption is not particularly easy to account for. Munro's postulated lacuna after 1011 would allow *qui* to refer specifically to *aestus*, but his suggestion that the lacuna contained, inter al., Ixion, we have seen to be improbable (1010 n.). Bailey's alternative lacuna after 1012, containing the sense 'are similarly told of by poets', gives no satisfactory reference for *qui*. Bailey later withdrew the suggestion, pointing to anacolutha like this one at e.g. 2. 342–8, 4. 123–8. The gender of *qui* remains as a slight difficulty, but on the whole it seems prudent, having registered misgivings, to allow the transmitted text to stand.

1011   iam uero 'and as for...'.

1012   The description would suit either a volcano belching fire or a cave exhaling noxious vapours: the ambiguity, and the inflated epicizing vocabulary, are no doubt designed to ridicule the vagueness and confusion of the underworld geography and popular superstitions in general. Tartarus appears to be figured as a monster, like Enceladus buried under Aetna (Virg. *A*. 3. 578–82).

1013   sùnt...pòssunt '*are* not and *can*not be'.

1014–17   The guilty mind creates for itself an image of punishments after death like those seen in life. The order of words in 1014–15 is manipulated in order to juxtapose *insignibus insignis* and to position *est* emphatically: 'But there *does* exist here on earth a fear of punishment, proportioned to a man's misdeeds, and there *does* exist expiation of crime – prisons...', etc. The gruesome inventory of Roman inhumanity to man that follows has its point also: it is the frightful particularity of what he can *see* that stimulates the guilty man to invent corresponding torments in the hereafter, even though here and now he escapes the consequences of his wrongdoing. (See p. 244.)

1015   luella 'expiation', hence 'punishment': the word occurs nowhere else. The MSS give *luela*; the correct orthography was restored by Lachmann.

1016   carcer: perhaps to be written *Carcer* as alluding to the State prison near the Forum; the list is throughout specifically Roman.

saxo: the Tarpeian Rock.

iactu' deorsum: Lambinus' conjecture is further from the MS reading than Heinsius' *iactu' reorum*, but gives much better sense. Mention of 'criminals' is not wanted in connexion with any one punishment, and the word *reus* occurs nowhere else in L.

1017   robur: probably, in view of the context, an instrument of torture, though the word is used nowhere else in such a sense: the *eculeus*, a sort of rack, has been suggested. The well-attested sense of 'dungeon', specifically the *Tullianum*, an apartment of the State prison, seems feeble after *carcer*.

pix lammina taedae: pitch, metal plates, torches, indicating various forms of torture by fire.

1018   facti: the usual construction of *sibi conscius* is with the genitive; for the dat. of the MSS, retained by all modern editors, there is no parallel, for 6. 393 *nulla sibi turpi conscius in re*, though itself an unusual construction, does not support *factis* here. The error was due to *factis* at 1014 ('Perseverationsfehler': cf. Reynolds and Wilson 159–60). With this verse and the next compare Juv. 13. 192–5 *cur tamen hos tu | euasisse putes, quos diri conscia facti | mens habet attonitos et surdo uerbere caedit | occultum quatiente animo tortore flagellum?*

1019   adhibet stimulos: sc. *sibi*. *stimulos* (for which cf. also 874) further develops the torture-image: the goad and the lash were the instruments of servile discipline, as frequent references in comedy remind us.

torretque flagellis: sc. *se*. The usual verb is *urere*: if the text is right L. has deliberately varied it, perhaps on the grounds of euphony. Lachmann's *terret* gives inappropriate sense, for the mind as L. portrays it is actually tormenting itself, not threatening to do so. Heinsius' *torquet* in the general sense 'torment' entails straining the language, for in this context it is the special sense 'rack' that would spring to mind, and that of course is at odds with *flagellis* (but cf. the passage of Juvenal quoted in the preceding n.).

1020   nec uidet interea 'and all the time it is unaware'.

1020–21   terminus...finis: i.e. death.

1023   Acherusia...uita 'death in life', a contradiction in terms to drive home the point. The phrase returns us to the point of departure in 978.

stultorum: the philosophically unqualified, Greek ἄφρονες, opp. to *sapientes*, σοφοί. This terminology was common to Epicureans and Stoics alike: when L. varies it at 1. 641, calling the Stoics *stolidi*, it is probably for the sake of the pun.

1024–1052

Even the good and the great have died. This is an expansion in rhetorical terms of what was said at 964–9. L. now returns to the sequence of the *consolatio*, as is indicated by the form of the section, a harangue placed by a fresh variation in the mouth of the imaginary and typical individual to whom the consolation is directed. The argument is none the less effective because it is hackneyed; indeed it is because it is hackneyed that it is effective: as Lattimore remarks, 'it is the consolation *par excellence* not only of classical but of modern times, representing as it does the ultimate if meagre solace which not even despair of immortality can take away' (250–51). (It is a variant or special case of the general consolatory commonplace 'non tibi hoc soli': Cic. *Tusc.* 3. 79; cf. Otto 328.) The examples quoted by Lattimore range over a wide field of literary and epigraphical texts and show the familiarity of the idea at all periods; see also Lavagnini, *Athenaeum* 25 (1947) 83–8; Nisbet and Hubbard on Hor. *C.* 1. 28. 7. The use of historical and mythological *exempla* was worked to death in the rhetoric of the schools (E. Norden, *Die antike Kunstprosa*[5] (1958) 276), but its power persisted, as can be seen from the poem that is most directly comparable with this passage of L., the Tenth Satire of Juvenal.

L.'s list is carefully selected and graded to exemplify particular attributes and to achieve a climax: Ancus = virtue, Xerxes = regal power, Scipio Africanus = military glory, Homer = literary genius, Democritus > Epicurus = wisdom. The key to the argument is the contrast between Epicurus, named here only in the entire poem, and the anonymous *tu* (1045): the procedure is entirely emotional and suggestive. Cf. Schrijvers 231–4. (See the stylistic analysis of this section, Introd. 27–8.)

1024 tibi tute: the suffix *-tĕ*, like *-met* and *-pte*, adds emphasis.

L. uses the phrase several times elsewhere; here it has an Ennian flavour (cf. next n.).

1025 Quoted from Enn. *Ann.* 149 V.[2] *postquam lumina sis oculis bonus Ancu' reliquit. sis* = *suis*; in spite of Festus (p. 387 L.) it seems best to take *sis oculis* as abl. not dat., 'has left the light with his eyes'. For the Romans Ancus was always the archetypal 'good king'. This introductory use of a quotation is quite in the manner of the diatribe: 'You know, of course, Ennius' famous line about Ancus; well, he is not the only great ruler who has died...'. Cf. 1034–5 n.

1026–35 The lofty phrasing throughout these verses, reinforced by alliteration, assonance, and the repetition of keywords (*multis, multi, magnis, magnum*) contrasts the deeds of these men with the insignificance of the complainant, *tu.*

1026　improbe 'shameless fellow'; the contrast with *bonus* underlines the man's presumption in somehow expecting not to have to share the common fate of all mankind. The phrasing and the sentiment recall, and are no doubt intended to recall, Homer, *Il.* 21. 107 (Achilles to Lycaon, before slaying him): 'even Patroclus is dead, a better man by far than you', κάτθανε καὶ Πάτροκλος, ὅ περ σέο πολλὸν ἀμείνων.

1027　inde 'since then'.

1028　occidērunt: 86 n.
　　imperitarunt: for the frequentative form cf. 352 n. The verse has an Ennian ring, but the 'framing' of it by the two verbs is Lucretian.

1029　ille: Xerxes, who built a bridge of boats across the Hellespont; not to name him emphasizes the uniqueness of his feat. Plutarch (*Cons. ad Apoll.* 15. 110d) quotes some verses from an unnamed poet which L. may well have had in mind; cf. also the last stanza of the *Aulodiae* in P. Oxy. xv. 1795 (= *Coll. Alexandrina*, ed. J. U. Powell (1925) 200).

1030　strauit 'calmed and paved', 'laid a smooth road', with a play on the senses of *sterno* (cf. *strata uiarum* at 1. 315, 4. 415).
　　iter: internal acc. after *ire* rather than direct object of *dedit*, which = *permisit.*

1031–2   An expansion of *legionibus*: not only the infantry but even the cavalry passed over.

1031   salsas...lacunas 'salt lakes', a mock-heroic periphrasis for the sea; we find the Auctor *Ad Herennium* objecting (4. 10. 15) to *Neptuniae lacunae*. L. repeats the phrase at 5. 794. The spelling *lucunas* is also offered by the MSS at 6. 538, 552; it may be merely a casual deviation which should not be ascribed to L.

super ire: in spite of the apparently inartistic repetition it is better to keep the reading of the MSS. The easy correction *superare* cannot justly be called 'weaker' (Bailey), but the word does not occur elsewhere in L. = 'pass over'.

1032   insultans: both 'prancing' and 'insulting'.

1033   lumine adempto ~ 1025. For the rhythm cf. 887 n.

1034   Scipiadas: a hybrid patronymic like *Memmiadae* (dat.) = 'the scion of the Memmii' at 1. 26. The nom. form is attested by Lucilius 1139 M. It is probably P. Cornelius Scipio Africanus Major who is meant rather than the younger Africanus: it was the Second Punic War and the invasions of Spain and Italy that constituted the supreme crisis for Roman power in the Mediterranean (cf. 833–7).

fulmen 'thunderbolt', but also 'stay' or 'support', with a Greek pun (σκηπτός = *fulmen*, σκῆπτρον = *scipio*) on the family name. Cf. Munro's note, and for the source of the idea in Ennius see O. Skutsch, *S.I.F.C.* 27–8 (1956) 536–40 = *Studia Enniana* (1968) 145–50.

1035   Compare Enn. *Ann.* 312–13 V.[2] *mortalem summum Fortuna repente | reddidit e summo regno ut famul infimus esset* (*infimus* Lipsius: *ultimus* T. Faber: *oltimus* W. M. Lindsay: *famul ut optimus* MS). *famul* for *famulus* is found nowhere else and seems to have been an arbitrary abbreviation by Ennius, suggested perhaps by Oscan *famel*; for Ennius spoke Oscan as well as Greek and Latin (Gell. 17. 17. 1). The allusion would have been immediately taken by a Roman reader. L. has transferred the thought from one commonplace, the mutability of human affairs (the *locus de Fortuna*) to another.

1036   repertores: great kudos attached to the status of inventor, πρῶτος εὑρετής. L. mentions philosophers and artists; he significantly makes no reference to the 'culture-heroes' who are prominent in Greek mythology. In Book v the invention of fire, for instance, is ascribed, not to the intervention of Prometheus, but to man's observation of natural phenomena (1091–1104); and in his summary of other cultural achievements (1447–57) he emphasizes that this was a slow and gradual process made up of many small steps.

leporum 'graceful arts' (Munro); the word takes this special colour (cf. e.g. 1006) as complementing *doctrinarum*. For its application to poetry cf. 1. 28 *aeternum da dictis, diua, leporem*, 934 *musaeo contingens cuncta lepore*.

1037 Heliconiadum comites: in the prooemium to Book 1 L. allusively but unambiguously rejected the traditional idea that he was a retainer of the Muses (Kenney 375–7). On the other hand he uses the traditional language without embarrassment when he speaks of his poem as *carmen Pierium* (1. 946 = 4. 21), and no sarcasm is necessarily intended here. We may however be justified in reading into this rather grandiloquent phrase, with its clear echo of Hesiod (*Theog.* 1 Μουσάων Ἑλικωνιάδων, 100 Μουσάων [θεράπων, 'servant of the Muses') the implication 'for all that they claim a special relationship with divinity, poets die like other men'.

unus 'alone', i.e. apart from and beyond all others.

1038 sceptra potitus 'though he achieved supremacy'; cf. 119n. For the acc. after *potior*, usual in L. (contrast however 1027, 2. 13, 2. 50), cf. 734n.

aliis = *ceteris* 'the rest'. For the condensed or compendious construction with *idem* cf. 4. 1174 *eadem facit...omnia turpi* 'she does all the same things as an ugly woman (does)', Hor. *A.P.* 467 *idem facit occidenti* 'does the same as a murderer (does)'. For the straightforward dat. cf. 2. 919 *animalia (sunt) mortalibus una eademque* 'living things are exactly the same as mortal things', i.e. are mortal because living. The rhythm of the verse is unusual, with two false verse-endings at the second and third diaereses: cf. 887, 893 nn.

1039 Democritum: treated with respect as the inventor of the atomic theory, therefore the *repertor doctrinae* par excellence. Cf. 371 n.

matura uetustas: according to one account he was 109.

1040 memores motus 'movements of memory', part of the *sensiferi motus*; Democritus' failing is described in the atomic terminology, emphasized by alliteration: he was fully aware of what was happening to him, and why.

1041   sponte sua: according to Athenaeus (2. 46 e) by refusing food, a classic method of self-ending (Sen. *Ep.* 77. 5–9); cf. D.L. 9. 43. L. is our oldest authority for Democritus' suicide, which allows him to draw an implicit contrast with the reluctance of the *stultus*, but it does not follow either that he invented the story or that he cited it because he was himself attracted by the idea of suicide: cf. Introd. 6–7, 943 n.

caput...obtulit: a more vivid version, as Heinze remarked, of the common *morti se offerre*: 'Death seems to be personified in the form of an executioner' (Smith).

1042   Epicurus: the only place in the poem where his name is mentioned. Possibly L. breaks his rule to make his point as starkly as possible: *ipse Epicurus obit* is direct writing.

obît = *obiit*; cf. 502 *redîtque.*

decurso lumine 'when his daylit race was run' (Latham), a remarkable 'mixed' metaphor. *decurrere aetatis/uitae spatium* is common enough; L.'s variation prepares us for the image of 1044.

1043   Cf. 15 *diuina mente.* For the metre cf. 174 n.

1044   A well-known epigram by Leonidas of Tarentum (*A.P.* 9. 24 = 2147–50 G.–P.) had applied this conceit to Homer, and there is reason to believe that L. had read the poets of Meleager's *Garland* (Kenney 381–8). In transferring the idea to Epicurus there may be some criticism of their values. Similar comparisons were at home in the tradition of panegyric: E. Doblhofer, *Die Augustuspanegyrik des Horaz...* (1966) 86–91; Nisbet and Hubbard on Hor. *C.* 1. 12. 47, 48. The use by L. of terminology also accounted appropriate to the deified rulers of the Hellenistic world might be interpreted as a reminder that Epicurus was the only true Deliverer, σωτήρ. For the recurrence of images of light and illumination in L. cf. 1 n.

aetherius sol: the ending occurs four times in Book v. The use of *sol* in this position is Ennian: *Ann.* 92 V.[2] *simul aureus exoritur sol*; in later poets it becomes something of a cliché.

1045–52   Who then are you to complain about dying – especially when you are to all intents and purposes dead already? The paradox was (and is) common; by using it to insist on the difference between (Epicurean) reality and the illusions of the *stultus* L. provides a transition to the next topic. There is a carefully contrived progression: sleep > daydreaming > empty fears > mental confusion.

1045 Again the phrasing recalls Achilles' address to Lycaon (Hom. *Il.* 21. 106): 'Come, my friend, you must die too; why do you grieve so?', ἀλλά, φίλος, θάνε καὶ σύ· τίη ὀλοφύρεαι οὕτως;

1046 **mortua...uita:** cf. Sall. *Cat.* 2. 8 *sed multi mortales, dediti uentri atque somno, indocti incultique uitam sicuti peregrinantes transiere. quibus profecto contra naturam corpus uoluptati, anima oneri fuit. eorum ego uitam mortemque iuxta aestumo, quoniam de utraque siletur*; Sen. *Ep.* 77. 18 *mortem times: at quomodo illam media boletatione contemnis! uiuere uis: scis enim? mori times: quid porro? ista uita non mors est?*; St Paul, 1 Tim. 5. 6 'But she that liveth in pleasure is dead while she liveth'.

   prope: take with *mortua*.

   iam uiuo atque uidenti 'while you are still alive and kicking': the effect of scorn is increased by the fact that the phrase was a cliché; cf. Cic. *Sest.* 59 *uiuus ut aiunt...et uidens.*

1047 **conteris** 'use up', generally, as here, in a bad sense, 'waste'.

1048 **uigilans stertis** is L.'s vivid variation on the usual *uigilans somniare* 'daydream': cf. Ter. *Eun.* 1079 *fatuos est, insulsu' tardu', stertit noctes et dies.*

   somnia: so in the prooemium to Book 1 (104–6) the idle tales (*somnia*) concocted by priests and seers (*uates*) are said to be able to ruin the life of reason.

1049 **geris** = *habes.*

1050 = *et saepe reperire non potes quid mali tibi sit.*

1050–52 **cum...urgeris...uagaris:** the temporal sense predominates: 'and all the time (what is wrong with you is that) you are the victim of causeless fears and of error'.

1051 **ebrius urgeris...undique:** the section, having begun with an image of torpor, ends in one of confusion (cf. 1045–52 n.), which is developed in the next verse by the accumulation of no fewer than four words connoting uncertainty. *ebrius* is elsewhere used of people who are a prey to their emotions (love, elation, etc.), but to speak of someone's being 'drunk' with cares and distractions is more daring. In *urgeris...undique* we have the further suggestion that the man is hemmed in and jostled by a crowd.

1052   animi: Lambinus' correction imparts order and elegance to what would otherwise be an uncouth arrangement of words; *animo* is due to anticipation of *incerto* (cf. Reynolds and Wilson 159). Bentley's *incertus* (construed with *animo*, which is retained) leaves *errore* less well supported.

1053–1075

Men are unhappy and restless because they do not understand the cause of their troubles. The only remedy for this ignorance is philosophy. Epicurus, as we have seen (40n.), taught that a correct understanding of nature was essential to happiness. The restlessness so vividly described in this passage is the exact converse of the freedom from disturbance, ἀταραξία, which it was the aim of the Epicurean system to attain; and high among the causes of 'disturbance' must rank the fear of death. At 58–98 it was argued that disturbing and destructive emotions such as ambition and avarice are due ultimately to the fear of death; and it might be concluded that that fear and the discontent now depicted are in fact one and the same thing (cf. 957n.). L. himself does not make this identification explicitly, but it may be suggested that he does so implicitly in 1054 by the *pondus*-image, in which both ideas are merged. However, the vividness and particularity of the illustration suggests that the influence of the diatribe here too predominates over Epicurean doctrine: for discontent with one's lot, μεμψιμοιρία, as a commonplace of popular philosophy see E. Fraenkel, *Horace* (1957) 92–4; N. Rudd, *The Satires of Horace* (1966) 20–22; Nisbet and Hubbard on Hor. *C.* 1. 1. 17. The adaptations of this passage by Horace and Seneca (1068–9n.) show that it made a strong impression.

1053   sentire uidentur 'one can see clearly that they feel'; *sentire* is contrasted with *noscere* in 1055.

1056   mali tamquam moles 'weight of woe', as we should say.

The figurative use of *moles* is fairly common, and it is not clear why L. should excuse it with *tamquam*; cf. 1054 *pondus inesse animo*.

1057-9 'They would not behave as we see they do, that is not knowing...': the construction, though slightly informal, is neither awkward nor irregular; *nescire* and *quaerere* are grammatically dependent on *uidemus*, but in sense they expand *agerent*.

1058 quid sibi quisque uelit nescire 'doesn't know what to do with himself'. The phrase and what follows are reminiscent of the Soldiers' Chorus in Ennius' *Iphigenia, Sc.* 234-41 V.[2] (195-202 Jocelyn):

> otio qui nescit uti
> plus negoti habet quam cum est negotium in negotio.
> nam cui quod agat institutumst non ullo negotio
> id agit, id studet, ibi mentem atque animum delectat suum.
> otioso in otio animus nescit quid uelit.
> hoc idem est: em neque domi nunc nos nec militiae sumus:
> imus huc, hinc illuc, cum illuc uentum est, ire illuc lubet.
> incerte errat animus, praeter propter uitam uiuitur

(on the text, which is very uncertain, see O. Skutsch, *R.M.* 96 (1953) 193-210 = *Studia Enniana* (1968) 157-65). That soldiers in a tragedy should moralize in this way shows the power of the semi-philosophical commonplace (already well established in Euripides). For the thesis that *otium* was responsible for the ills of society cf. Fraenkel, op. cit. (1053-75n.) 212-13.

1059 That change of situation solves no problems is a favourite theme of Horace and Seneca: cf. the famous *caelum non animum mutant qui trans mare currunt* (Hor. *Ep.* 1. 11. 27).

1060-67 L.'s choice of illustration was in a manner forced upon him, since, as Ernout remarks, 'le spleen est une maladie des riches'. However, this is not a generalized declamatory example, but a sharply focused contemporary portrait: a well-to-do Roman, with a large town house and a country estate – a man such as Memmius and many of L.'s other (hoped-for) readers. In spite of political troubles and civil war, the last century of the Republic was an age of enormous private fortunes and much conspicuous consumption.

1060   exit 'he is off': the position of the verb and the metre convey the suddenness of the action.

1061   pertaesumst 'is thoroughly sick'; in the pf. tense only the passive form of *pertaedet* occurs. For the force of the compound cf. 179n. There is a 'concealed' caesura after *per-* (174n.), but the position of the word is emphatic, and the slightly lumpy rhythm of the verse is probably descriptive.

reuertit 'comes back indoors'. Politian's is the most obvious and easy supplement and is accepted *exempli gratia*. For the intr. use of the verb cf. 5. 1153 *unde exortast, ad eum plerumque reuertit.*

1062   melius: with *esse*, sc. *sibi*; cf. 597n. 'He feels no better off.'

1063   mannos: Gaulish ponies much prized for their speed. This is an extra detail in the picture: he shares a common passion for fast driving, here interpreted as a symptom of the desire to 'escape himself'.

praecipitanter 'hell-for-leather'; cf. 779n.

1064 A homely comparison in the diatribe manner.

1064–5   instans; oscitat...: an abrupt change from frantic activity to languor.

1066   grauis 'heavily', predicative.

1068–9 'In this way each man tries to escape himself, but in his own despite (*ingratis*) he clings to that self, which we know he can never (*scilicet, ut fit*) succeed in escaping, though he hates it.' With *haeret* an antecedent *ei* must be extracted from *quem*; *haeret et odit* is to be read as a single phrase incorporating two contradictory ideas, hence conferring an adversative force on *et*. Madvig's *fugitat* (an interpretation rather than a correction of the transmitted text, since word-division was unknown in ancient MSS: Reynolds and Wilson 151–2) spoils the rhetorical contrast in *fugere...effugere* 'try to escape'... 'succeed in escaping' (cf. Greek φυγεῖν, ἐκφυγεῖν), and further complicates the construction of the sentence. It is clear that Seneca, who quotes and comments on the passage in the *De Tranquillitate Animi* (cit. below), read the words as *fugit, at.*

The idea expressed in these lines is one with which we have been made familiar by later writers: Horace exploited it with his usual happy concision at *C.* 2. 16. 18–20 *quid terras alio calentis | sole mutamus? patriae quis exsul | se quoque fugit?*, and elsewhere (cf. *Satires*, ed. P. Lejay (1911) 555); and in Seneca it becomes a commonplace (*Ep.* 2. 1, 69. 1, 104. 8). A similar sentiment is ascribed by Seneca to Socrates (*Ep.* 28. 2), but elsewhere he seems to associate the idea particularly with L. (*De Tranqu. An.* 2. 14). Plato had expounded the theory that the wicked man hates and is at odds with himself (*Rep.* 1. 352 a); and Aristotle in discussing friendship had observed that the wicked shun their own society (literally, as in L., 'flee themselves') and seek the companionship of others (*E.N.* 9. 1166 b. 13–14). It does not necessarily follow that L. had Aristotle in mind, and at the very least he gave the conceit a new and effective twist. The reception of the idea by his successors is a striking illustration of his position near the source of the Roman tradition of diatribe satire.

1069   ingratis 'against his will'. The *ingratius* of the MSS gives no satisfactory sense; the same corruption occurs at 6. 216, and this may indicate that the original spelling *ingratiis* (abl. pl. of *ingratia*) was used by L. or by his early editors; it would be pronounced as a trisyllable, *ingratĩis*, by synizesis.

1070–75   If men understood the causes of their discontents they would turn to philosophy, for our concern is not with a single hour but with eternity: when we die, we die for ever. The contrast between *una hora* and *tempus aeternum* is ingeniously used to relate the passage to the main argument of the book, death and man's attitude to it. Strictly speaking, however, the connexion is not very close: cf. 1053–75 n.

1070   tenet 'grasps', 'understands'.
   aeger is predicative: 'he is sick and does not know why'.

1071   rebus...relictis: sc. *ceteris*, 'he would drop everything else and...'; the phrase is colloquial.

1073   unius horae: one of the hours that the restless man is at a loss to fill. L.'s implication is apparently that if we fix our attention on the great questions of philosophy, which include death and the eternal extinction of body and soul, we shall achieve ἀταραξία and boredom will disappear.

1074   ambigitur status 'it is a matter of the condition...', but the phrase can also mean 'the legal point before the court is...' (for *status* as the issue on which a case was fought see M. L. Clarke, *Rhetoric at Rome* (1953) 26–7, 67–8). In view of L.'s use of legal phraseology elsewhere (971 n.) the ambiguity may be deliberate.

   sit: subjunctive because the clause is in effect an indirect question after *ambigitur*.

1074–5   'The condition of the whole time that remains to be expected by mortals after death': *in quo sit...omnis aetas* restates the idea of *temporis aeterni. mortalibus* belongs in sense with *manenda*; this is preferable to placing a comma after *cumque* and construing *manenda* with *sit*, as recent editors have tended to do.

1075   quae...cumque: cf. 550, 940.

1076–1094

To crave long life is a mistake: it does not confer greater happiness nor does it make death, when it comes, any less eternal. This final passage has been criticized as an inadequate ending to the book. Some of the arguments we have admittedly met before, but some are new. Perhaps it suffices to say that it seems as good a way to end the book as any; only Book I, as Heinze remarks, is rounded off with anything like a formal epilogue.

1076–84   These verses echo, without repeating in so many words, things said by Nature at 931–62.

1076   dubiis...periclis ~ 55.

1077   mala 'destructive'.

1078   certa 'irreversible', not 'ordained by fate', an un-Epicurean idea.

1079   pote = *potest*. The form occurs nowhere else in L.'s MSS (it was restored by Lachmann at 5. 836); elsewhere he uses *potis est* (e.g. 468, 1069), but *pote* is not uncommon in other Republican authors and later colloquial Latin (Neue–Wagener II 174–6).

1080 ibidem 'in the same place', hence = *in isdem* 'in doing the same things', but perhaps with the suggestion of standing still and never progressing; the word qualifies both verbs. There is a false verse-ending after the fourth foot: cf. 893, 1033 nn.

1081 procuditur 'is forged'; L. is fond of the metaphorical use of this word.

1082 sed dŭm abest: this metrical licence, the so-called 'prosodic hiatus', that is, shortening (better, lightening) of a long open or 'middle' syllable before a vowel, is relatively frequent in comedy, rare in hexameter poetry. L. offers ten certain instances; the fragments of Lucilius three; other hexameter poetry not half-a-dozen in all (Soubiran 374). Only a monosyllable occupying the first *breue* of the dactyl is so treated. The usage is to be distinguished from 'epic shortening', *correptio epica*, of the second *breue*; both licences are found together at 6. 716 *tempore eo quĭ etesiǎe esse feruntur*.

For the sentiment of the verse cf. 957 n.

1083 post 'afterwards', 'then', adverbial.

1084 sitis...hiantis: a fresh twist to the image of the unsatisfied guest (938 n.).
aequa 'undiminished'.

1085 uehat 'may bring'. Here too there is the echo of a proverb: Varro called one of his satires *Nescis quid uesper serus uehat*, and Virgil borrowed the phrase (*G.* 1. 461); cf. Otto 369. The mutability of Fortune was a declaimer's *locus* (cf. 1035 n.), perfectly at home in a *consolatio*, but L. does not attempt to develop it here.

1087–94 A new thought – or rather a new twist to a thought already expressed (869 n.) – to conclude the book: however long a man lives, he will still be dead for ever. In using this as his final argument to ridicule those who cling to life L. rides roughshod over human psychology: it would be an oddly constituted man who received any real comfort from such reflections. Cf. Introd. 32–3.

1087 hilum: 220 n.

1089 minus...diu: take together, as also in 1092.

forte 'perhaps', ironical. The suggested corrections are no improvement.

1090 condere 'see laid to rest': for the idiom cf. 490 n. *condere saecla* seems to be used in the double sense of 'see out' a period of time, as in Virgil's *longos | ...condere soles* (*E.* 9. 51–2), and also 'bury' the defunct generations: *uiuendo* assists the word-play. It seems unlikely that L. had the technical term *lustrum condere* in mind.

1091 mors aeterna: cf. 869 n.

1092 iam non erit 'will from that moment be dead'.

1092–3 ex hodierno lumine 'from today's date', since *finem uitae fecit* = *mortuus est, occidit.*

1093 et 'than', after *minus*, a usage analogous to *alius ac/atque* but much rarer. Cf. 5. 1081–2 *longe alias alio iaciunt in tempore uoces | et cum de uictu certant praedaeque repugnant*; and *T.L.L.* v. 2. 894. 4–29.

Addendum

1014 poenarum ∼ 1011 *Furiae*, also called *Poenae*: cf. Cic. *Pis.* 91 *o Poena et Furia sociorum* and, for the pl., *Clu.* 171.

BIBLIOGRAPHY

This list consists for the most part of works cited in Introduction and Commentary by the name of editor or author alone. For a catalogue of editions and translations see C. A. Gordon, *A bibliography of Lucretius* (1962); and for a classified bibliography of modern Lucretian scholarship see Boyancé 329–47.

1. *Editions, Commentaries and Translations*

Bailey, C. 3 vols, 1947. Prolegomena, critical text, translation and commentary.

Büchner, C. 1966. Critical text.

Creech, T. 1695. Text, paraphrase and notes (in Latin).
 1682 (and often reedited). English verse translation.

Diels, H. 1923–4. Critical text and German translation.

Duff, J. D. (Book III) 1903. Introduction, text and commentary.

Ernout, A. 1920 (and often reedited). Critical text and French translation.

Ernout, A. and Robin, L. *Lucrèce de rerum natura*. 3 vols, 2nd ed. 1962. Introduction and commentary (in French).

Giussani, C. 4 vols, 1896–8. Introduction, text and commentary (in Italian).

Heinze, R. (Book III) 1897. Critical text and commentary (in German).

Lachmann, C. 1850. Critical text and commentary (in Latin).

Lambinus, D. 1563–4, 1570, 1583. Critical text and commentary (in Latin).

Latham, R. E. 1951. English translation.

Leonard, W. E. and Smith, S. B. 1965 (1942). Introduction, text and commentary.

Martin, J. 5th ed. 1963. Critical text.

Merrill, W. A. 1917. Critical text.

Munro, H. A. J. 3 vols, 4th ed. 1893. Introduction, critical text, translation and commentary.

Sinker, A. P. *Introduction to Lucretius*. 1937. Introduction and anthology, with commentary.

Smith, *see* Leonard.

Smith, M. F. 1969. English translation.

Wakefield, G. 3 vols, 1796–7; 4 vols, 1813. Critical text and commentary (in Latin).

2. *Other works*

Amory, A. '*Obscura de re lucida carmina*: Science and poetry in *De Rerum Natura*', *Y.C.S.* 21 (1969), 145–68.

Bell, A. J. *The Latin dual and poetic diction.* 1923.

Bennett, C. E. *Syntax of early Latin.* 1 *The verb.* 1910. 11 *The cases.* 1914.

Boyancé, P. *Lucrèce et l'Épicurisme.* 1963.

Chilton, C. W. (ed.) *Diogenis Oenoandensis fragmenta.* 1967.

Classen, C. J. 'Poetry and rhetoric in Lucretius', *T.A.P.A.* 99 (1968) 77–118.

Cox, A. 'Didactic poetry', in *Greek and Latin literature*, ed. J. Higginbotham. 1969.

Crawley, L. W. A. *The failure of Lucretius* (Univ. Auckland Bull. 66, Classics Series 5). 1963.

De Witt, N. W. *Epicurus and his philosophy.* 1954.

Dudley, D. R. (ed.) *Lucretius.* 1965.

Farrington, B. *The faith of Epicurus.* 1967.

Festugière, J.-A. *Épicure et ses dieux.* 2nd ed. 1968.

Fletcher, G. B. A. 'Lucretiana', *Latomus* 27 (1968) 884–93.

Fordyce, C. J. *Catullus: a commentary.* 1961.

Friedländer, P. 'Pattern of sound and atomistic theory in Lucretius', *A.J.P.* 62 (1941) 16–34 (= *Studien zur antiken Literatur und Kunst* (1969) 337–53).

Guthrie, W. K. C. *A history of Greek philosophy.* 1, 1962; 11, 1965; 111, 1969.

Hadzits, G. P. *Lucretius and his influence.* 1935.

Hense, O. (ed.) *Teletis reliquiae.* 2nd ed. 1909.

Hofmann, J. B. and Szantyr, A. *Lateinische Syntax und Stilistik.* 1965.

Jocelyn, H. D. *The tragedies of Ennius.* 1967.

Kenney, E. J. 'Doctus Lucretius', *Mnemosyne* 4, 23 (1970) 366–92.

Kühner, R. and Stegmann, C. *Ausführliche Grammatik der lateinischen Sprache.* 3rd ed. rev. A. Thierfelder. 2 vols, 1955.

Lattimore, R. *Themes in Greek and Latin epitaphs.* 1962.

Martha, C. *La poëme de Lucrèce.* 1867 (and often reedited).

Minadeo, R. 'The formal design of *De rerum natura*', *Arion* 4 (1965) 444–61.

Neue, F. and Wagener, C. *Formenlehre der lateinischen Sprache.* 4 vols, 1892–1905.

Nisbet, R. G. M. and Hubbard, M. *A commentary on Horace: Odes Book 1.* 1970.

Oltramare, A. *Les origines de la diatribe romaine.* 1926.

Otto, A. *Die Sprichwörter und sprichwörtlichen Redensarten der Römer.* 1890. [Supplement by R. Häussler. 1968.]

Owen, W. H. 'Structural patterns in Lucretius' *De Rerum Natura*', *Class. World* 62 (1968–69) 121–7, 166–72.

Paratore, H. *Lucreti De Rerum Natura locos praecipue notabiles collegit et illustravit.* Commentariolo instruxit H. Pizzani. 1960.

Pearce, T. E. V. 'The enclosing word order in the Latin hexameter', *C.Q.* N.S. 16 (1966) 140–71, 298–320.

Real, H. J. *Untersuchungen zur Lukrez-übersetzung von Thomas Creech.* 1970.

Reynolds, L. D. and Wilson, N. G. *Scribes and scholars. A guide to the transmission of Greek and Latin literature.* 1968.

Roberts, L. *A concordance of Lucretius.* Supplement to ΑΓⲰΝ. 1968.

Rozelaar, M. *Lukrez: Versuch einer Deutung.* 1943.

Santayana, G. *Three philosophical poets: Lucretius, Dante, and Goethe.* 1935.

Schmid, W. 'Lukrez und der Wandel seines Bildes', *Antike und Abendland* 2 (1946) 193–219.

Schrijvers, P. H. *Horror ac divina voluptas. Études sur la poétique et la poésie de Lucrèce.* 1970.

Sellar, W. Y. *The Roman poets of the Republic.* 3rd ed. 1889.

Sikes, E. E. *Lucretius, poet & philosopher.* 1936.

Soubiran, J. *L'élision dans la poésie latine.* 1966.

Sykes Davies, H. 'Notes on Lucretius', *The Criterion* 11 (1931–2) 25–42.

Us(ener), H. *Epicurea.* 1887.

West, D. *The imagery and poetry of Lucretius.* 1969.

INDEXES TO THE COMMENTARY

References are to lines of the text

1. *Latin words*

ab 74, 271, 323, 813, 820
abhinc 955
ac (disjunctive) 164, 442; (= 'than')
  96
adcredo 856
adhaesus 381–2
aegreo 106
aer 121–2
aeuus 605
agedum 962
algus 732
alienus (w. gen.) 821
alius (forms of) 918, 970
ancido 660
anima 35–6, 94, 117, 143, 150, 216,
  228, 277, 422–3, 597, 796,
  798–9
animans (gender of) 666
animus 35–6, 94, 175, 177, 237, 277,
  398, 422–3, 461, 464, 561, 680,
  705–8, 788, 796, 798-9
atque (disjunctive) 333–4; (emphatic)
  573-5; ('explicative') 793;
  (postponed) 531
augeo 626
augmen 268

baratre 955

cado (construction w.) 836
caput 138
caula 255, 702
causa 486
cerno 363
cinefactus 906
clueo (= *sum*) 207
comptus (subst.) 845-6

concilio 865
concilium 805
concrucio 148
coniugium 845–6
consentio 153
contages 734
contagium 345
contamino 882–3
conubia (prosody of) 776
conuenit 455
cum (causal w. indic.) 363; (concessive w. indic.) 107, 112; (concessive w. subj.) 101
cuppedo 994

deerro (prosody of) 861
defluo 517–18
dementio 464
desipientia 499
de subito 643
dies (gender of) 899
discrepito 802–5
disiectus (subst.) 928
dispargo (spelling of) 539
dissicio (spelling of) 638
dissoluo (prosody of) 330
distraho 492–4
do 355, 875
dum (concessive) 592

edo 560
enim 357
eo (= 'die') 526
ergo (= *causā*) 78
et (disjunctive) 694, 1068–9; (negative) 411; (= 'than') 1093
exos 721

2. Greek words

θυμός 94
θυρίδες 360

καλοῦμαι (= εἰμί) 207

λεπτομερές 179–80
(τὸ) λογικόν 95

μέλλω 594
μεμψιμοιρία 957, 1053–75

νεῦσις 144
νοῦς 94

πάσχω 168
περιέχω 323

περικοπή 219
πόροι 255, 442, 702

ῥοπή 144

σοφός 1023
στεγάζω 323, 576–7
συμπάθεια, συμπάσχω 153, 740, 801
συνέχω 323

ψυχή 94, 143, 161, 175, 237, 277

ὠγαθέ 206
Ὧραι, ὡραῖος 1008

3. General